GW00399870

THE HIDDEN

LIFE IN

FREMASONRY

CHARLES LEADBEATER

COPYRIGHT 2018

Premium Classic Books

Premiumclassicbooks@gmail.com

FOREWORD

IT is once more my privilege to usher into the world, for the helping of the thoughtful, another volume of the series on the hidden side of things written by Bishop Charles W. Leadbeater. True Mason that he is, he is ever trying to spread the Light which he has received, so that it may chase away the darkness of Chaos. To look for the Light, to see the Light, to follow the Light, were duties familiar to all Egyptian Masons, though the darkness in that Ancient Land never approached the density which shrouds the West today.

This book will be welcomed by all Freemasons who feel the beauty of their ancient Rite, and desire to add knowledge to their zeal. The inner History of Masonry is left aside for the present, and the apprentice is led by a trustworthy guide through the labyrinth which protects the central Shrine from careless and idle inquirers. Places that were obscure become illuminated; dark allusions are changed to crystal clarity; walls which seem solid melt away; confidence replaces doubt; glimpses of the goal are caught through rifts in the clouds; and the earth-born mists vanish before the rays of the rising sun. Instead of fragments of half-understood traditions, confused and uninterpreted, we find in our hands a splendid science and a reservoir of power which we can use for the uplifting of the world. We no longer ask: "What is the Great Work? We see "that it is nothing less than a concerted effort to carry out the duty that is laid upon us, as those who possess the Light, to spread that Light abroad through the World, and actually to become fellow-labourers with T.G.A.O.T.U. in His great Plan for the evolution of our Brn".

The detailed explanations of the ceremonies are profoundly interesting and illuminative, and I commend them very heartily to all true Freemasons. Our V .·. I .·. Brother has added a heavy debt of gratitude by this book to the many we already owe him. Let us be honest debtors.

Adyar

ANNIE BESANT

December 25, 1925

AUTHOR'S PREFACE

THE Masonic fellowship differs from all other societies in that candidates for membership have to join it blindfold, and cannot receive much information about it until they actually enter its ranks. Even then the majority of Masons usually obtain only the most general idea of the meaning of its ceremonies, and seldom penetrate further than an elementary moral interpretation of its principal symbols. In this book it is my object, while preserving due secrecy upon those matters which must be kept secret, to explain something of the deeper meaning and purpose of Freemasonry, in the hope of arousing among the Brn. a more profound reverence for that of which they are the custodians and a fuller understanding of the mysteries of the Craft.

Although the book is primarily intended for the instruction of members of the Co-Masonic Order, whose desire, as is expressed in their ritual, is to pour the waters of esoteric knowledge into the Masonic vessels, I hope nevertheless that it may appeal to a wider circle, and may perhaps be of use to some of those many Brn. in the masculine Craft who are seeking for a deeper interpretation of Masonic symbolism than is given in the majority of their Lodges, showing them that in the ritual which they know and love so well are enshrined splendid ideals and deep spiritual teachings which are of the most absorbing interest to the student of the inner side of life.

Before we can gain this fuller understanding we must have at least some slight acquaintance with certain facts concerning the world in which we live - a world only half of which we see or understand. Indeed, undignified as the statement sounds, it is quite true that our position resembles very closely that of a caterpillar feeding upon a leaf, whose vision and perception extend but very little beyond the leaf upon which he crawls. How difficult it would be for such a caterpillar to transcend his limitations, to take a wider view, to understand that his leaf is part of a huge tree with millions of such leaves, a tree with a life of its own - a life outlasting a thousand generations of lives such as his; and that tree in turn only a unit in a vast forest of dimensions incalculable to his tiny brain! And if by some unusual development one caterpillar did catch a glimpse of the great world around him and tried to explain his vision to his fellows, how those other caterpillars would disbelieve and ridicule him, how they would adjure him to waste no time on such unprofitable imaginings, but to realize that the one purpose of life is to find a good position on succulent leaf, and to assimilate as much of it as he can!

When later on he becomes a butterfly, his view widens, and he comes into touch with a beauty, a glory and a poetry in life of which he had no conception before. It is the same world, and yet so different, merely because he can see more of it, and move about in it in a new way. Every caterpillar is a potential butterfly; and we have the advantage over these creatures in that we can anticipate the butterfly stage, and so learn much more about our world, come much nearer to the truth, enjoy life much more, and do much more good. We should study the hidden side of every-day life, for in that way we shall get so much more out of it. The same truth applies to higher things - to religion, for example. Religion has always spoken to mankind of unseen things above - not only far away in the future, but close around us here and now. Our life and what we can make of it largely depend upon how real these unseen things are to us. Whatever we do, we should think always of the unseen consequences of our action. Some of us know how useful that knowledge has been to us in our Church Services; and it is just the same in freemasonry.

Though this vast inner world is unseen by most of us, it is not therefore invisible. As I wrote in *The Science of the Sacraments*:

There are within man faculties of the soul which, if developed, will enable him to perceive this inner world, so that it will become possible for him to explore and to study it precisely as man has explored and studied that part of the world which is within the reach of all. These faculties are the heritage of the whole human race; they will unfold within every one of us as our evolution progresses; but men who are willing to devote themselves to the effort map gain them in advance of the rest, just as a blacksmith's apprentice, specializing in the use of certain muscles, may attain (so far as they are concerned) a development much greater than that of other youths of his age. There are men who have these powers in working order, and are able by their use to obtain a vast amount of most interesting information about the world which most of us as yet cannot see. ... Let it be clearly understood that there is nothing fanciful or unnatural about such sight. It is simply an extension of faculties with which we are all familiar, and to develop it is to make oneself sensitive to vibrations more rapid than those to which our physical senses are normally trained to respond.* (*Op. cit., pp. 9, 10.)

It is by the use of those perfectly natural but super-normal faculties that much of the information given in this book has been obtained. Anyone who, having developed such sight, watches a Masonic ceremony, will see that a very great deal more is being done than is expressed in the mere words of the ritual, beautiful and dignified as they often are. Of course, I fully understand that all this may well seem fantastically impossible to those who have not studied the subject at first-hand; I can but affirm that this is a clear and definite reality to me, and that by long and careful research, extending over more than forty years, I am absolutely certain of the existence and reliability of this method of investigation.

It is no new discovery, for it was known to the wise men of old; but, like so much else of the ancient wisdom, it has been forgotten during the darkness of the early Middle Ages, and its value is only gradually being rediscovered; so to many it appears unfamiliar and incredible. We have only to remember how utterly inconceivable the wireless telegraph, the telephone, the aeroplane or even the automobile would have seemed to our great-grandfathers, in order to realize that we should be foolish to reject an idea merely because we have never heard of it before. Only a few years ago the powers of research put at our disposal by the invention and development of the spectroscope were as far beyond popular thought as those of clairvoyance are now. That by it we could discover the chemical constitution and measure the movements of stars thousands of millions of miles away might well have been regarded as the baseless fabric of a dream. May not other discoveries be impending?

Men of high scientific attainments, such as Sir Oliver Lodge, Sir William Crookes, Professor Lombroso, M. Camille Flammarion and the late Professor Myers, who have taken the trouble to inquire into this matter of inner sight, have convinced themselves that this faculty exists; so if there be those among the Brn. to whom this claim seems ridiculous, I would ask them notwithstanding to read on and see whether the knowledge obtained by a means which is strange to them does not nevertheless supply for obscure or incomprehensible points in our ritual an explanation which commends itself to their reason and common sense. That which gives them a better grasp of the meaning underlying the mysteries of our Craft, and thereby increases their veneration and love for it, cannot be unworthy or absurd. Any student who wishes to know more of this fascinating subject may be referred to a little book entitled *Clairvoyance*, which I wrote some years ago.

I should like strongly to recommend for the perusal of my Brn. Of the Craft two books by Wor. Bro. W. L. Wilmhurst - *The Meaning of Masonry* and *The Masonic Initiation*; I have myself read them with great delight and profit, and have gathered many gems from their pages.

I desire to offer my heartiest thanks to the Rev. Herbrand Williams, M.C., B.A., for his kindness in placing at my disposal his vast stores of Masonic erudition, and for many arduous months of patient and painstaking research; also to the Rev. E. Warner and Mrs. M. R. St. John for the careful drawing of the illustrations, and to Professor Ernest Wood for his untiring assistance and cooperation in every department of the work, without which the production of the book would not have been possible.

C. W. L.

CHAPTER I.
INTRODUCTORY
PERSONAL EXPERIENCE

THE origins of Freemasonry are lost in the mists of antiquity. Last century there were many who thought that it could be traced no further back than the mediaeval guilds of operative masons, though some regarded these in turn as relics of the Roman Collegia. There may still be some who know no better than that, but all students of the Ancient Mysteries who are also Freemasons are aware that it is along that line that we find our true philosophical ancestry; for there is much in our ceremonies and teachings which could have had no significance for the mere operative mason, though when examined by the light of the knowledge received in the Mysteries it is seen to be pregnant with meaning. Many Masonic writers claim various degrees of antiquity for the Craft, some assigning its foundation to King Solomon, and one at least boldly stating that its wisdom is all that now remains of the divine knowledge which Adam possessed before his fall. There is, however, plenty of evidence less mythical than that, and to that evidence I happen to be able to contribute a fragment of personal experience of a rather unusual kind.

By devoting some years to the effort and many more years to practice, I have been able to develop certain psychic faculties of the kind mentioned in the Foreword, which, among other things, enable me to remember the previous existences through which I have passed. The idea of pre-existence may be new to some of my readers.[1] I do not propose now to advance arguments in its favour, though they exist in abundance, but simply to state that for me, as for many others, it is a fact of personal experience. The only one of those previous lives of mine with which we are here concerned was lived some four thousand years before Christ in the country which we now call Egypt.

When I was initiated into Freemasonry in this life, my first sight of the Lodge was a great and pleasant surprise, for I found that I was perfectly familiar with all its arrangements, and that they were identical with those which I had known six thousand years ago in the Mysteries of

---

[1] Those who wish to learn more about this most fascinating subject should read *Reincarnation*, by the V ∴ Ills ∴ Bro ∴ A. Besant, and the chapter on Reincarnation in my *Textbook of Theosophy*

Egypt. I am quite aware that this is a startling statement; I can only say that it is literally true. No mistake is possible; coincidence will not serve as an explanation. The placing of the three chief officers is unusual; the symbols are significant and distinctive, and their combination is peculiar; yet they all belonged to ancient Egypt, and I knew them well there. Almost all the ceremonies are unchanged; there are only a few differences in minor points. The s ... ps taken, the k ... s given - all have a symbolical meaning which I distinctly remember.

EGYPTIAN EVIDENCES

Knowing these facts to be so from my own experience, I set to work to collect ordinary physical-plane corroborative evidence for them from such books as were within my reach, and found even more than I had hoped. The explanation of the First Degree t ... b ... begins by remarking that the usages and customs among Freemasons have ever borne a near affinity to those of the ancient Egyptians, but does not furnish us with any illustrations of the points of similarity. These are to be found in Bro. Churchward's most illuminative books, *Signs and Symbols of Primordial Man* and *The Arcana of Freemasonry*, also in *The Arcane Schools*, by Bro. John Yarker, and *Freemasonry and the Ancient Gods*, by Bro. J. S. M. Ward. I will proceed to summarize, with grateful acknowledgment, the information derived from these volumes. Masons of various degrees will be able to select from it the features which remind them of their own ceremonies.

Some interesting illustrations have been collected from the wall-pictures of ancient Egypt, and from vignettes on various papyri, chiefly from *The Book of the Dead*, of which there are many recensions. It is clear from these sources that the formation of the temple in Egypt was a double square, and in the centre were three cubes standing one upon another, forming an altar* (*Churchward, *The Arcana of Freemasonry*, p. 43.) upon which were laid their Volumes of the Sacred Lore - not the same as our own, of course, for ours had not yet been written. Those cubes represented the three Aspects or Persons of the Trinity - Osiris, Isis and Horus - as may be seen from the signs engraved on them (see Fig. 1) which, however, is copied not from an Egyptian altar, but from an illustration in Mr. Evans' book on Crete; but at a later period we find only a double cube.

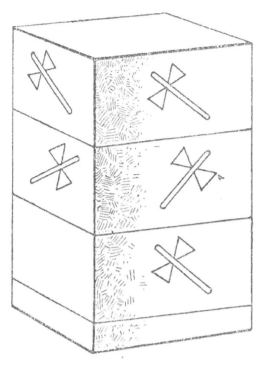

Fig. 1

There were two pillars at the entrance to the temple, and on them were squares representing earth and heaven.* (*Ibid., p. 44.) One of them bore a name which signified "in strength" while the name of the other signified "to establish".* (*Ibid., p. 121.) This gateway was regarded as leading to the higher world of Amenti, the world where the soul was blended with immortal spirit, and thereafter established for ever; so this was the figure of stability. At the entrance of the Lodge there were always two guards armed with knives; the outer was called the Watcher, the inner was known as the Herald.* (*Ibid., p. 47.) The candidate was divested of most of his clothing, and entered with a c ... t ... and h ... w ... He was led to the door of the temple, and there asked who he was. He replied that he was Shu, the "suppliant" or "kneeler," coming in a state of darkness to seek for Light. The door was an equilateral triangle of stone, which turned on a pivot on its own centre.

As the candidate entered he trod on the square, and, in so doing, it was supposed that he was treading on, and leaving, the lower quaternary or personality of man, in order to develop the higher triad, the ego or soul. (In modern Masonry the same idea is expressed in the First Lecture, where it is stated that a Mason comes to the Lodge "to learn to rule and subdue his passions, and to make further progress in Masonry".) He was conducted through long passages, and led round the Lodge seven times; and, after having replied to many questions, he was eventually brought to the centre of the Lodge, and there asked what he required. He was told to answer: "Light". In all his perambulations, he had to begin with the left foot. If the candidate violated his O., so it is stated in *The Book of the Dead*, his throat was cut and his heart torn out. Another degree is mentioned in the papyrus of Nesi-Amsu, where it is said that the body was cut to pieces and burnt to ashes, and these were spread over the face of the waters to the four winds of heaven.

There is in the temple of Khnumu in the island of Elephantine, just off Assouan, a bas-relief which shows us two figures, one of the Pharaoh and the other of a priest wearing the ibis head-dress of Thoth, standing in an attitude strongly suggestive of the f ... p ... of f ..., though not exactly agreeing with our present practice. (See Plate II a.) It is intended to represent an initiation, and the word given is "Maat-heru," which means "true of voice" or "one whose voice must be obeyed".* (*Churchward, *The Arcana of Freemasonry*, p. 49.) I have also seen a painting in which four attendants are depicted saluting a Pharaoh with the p ... s ... of an I.M., and the s ... of s ... is often to be found on the monuments, and is characteristic of Horus. The gavel was then made of stone, and was a model of the double-headed axe.

In those days the aprons were made of leather, and were triangular. That of the First Degree was pure white, as it is now; but the M.M.'s apron was brilliantly coloured and heavily jewelled, with tassels of gold. (See Plate I.) Our t ... f ... i ... g ... was represented by a cubit of twenty-five inches. The Blazing Star in the centre of the Lodge existed, but it had eight points instead of six or five. It was called "The Star of Dawn" or "The Morning Star," and represented Horus of the Resurrection, who is pictured as bearing it upon his head and as having given it to his followers.

The Masonic square was well-known, and was called *neka*. It is to be found in many temples, and also appears in the great pyramid. It is said that it was used for squaring stones, and also symbolically for squaring conduct, which once more resembles the modern interpretation. To build on the square was to build for ever, according to the teachings of ancient Egypt; and in the Egyptian Hall of Judgment Osiris is seen seated on the square while judging the dead. (See Plate II b.)

Plate I

AN EGYPTIAN APRON

Plate II

(a) AN EGYPTIAN INITIATION   (b) OSIRIS ON THE SQUARE

Thus the square came to symbolize the foundation of eternal law.*
(*Churchward, The Arcana of Freemasonry, p. 59.)

The Egyptians used the rough and the smooth ashlars with much the same meaning that Masons attach to them today.* (*Ibid., p. 60.) A wand surmounted by a dove is represented, not only in ancient Egypt, but also in some of the monuments in Central America, and those who bore it were called "conductors". It is a curious fact, also, that the descendants of the Nilotic negroes, who emigrated long ago from Egypt to Central Africa, when called to take an oath in a court of law, still do so with a gesture which, still do so with a gesture, were I at liberty to describe it in writing, would be universally recognized by the Craft.

Another point that struck me much on looking at engravings of vignettes in *The Book of the Dead* is that the h ... s ... of the F.C. is depicted perfectly clearly; a group of people is shown as worshipping the setting sun, or paying respect to it, in that attitude.

This *Book of the Dead*, as it has been somewhat unfortunately called, is part of a manual which in its entirety was intended as a kind of guide to the astral plane, containing a number of instructions for the conduct both of the departed and the initiate in the lower regions of that other world. The chapters which have been collected from the various tombs do not give us the whole of that work, but only one section of it, and even that is much corrupted. The mind of the Egyptian seems to have worked along exceedingly formal and orderly lines; he tabulated every conceivable description of entity which a dead man could by any possibility meet, and arranged carefully the special charm or word of power which he considered most certain to vanquish the creature if he should prove hostile, never apparently realizing that it was his own will which did the work, but attributing his success to some kind of magic. *The Book of the Dead* was originally intended to be kept secret, although in later days certain chapters were written on papyrus and buried with the dead man. As is said in one of the texts: "This Book is the greatest of mysteries. Do not let the eye of anyone look upon it - that were abomination. *The Book of the Master of the Secret House* is its name."* (*W. Marsham Adams, *The Book of the Master*, p. 96.)

In ancient Egypt they recognized seven souls, or life-forces, coming forth from the Most High. Students of Eastern philosophy call them the primordial seven, and they are mentioned in *The Book of Dzyan*.* (*See *The Secret Doctrine*, by H. P. Blavatsky.) Six of these were prehuman; the seventh was our humanity, and was brought forth from the virgin Neith. The symbol attached to that bringing forth was that of the pelican, who was fabled to draw blood from her own breast in order to feed her young;

this later became a prominent symbol in the Rosicrucian philosophy, which seems to have been derived largely from Egyptian teaching. We read in Egyptian hieroglyphics of "the One and the Four," referring to Horus and his four Brothers. Of that we also read in *The Stanzas of Dzyan*; and another expression common to both is "The One from the Egg". In Egypt the egg was the symbol for the setting sun, which is often seen in that shape when about to touch the horizon. That egg passed into the underworld, and was hatched there, and out of it came the young sun the next morning, rising in his strength, which was called "the flame born of a flame". All this bore a deeply mystical significance, which was explained in the Mysteries.

When Osiris died, Isis and Nepthys - in turn tried to raise him, but it proved a failure; then Anubis attempted it and succeeded, and Osiris returned to the world with the secrets of Amenti - a significant statement which seems to suggest that the secrets which we possess are closely connected with the underworld and the life after death.

These are some of the most striking of the evidences which I have been able to collect; and there are others which may not be written. I feel that many more can probably be found, but even these, when taken together, make any theory of coincidence impossible. There is no doubt that this to which we have the honour to belong today is the same fraternity which I knew six thousand years ago, and it can indeed be carried back to a far greater antiquity still. Bro. Churchward claims that some of the signs are six hundred thousand years old; that is quite likely to be true, for the world is very ancient, and assuredly Freemasonry has one of the very oldest rituals existing. We must of course admit that the mere appearance of one of our symbols does not necessarily involve the existence of a Lodge, but at least it shows that, even so long ago as that, men were thinking along somewhat the same lines, and trying to express their thoughts in the same language of symbol that we employ today.

PRESERVATION OF RITUALS AND SYMBOLS

That the rituals and symbols should have been preserved to us with so wonderfully little alteration is surely a marvellous thing; it would be inexplicable but for the fact that the Great Powers behind evolution have taken an interest in the matter, and gradually brought people back to the true lines when they had swerved somewhat away from them. This business was always in the hands of the Chohan of the Seventh Ray, for that is the ray most especially connected with ceremonial of all kinds, and its Head was always the supreme Hierophant of the Mysteries of ancient

Egypt. The present holder of that office is that Master of the Wisdom of whom we often speak as the Comte de S. Germain, because He appeared under that title in the eighteenth century. He is also sometimes called Prince Rakoczi, as He is the last survivor of that royal house. Exactly when He was appointed to the Headship of the Ceremonial Ray I do not know, but He took a keen interest in Freemasonry as early as the third century A.D.

We find him at that period as Albanus, a man of noble Roman family, born at the town of Verulam in England. As a young man he went to Rome, joined the army there, and achieved considerable distinction in it. He served in Rome for some seven years at any rate, perhaps longer than that. It was there that he was initiated into Freemasonry, and also became a proficient in the Mithraic Mysteries, which were so closely associated with it.

After this time in Rome he returned to his birthplace in England, and was appointed governor of the fortress there. He also held the position of "the Master of the Works", whatever that may have meant; he certainly superintended the repairs and the general work in the fortress at Verulam, and he was at the same time the Imperial Paymaster. The story goes that the workmen were treated as slaves and wretchedly paid, but that S. Alban (as he was afterwards called) introduced Freemasonry and changed all that, securing for them better wages and greatly improved conditions generally. Many of our Brn. must have heard of the Watson MS of 1687. In that a good deal is said about S. Albans work for the Craft, and it is specially mentioned that he brought from France certain ancient charges which are practically identical with those in use at the present time. He was beheaded in the persecution by the Emperor Diocletian in the year 303, and the great abbey of S. Alban was built over his remains some five hundred years later.

In the year 411 he was born in Constantinople and received the name of Proclus - a name which in after life he was destined to make famous. He was one of the last great exponents of Neo-Platonism, and his influence overshadowed to a great extent the medieval Christian Church. After that there is a gap in his list of incarnations, as to which at present we know nothing. We find him reborn in the year 1211, and in that life he was Roger Bacon, a Franciscan friar, who was a reformer both of the theology and the science of his day. In 1375 came his birth as Christian Rosenkreutz. That also was an incarnation of considerable importance, for in it he founded the secret society of the Rosicrucians. He seems some fifty years later, or a little more than that, to have used the body of Hunyadi Janos, an eminent Hungarian soldier and leader. Also we are told that about 1500 he had a life as the monk Robertus, somewhere in middle Europe. We know practically nothing about that, as to what he did or in what way he distinguished himself.

After that comes one of the greatest of his births, for in the year 1561 he was born as Francis Bacon. Of that great man we hear in history little that is true and a great deal that is false. The real facts of his life are gradually becoming known, largely by means of a cipher story which he wrote secretly in the many works which he published. That story is of entrancing interest, but it does not concern us here. A sketch of it may be found in my book *The Hidden Side of Christian Festivals*, from which I am epitomizing this account.* (*Op. cit.., p. 303.)

A century later we are told that he took birth as Jozsef Rakoczi, a prince of Transylvania. We find him mentioned in the encyclopedias, but not much information is given. After that considerable mystery surrounds his movements. He seems to have travelled about Europe, and he turns up at intervals, but we have little definite knowledge about him. He was the Comte de S. Germain at the time of the French Revolution, and worked much with Madame Blavatsky, who was at that period in incarnation under the name of Père Joseph. He also appears to have disguised himself as Baron Hompesch, who was the last of the Knights of St. John of Malta, the man who arranged the transfer of the island of Malta to the English. This great saint and teacher still lives, and His present body has no appearance of great age. I myself met Him physically in Rome in 1901, and had a long conversation with Him.

In Co-Masonry we refer to Him as the Head of all True Freemasons throughout the world (abbreviated as the H.O.A.T.F.) and in some of our Lodges His portrait is placed in the east, above the chair of the R.W.M., and just beneath the Star of Initiation; others place it in the north, above an empty chair. Upon His recognition and assent as Head of the Seventh Ray the validity of all rites and degrees depends. He often selects pupils from among the Brn. of the Masonic Order, and prepares those who have fitted themselves in the lower mysteries of Masonry for the true Mysteries of the Great White Lodge, of which our Masonic initiations, splendid though they be, are but faint reflections, for Masonry has ever been one of the gates through which that White Lodge might be reached. Today but few of His Masons acknowledge Him as their Sovereign Grand Master, yet the possibility of such discipleship has ever been recognized in the traditions of the Order. It is said in an ancient catechism of masculine Masonry:

Q. As a Mason whence come you?

A. From the W ... t.

Q. Whither directing your course?

A. To the E ... t.

Q. What inducement have you to leave the W ... t and go to the E ... t?

A. To seek a Master, and from Him to gain instruction.

Fortunately our ancestors have recognized the importance of handing down the working unchanged. Some few points have been dropped during that vast lapse of time; a few others have been slightly modified; but they are marvellously few. The charges have become longer, and the non-officials take less part in the work than they used to do; in the old days they constantly chanted short versicles of praise or exhortation, and each one of them understood himself to be filling a definite position, to be a necessary wheel in the great machine.

From this knowledge several points emerge. It is noteworthy that the Masonic ceremonies, which have so long been supposed to be rather in opposition to the received religion of the country, are seen to be themselves a relic of the most sacred part of a great ancient religion. Like every product of these ancient and elaborately perfected systems, these rites are full of meaning, or rather of meanings; for in Egypt we attributed to them a fourfold signification. Since every detail is thus full of import, it is obvious that nothing should ever be changed without the greatest care, and only then by those who know its full intent, so that the symbology of the whole may not be spoiled.

THE EGYPTIAN OUTLOOK

It is exceedingly difficult to explain to twentieth century readers all that this work meant to us in the sunny land of Khem; but I will try to describe the four layers of interpretation as they were taught when I myself lived there.

The first idea of its meaning was that it conveyed to us and symbolized in action the way in which the Great Architect had constructed the universe - that in the movements made and in the plan of the Lodge were enshrined some of the great principles on which that universe had been built. The vortical movement in the censing, the raising and lowering of the columns, the cross, the anchor and the cup upon the ladder of evolution - all these things and many more we interpreted in that way. The different degrees penetrated further and further into the knowledge of His methods and of the principles upon which He works. For we not only held that He worked in the past, but that He is working now, that His universe is an active expression of Him. In those days, books filled a far less prominent place in our lives than they do now, and it was considered that to record knowledge in a series of appropriate and suggestive actions made a more powerful appeal to a man's mind, and established that knowledge better in memory, than to read it from a book. We are, therefore, preserving by our unvarying actions the memory of certain facts and laws in nature.

Because that is so, and because the laws of the universe must be universal in their application and must act down here as well as above, we held that the Great Architect expected from us a life in accordance with the law which He had made. The square was to be applied literally to stones and buildings, but symbolically to man's conduct, and man must arrange his life in agreement with what obviously followed from these considerations; therefore the strictest probity was demanded, and a high level of purity, physical, emotional and mental. Perfect rectitude and justice were required, and yet at the same time loving-kindness and gentleness, and in all cases "doing unto others what ye would that they should do unto you." So Masonry is indeed "a system of morality veiled in allegory and illustrated by symbols," but it is a system based not on an alleged commandment, "Thus saith the Lord," but on definite facts and laws in nature which cannot be doubted.

The work is a preparation for death, and for what follows it. The two pillars B. and J. were supposed to stand at the entrance to the other world, and the various experiences through which the candidate passed were intended to symbolize those which would come to him when he passed out of this physical world into the next stage. There is a vast amount of information about the life after death to be derived from an intelligent consideration of Masonic ceremonies, and through constantly practising them these worlds will become really familiar to us; so that when we shall pass beyond the grave, no longer in figurative death, we shall feel ourselves quite at home in repeating once more what we have so often enacted in symbol within the Lodge. Above all, it is emphasized that the same laws hold good on the other side of the grave as on this, that in both states we are equally in the presence of God, and that where that holy Name is invoked there can be no cause for fear.

The fourth intention is the hardest of all to explain. To make you understand that, I must try to take you back, if I can, into the atmosphere of old Egypt, and to the attitude that religious men held there. I do not know whether it is possible to reconstruct that in these modern days, which are so hopelessly, so fundamentally different.

The religion which we know best at the present day is intensely individualistic; the great central objective put before most Christians is that of saving their own souls. That duty is represented to be of primary importance. Can you picture to yourselves a religion, just as much a religion in every way, in every respect as earnest, as fervid, as real, from which that idea was entirely absent, to which it would have been utterly inconceivable? Can you think, as a beginning, of a condition of mind in which no one feared anything excepting wrong, and its possible results in delaying unfoldment; in which men looked forward with perfect certainty to their progress after death, because they knew all about it; in which their one desire was not for salvation but for advancement in evolution, because such advancement brought them greater power to do effectively the hidden work which God expected of them?

I am not suggesting that every one in ancient Egypt was altruistic, any more than are all the people in modern England. But I do say that the country was permeated with joy and fearlessness so far as its religious ideas were concerned, and that every one who by any stretch of courtesy could be described as a religious man was occupied not with thoughts of his personal salvation, but with the desire to be a useful agent of the divine Power.

The outer religion of ancient Egypt - the official religion in which everyone took part, from the King to the slave - was one of the most splendid that have ever been known to man. Gorgeous processions perambulating avenues miles in length, amid pillars so stupendous that they seemed scarcely human work, stately boats in a medley of rainbow colours sweeping majestically down the placid Nile, music triumphant or plaintive, but always thrilling - how shall I describe something so absolutely without parallel in our puny modern times? The common dress of all classes in Egypt was white; but in contradistinction their religious processions were masses of splendid, glowing colour, the priests wearing vestments of crimson and a gorgeous blue supposed to represent the blue of the sky, and many other brilliant colours also. The life of ancient Egypt, as indeed of modern Egypt, centred round the river Nile, slow-flowing and majestic, and richly decorated barges were used for all purposes of transit, and also for the celebration of religious festivals. On these the priests were arranged in certain symbolical figures, standing or sitting; and all wore the colours appropriate to the particular aspect of the Deity which they symbolized.

Not only were solemn sacrifices offered to the gods upon these barges at altars wonderfully adorned with flowers and precious embroideries, sometimes built up by stages to a hundred feet or more in the air; but living pictures or scenes were also enacted upon them, having a symbolical meaning connected with the festival which was being celebrated. In such ways was represented the judgment of the dead, with the weighing of the heart by Anubis against the feather of Maat, the characters of Anubis and Thoth being played by priests who wore the appropriate masks. I remember also a very gruesome performance of the dismemberment of Osiris, in which His body was cut into pieces and then put together again - not the body of a real person, of course, but none the less very realistically enacted. These splendid processions swept down the river between the thronging multitudes of worshippers, shedding the benediction of the gods as they passed by, and evoking tremendous enthusiasm and devotion in the people.

The ancient Egyptians have often been accused of polytheism, but in reality they were no more guilty of the charge than are the Hindus. All men knew and worshipped the One God, Amen-Ra, the "One without a Second", the centre of whose manifestation on the physical plane is the sun; but they worshipped Him under different aspects and through different channels. In one of the hymns addressed to Him it was said:

The gods adore Thee, They greet Thee, O Thou the One Dark Truth, the Heart of Silence, the Hidden Mystery, the Inner God seated within the shrine, Thou Producer of Beings, Thou the One Self. We adore the souls that are emanated from Thee, that share Thy Being, that are Thyself. O Thou that art hidden, yet everywhere manifest, we worship Thee in greeting each God-soul that cometh forth from Thee and liveth in us.

The "gods" were not considered to be equal with God, but rather to have attained union with Him at various levels, and therefore to be channels of His infinite power to mankind.

The cult of the gods was in reality but little different from the cult of Angels and Saints in the Catholic Church. Just as Christians look to St. Michael and to Our Lady as real personages and hold festivals in their honour, so in ancient Egypt adoration was offered to Isis and Osiris, and to other deities likewise. In the ultimate these august names referred to Aspects of the Godhead, Amen-Ra, for the Trinity in Egypt was represented by Father, Mother, Son - Osiris, Isis and Horus instead of the Christian presentation of Father, Son, and Holy Spirit; but below that divine level there were then, as there are now, great Beings in whom the Ideal was embodied, who acted as representatives and as channels of God's threefold power and grace to man. Furthermore there are hierarchies of Angels belonging to these different lines, just as there are hierarchies of Angels who follow the leadership of St. Michael and of Our Lady - each of whom is a channel and representative of his Order according to the level of his development. The celebration of the ritual of Isis, for instance, always attracted her attention, and invoked the presence of Angels of Her Order, who acted as channels of the divine blessing in that wondrous aspect of the Hidden Truth which she represented.

THE HIDDEN WORK

No doubt the really religious man took his part in all the outward pomp which I have described; but what he prized far above all its amazing magnificence was his membership in some Lodge of the sacred Mysteries - a Lodge which devoted itself with reverent enthusiasm to the hidden work which was the principal activity of this noble religion. It is of this hidden side of the Egyptian cult, not of its outer glories, that Freemasonry is a relic, and the ritual which is preserved in it is a part of that of the Mysteries. To explain what this hidden work was, let us draw a parallel from a more modern method of producing a somewhat similar result.

The Christian plan for spreading abroad the divine power or grace is principally by means of the celebration of the Holy Eucharist, commonly called by our Roman brethren the Mass. We must not think of that grace as a sort of poetical expression, or as in the least degree vague and cloudy; we are dealing with a force as definite as electricity - a spiritual power which is spread abroad over the people in certain ways, which leaves its own effect behind it, and needs its own vehicles, just as electricity needs its appropriate machinery.

It is possible by clairvoyance to watch the action of that force, to see how the service of the Eucharist builds up a thought-form, through which that force is distributed by the priest with the aid of the Angel invoked for that purpose. It has been so arranged that the attitude of the priest, his knowledge - even his character - does not in any way interfere with the due effect of the Sacrament. (See No. 26 of the Thirty-nine Articles of the

Church of England in *The Book of Common Prayer*.) There is, in any case, an irreducible minimum which is transmitted. So long as he performs the prescribed ceremonies the result is achieved.[2] If he is also a devout man, those who receive the Sacrament at his hands have the additional benefit of a share in his love and devotion, but that in no way affects the value of the Sacrament itself; whatever his failings, the divine strength is outpoured upon the people.

The old Egyptian religion had the same idea of pouring out spiritual force upon all its people, but its method was altogether different. The Christian magic can be performed by the priest alone, and may even be done quite mechanically; but the intelligent assistance of the laity greatly increases its power and the amount of force which can be outpoured. The Egyptian plan, however, positively required the earnest and intelligent co-operation of a considerable number of people. It was, therefore, much more difficult to achieve perfectly, but when thoroughly done it was far more powerful, and covered a much wider range of country. The Christian scheme needs a vast number of churches dotted all over the land; the Egyptian plan required only the action of a few Grand Lodges established in the principal cities in order to flood the whole kingdom with the Hidden Light - the work of the ordinary Lodges being regarded as subsidiary to these, and rather as a training ground for membership in the Grand Lodges.

The central doctrine of the religion of the ancient Egyptians was that the divine power dwelt in every man, even the lowest and most degraded, and they called that power "The Hidden Light". They held that through that Light, which existed in all, men could always be reached and helped, and that it was their business to find that Light within every one, however unpromising, and to strengthen it. The very motto of the Pharaoh was "Look for the Light," implying that his supreme duty as King was to look for that Hidden Light in every man around him, and strive to bring it forth into fuller manifestation. The Egyptians held that this divine spark, which exists in every one, could most effectively be fanned into flame by transmuting and bringing down to the three lower worlds the tremendous spiritual force which is the life of the higher planes, and then pouring it out over the country as has been described. Knowing that spiritual force to be but another manifestation of the manifold power of God, they gave to it also the name of the Hidden Light; and from this double use of the

---

[2] See *The Canons and Decrees of the Council of Trent*, by T. Waterworth, p. 55 (Session VII, Canon xii)

term confusion sometimes arises. They fully recognized that such a downpour of divine grace could be evoked only by a supreme effort of devotion on their part; and the making of such an effort, together with the provision of suitable machinery for spreading the force when it came, was a great part of the hidden work to which the noblest of the Egyptians devoted so much of their time and energy; and this was the fourth of the objects intended to be served by the sacred and secret ritual, of which that of Masonry is a relic.

THE EGYPTIAN RACE

The Egyptian race of the period of which I have been speaking was of mixed blood, but dominantly Aryan. Our researches show that about 13,500 B.C. a band of men and women belonging to the highest classes of the great South Indian empire which then existed set out on an expedition to Egypt, by way of Ceylon, having been directed to do so by the Manu. The ruling race in Egypt in those days was a branch of what has been called in Theosophical books the Toltec sub-race - a branch probably identical with that Cro-Magnon race which inhabited Europe and Africa somewhere about 25,000 B.C. In *Ancient Types of Man*, p. 71, Sir Arthur Keith remarks that this race was mentally and physically one of the finest that the world has ever seen. Broca has noted that the brain content of the skull of the Cro-Magnon woman surpasses that of the average male of today. The average height of the men of this race was six feet one and a half inches; the shoulders were exceedingly broad and the arms short as compared with the legs; the nose was thin but prominent, the cheek-bones high, and the chin massive.

It happened that the King or Pharaoh on the throne at the time when the expedition from South India arrived had a daughter but no son, his wife having died in child-birth. The newcomers were received with great cordiality by both King and High-Priest, and intermarriage with the strangers became a coveted honour in the Egyptian families, especially as the King had approved the marriage of his daughter with the leader of the band, who was a Prince of India.

In a few generations the Aryan blood had tinged the entire Egyptian nobility, and this produced the type, well known from the monuments, which had Aryan features, but the Toltec colouring. After many centuries there came a ruler who was influenced by a foreign princess, whom he had espoused, to cast aside the Aryan traditions and establish lower forms of worship; but the clan drew together and, by strictly marrying only among themselves, preserved the old customs and religion as well as their purity of race. Nearly four thousand years after the arrival of the Indians, there arose in Egypt certain prophets who foretold a great flood, so the clan in a body took ship across the Red Sea and found a refuge among the mountains of Arabia.

In 9,564 B.C. the prophecy was fulfilled; the island of Poseidonis sank beneath the Atlantic Ocean in the deluge mentioned in the *Timaeus* of Plato; at the same time the land rose and made theSahara Desert where a shallow sea had been before, and a vast tidal wave swept over Egypt, so that almost its entire population was destroyed. Even when everything settled down, the country was a wilderness, bounded on the west no longer by a peaceful sea but by a vast salt swamp, which as the centuries rolled on dried into an inhospitable desert. Of all the glories of Egypt there remained only the pyramids towering in lonely desolation - a state of things which endured for fifteen hundred years before the clan returned from its mountain refuge, grown into a great nation.

But long before this half-savage tribes had ventured into the land, fighting their primitive battles on the banks of the great river which had once borne the argosies of a mighty civilization, and was yet to witness a revival of those ancient glories, and to mirror the stately temples of Osiris and Amen-Ra. The first of the several races that entered the country was a negroid people from Central Africa; they had, however, been displaced by various others before the Aryo-Egyptians returned from Arabia, settled near Abydos, and gradually in a peaceful manner became once more the dominant power. Two thousand four hundred years later the Manu (under the name of Menes) incarnated, united the whole of Egypt under one rule, and founded at the same time the first dynasty and his great city of Memphis. This empire had already flourished for more than a millennium and a half before the reign of Rameses the Great, who was himself the Master of one of the principal Lodges at the time when I had the Honour to belong to it.

THE GRAND LODGES

During the time when I was living in Egypt, the government of the country was directed from within the organization of the Mysteries. Egypt was divided into forty-two nomes or counties, and the nomarch or ruler of the county was the Master of the principal Lodge of the nome. There was a Grand Lodge - not to be confused with the three Grand Lodges of Amen to be described later - which consisted of all the nomarchs, and of which the Grand Master was the Pharaoh. This Grand Lodge was convened at Memphis, and worked a different ritual from those of the lower grades. It was to this body that the Pharaoh announced his decrees; for although his power in the land was almost absolute, yet before any serious decision was made he always took counsel with his nomarchs - and, judging by their decisions, they were a very capable body of men. Lesser matters were settled by an executive committee of this Lodge over which the Pharaoh presided; but important steps were always discussed in Grand Lodge itself. Thus the Mysteries entered into political as well as into religious life in the old days; and politics were much less selfish in consequence.

There were in Egypt in those days three Grand Lodges of Amen, each of which was strictly limited to forty members, every one of whom was a necessary part of the machine. Including the officers, whose business was the recitation of the Office and the magnetization of the Lodge, each member was the representative of a particular quality. One was called the Knight of Love, another the Knight of Truth, another the Knight of Perseverance, and so on; and each was supposed to become a specialist in thinking and expressing the quality assigned to him. The idea was that the forty qualities, thus expressed through the Lodge as a whole, would make the character of a perfect man, a kind of heavenly man, through whom the power behind could be poured out upon the whole country.

These three Grand Lodges worked three distinct types of Masonry, of which only one has come down to us in the twentieth century. The Master of the first Grand Lodge represented wisdom, and his two Wardens strength and beauty, as in our Lodges today. The predominant power outpoured was that wisdom which is perfect love, the quality that is indeed most needed in the world at the present time. The Master of the second Grand Lodge represented strength, and his Wardens wisdom and beauty, and the strength of the First Aspect of the Trinity was the predominant quality of the Lodge. The Master of the third Grand Lodge typified beauty, and the wisdom and the strength were made subordinate to that third aspect of the Hidden Light.

As every one present had to bear his part in building the form, exact co-operation and perfect harmony were absolutely necessary, and only people who could forget themselves entirely in the great work were selected from the ordinary Lodges to become members of these three Grand Lodges, whose power was such that their influence covered the entire country. The slightest flaw in the character of one of the forty members would have seriously weakened the form through which all the work was being done. It is perhaps a relic of this paramount necessity which dictates our present regulation that any Brn. who are not in perfect harmony with each other should not put on their aprons until they have settled their differences. In ancient Egypt there was an intensity of brotherly feeling between the members of a Lodge which is probably rarely attained now; they felt themselves bound together by the holiest of ties, not only as parts of the same machine, but actually as fellow-workers with God Himself.

The ritual worked by the Grand Lodges was known as *The Building of the Temple of Amen*; a translation of its actual wording will be given in another part of this book. It was indeed one of the most splendid and powerful sacraments known to man. It was celebrated for thousands of years, during which Egypt was a mighty land, but a time came when the egos most advanced in evolution began to seek incarnation in new nations, in which, as in different classes in the world-school, they might learn new lessons. Then this portion of the Egyptian Mysteries fell into abeyance, while the Egyptian civilization grew degenerate and formalized as it became a theatre for the activities of less evolved men.

THE ORDINARY LODGES

There were also dotted all about the country numerous other Lodges, which more closely resembled those of modern times. Their work was much more varied than that of the three Grand Lodges, and they met more frequently, for to them was entrusted the work of preparing their members for higher things, and giving them a liberal education. Their purpose was the same as that of the Mysteries everywhere, to provide a definite system of culture and education for adults, a thing which is not done on a large and public scale in our present day, when the rather curious belief is widely spread that education ends with school or college. The Mysteries were the great public institutions, centres of national and religious life, to which people of the better classes flocked in thousands, and they did their work well, for one who had passed through their degrees - a process of many years - thereby became what we should now call a highly educated and cultured man or woman, with, in addition to his knowledge about this world, a vivid realization of the future after death, of man's place in the scheme of things, and therefore of what was really worth doing and living for.

Even in these ordinary Lodges every member took part in the work, and the labour of those in the columns was regarded as more arduous than that of the officers. Though the latter had special physical actions through which they must go with great accuracy, the former had to use their thought-power all the time. They had all to join at certain points in the ritual in sending out streams of thought, more in the nature of will-power than of meditation, the object of the whole effort being to erect over and around the Lodge a magnificent and radiant thought-form of perfect proportions, specially constructed to receive and transmit in the most effective way the Divine Force which was called down by their act of devotion. If any member's thought was ineffectual, the mighty temple-like thought-form was correspondingly defective in one part; but the Master of the Lodge was usually a clairvoyant priest or priestess who could see where the defect lay, and so could keep his Lodge strictly up to the mark. Thus these Lodges also shared in the same great work of force-distribution, though on a smaller scale than the three Grand Lodges which were specially entrusted with that task.

Without some purpose such as this our great Masonic effort seems unintelligible. We have in nearly all Masonic Lodges a beautiful opening ceremony, full of deep symbolical meaning, and when understood it is seen to be no mere form, but a wonderfully effective formula, calling to our aid various entities, and preparing the way for the performance of a very definite service to mankind. Yet, having opened our Lodge and made all these preparations, we proceed at once to close down, unless we have a candidate to initiate or pass or raise, or a lecture to deliver to our own people. Surely such a wonderful preparation should end in something definite, in a real piece of work for the benefit of mankind.

In ancient Egypt there was this splendid work, the culmination to which all the preparations led up. Our true purpose should be the same. We meet and go through certain ceremonies, and give them the name of work - a name that is quite inappropriate as applied to the mere ceremonies, no matter how full of meaning they may be. But if we are building a grand and beautiful form as a channel for the divine energy, through which the world may be helped, then most assuredly we are doing work, collecting, concentrating and storing up great superhuman forces, and then, with the closing blessing, pouring all that out upon the world. Without this, all the preliminaries are, as it says in the Co-Masonic mystic charge, "like massive doorways, leading nowhither".

There is no reason why we in the present day should not do as much with our ritual as did the ancient Egyptians. Any defects that may stand in the way are to be found not in the outer world, but in the failure on the part of the Brn. to realize the seriousness of the work which they have undertaken, or to rise to the degree of unselfishness that is requisite to ensure regular attendance for the sake of humanity. In Egypt no one troubled the Bro. Secretary with letters of excuse; the Brn. considered their membership the most valuable privilege and blessing of their lives, and were always in the Lodge at the proper time, unless too ill to move. Let us hope that Freemasonry will have a future worthy of its past, and that before long such Lodges as they had in Egypt will be working in many parts of the world.

There are various lines along which the recollection of the way in which the work was done in ancient Egypt may be of use to us, for those people performed their ceremonies with full knowledge of their meaning, and so the points upon which they laid great stress are likely to be important to us also.

Deep reverence was their strongest characteristic. They regarded their temple much as the most earnest Christians regard their church, except that their attitude was dictated by scientific knowledge rather than by feeling. They understood that the temple was strongly magnetized, and that to preserve the full strength of that magnetism great care was necessary. To speak of ordinary matters in the temple would have been considered as sacrilege, as it would mean the introduction of a disturbing influence. Vesting and all preliminary business was always done in the anteroom, and the Brn. entered the Lodge in procession, singing, as Co-Masons do now.

THE HISTORY OF MASONRY

The Mystery teaching of Egypt was very closely guarded, and it was only with great difficulty and under special conditions that anyone not an Egyptian born could be allowed to receive it. Still, it was given to various distinguished foreigners, and among others to Moses, of whom it is said in the biblical story that he was "learned in all the wisdom of the Egyptians". He passed on his knowledge to the Jewish priestly line, and thus it survived in a more or less defective form till the time of David and Solomon.

When Solomon built his temple he erected it on Masonic lines, and made it a centre of Masonic symbolism and work. He unquestionably intended his temple to demonstrate and to preserve for his people a certain set of measurements, in the same sort of way in which all kinds of astronomical and geodetic facts were enshrined in the measurements of the great pyramid.* (*See Ch. II, on the Pillars.) He did not succeed, because much of the tradition had been lost; or it would perhaps be truer to say that while external ceremonial and even the traditional ornamentation had been very fairly preserved, the clue to the meaning of it all was no longer known. Until that time initiates of the Jewish Mysteries had had their attention directed to the House of Light in Egypt; but King Solomon resolved to keep their thoughts and feelings strictly focused upon the building which he had himself erected, and therefore instead of speaking to them of the symbolical death and resurrection of Osiris in Egypt he invented the original form of our present traditional history to take its place. In fact, he Judaized the entire ritual, substituting Hebrew words for the original Egyptian, though in some cases at least preserving the original meaning.

It should be remembered that in doing this he was only bringing the practice of his people into line with that of neighbouring tribes and nations. There were many lines of Mystery tradition, and though the Jews had brought with them across the desert of Sinai much of the Egyptian form, the Tyrians and others preserved rather the story of the descent of Tammuz or Adonis than that of the dismemberment of Osiris. Indeed, Bro. Ward in his latest book on this subject seems inclined to advocate the theory that we as Masons owe comparatively little to Egypt and very much to Syria. In this briefest of outlines of Masonic history I cannot pursue the question further, but I hope to say more upon it in my next volume, *Glimpses of Masonic History*.

It is principally along this line of Jewish descent that Masonry has come down to us in Europe, though there have been other infiltrations. Numa Pompilius, the second King of Rome, who founded the Roman Collegia, established in connection with them a system of the Mysteries which derived its Masonic succession from Egypt; but its ceremonies and teachings were somewhat modified by the migration of the rites of Attis and Cybele to Rome about 200 B.C., and again through the medium of the soldiers returning from the campaigns of Vespasian and Titus. From the Collegia this mingled tradition was handed on through the Comacini and various other secret societies through the dangerous times of the Middle Ages; and when a better age dawned and persecution became less fierce it came to the surface once more. Certain fragments of it were gathered together in 1717 to form the Grand Lodge of England, and so it has come down to us unto the present day.

It should be understood, however, that there is no one line of Masonic orthodoxy. A parallel tradition, coming originally from Chaldean sources, has given rise to Masonry as worked upon the continent of Europe. And yet another line seems to have been brought back by the Knights Templars on their return from the crusades.

The whole subject of Masonic history is one of exceeding interest; but, owing to the fact that Masonry is after all a secret society, it is often almost impossible to trace the line of its descent by means of any documents which are now available, and consequently there is great confusion and contradiction among the various accounts. We have ourselves devoted a good deal of investigation and research to this matter, and I have published some of its results in the book just mentioned, *Glimpses of Masonic History.*

Much of the ancient wisdom has been allowed to slip into oblivion, and so some of the true secrets were lost to the great body of the Brn. But among the Hierophants of the Great White Brotherhood the true secrets have ever been preserved, and they will always reward the search of the really earnest Mason. We, of these later sub-races, may prove ourselves just as unselfish and capable of just as good work for our fellowmen as were the people of old. Indeed, we ourselves may well be those men of old, come back in new bodies, and bringing with us the old attraction to the form of faith and work which then we knew so well. Let us try to revive under these far different conditions the unconquerable spirit which distinguished us so long ago. It means a good deal of hard work, for every officer must do his part quite perfectly, and that involves much training and practice. Yet I feel sure that there are many who will respond to the Master's call and come forward to join in preparing the way for those who are to come.

Let each Lodge make itself a model Lodge, thoroughly efficient in its working, so that when anyone visits it he may be impressed by the good work done and by the strength of its magnetic atmosphere, and may thereby be induced to share in this vast undertaking. Our members must also be able, when they in turn visit other Lodges, to explain our method of working, and show how, from the occult point of view, the ceremonies should be performed. Above all, they must carry with them everywhere the strong magnetism of a completely harmonious centre, the potent radiation of brotherly love.

To us also, as to the ancient Egyptians, the Lodge should be holy ground, consecrated and set apart for Masonic work, never to be used for any secular purpose. It should have an atmosphere of its own, just as have the great medieval cathedrals; as they are permeated by the influence of centuries of devotion, so should the very walls of our Temple radiate strength, broadmindedness and brotherly love.

CHAPTER II.
THE LODGE

FORM AND EXTENSION

IT is customary in speaking of the Freemasonic Lodge to which one belongs to think of a hall or room in an ordinary building in the physical world. Therefore, when its extension is mentioned, the ordinary ideas of its measurements in length, breadth and height come up in the mind. It is necessary, however, to think of much more than that, for the Lodge represents the universe at large, as is explained in the ritual of the Craft degrees of Universal Co-Masonry. In the description of the t ... b ..., we are told that the Lodge is in length from east to west, in breadth from north to south, and in depth from the zenith to the centre of the earth, which shows that it is a symbol for the whole world.

Plate III. PLAN OF THE LODGE

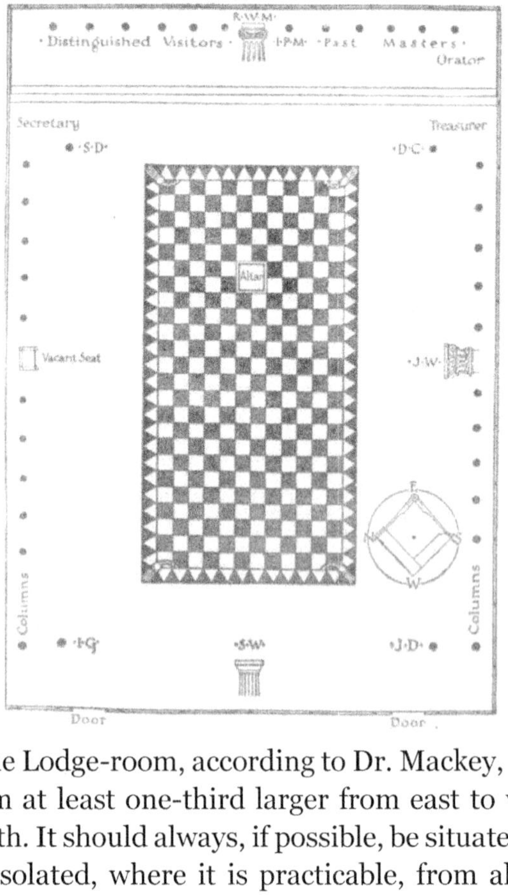

The form of the Lodge-room, according to Dr. Mackey, should be that of a parallelogram at least one-third larger from east to west than it is from north to south. It should always, if possible, be situated due east and west, should be isolated, where it is practicable, from all surrounding buildings, and should be lofty, to give dignity to the appearance of the hall, as well as for purposes of health. The approaches to the Lodge room from without should be angular, for, as Oliver says, "a straight entrance is unmasonic, and cannot be tolerated." There should be two entrances to the room, which should be situated in the west, and on each side of the W.S.W.'s station. That on his right hand is for the introduction of visitors and members and, leading from the T.'s room, is called the T.'s or the outer door; the other, on his left, leading from the preparation room, is known as the "inner door" and sometimes is called the north-west door. Plate III shows the form of the Lodge and the positions of the principal objects in it, as usually arranged by Co-Masons of the British jurisdiction.

The floor of the Lodge, technically speaking, is the mosaic pavement, which will be described among the ornaments of the Lodge. The correct shape for this is a double square - that is to say, a rectangle having a length double its breadth - and the Lodge may be thought of as a double cube standing on this floor. Considered as the entire room, the Lodge is a temple of humanity, and as such it may be taken to symbolize a man lying upon his back. In this position the three great supports correspond to important centres in the human body. The column of the R.W.M. is in the place of the head or brain; that of the W.S.W, corresponds to the generative organs, symbols of strength and virility, and also to the solar plexus, the great ganglionic centre of the sympathetic system; and that of the W.J.W. corresponds to the heart, anciently regarded as the seat of the affections.

ORIENTATION

Three reasons are given in the ritual to explain why our Lodges are set east and west. In the first place, the sun rises in the east, and the sun is regarded in Masonry as a symbol of divinity. Secondly, all the western nations look to the east as the source of their wisdom. Thirdly, the Masons follow the precedent of the temple of King Solomon, which was set east and west in imitation of the arrangement of the tabernacle which was carried by the Israelites in their wanderings through the desert, and was always placed east and west when put down. It is certainly not sufficient to say that the early Masons oriented their Lodges merely because all churches and chapels ought to be so; rather the ecclesiastical rule *spectare ad orientem* was also a rule for the Masons.

As we have already said, the Egyptian origin of Masonry has been somewhat obscured by Jewish influence. When Moses introduced the Egyptian wisdom to the Jews they quickly gave their own colouring to it.

They are a very remarkable race, in that they assimilate readily, but stamp their own decided characteristics upon whatever they take up. In this case, the Egyptians spoke of the great pyramid of Gizeh as the "House of Light", or more commonly "The Light" but the Jews were taught to interpret it as referring to the temple of King Solomon.

The real reason, however, for the careful orientation of the Lodge is magnetic. There is a constant flow of force in both directions between the equator and each of the poles of the earth, and there is also a current flowing at right angles to that, moving round the earth in the direction of its motion. Both of these currents are utilized in the working of the Lodge, as will be explained when we come to deal with the ceremonies. The world at large does not recognize the presence of these forces, which are not of the same order as those which influence a common steel or iron magnet, but there are some people who are sensitive to them to such an extent that they cannot sleep comfortably if they lie across them. Some of these people sleep best with the head to the north, others with the head to the south. Among the Hindus it is considered that only an ascetic should sleep with his head to the north. The householder, the man of the world, should lie with his head to the south.

THE CELESTIAL CANOPY

The ritual tells us that the covering of a, Freemason's Lodge is a celestial canopy of divers colours. This may very well symbolize the star-lit heavens which canopy the true temple of humanity, when we regard the Lodge as universal; but the reference to divers colours indicates another meaning, for the vault of the sky is not of various hues, except at sunrise and sunset, but is blue. The real celestial canopy is the aura of the man whom we have thought of as lying on his back; it is the vividly tinted thought-form that is made during the working of the Lodge. We see this symbolism appearing elsewhere also, in Joseph's coat of many colours in the V.S.L., in the Robe of Glory which the initiate puts on, according to the Gnostic hymn; and also in the Augoeides of the Greek philosophers, the glorified body in which the soul of man dwells in the subtle invisible world. Bro. Wilmshurst in *The Meaning of Masonry* also interprets the canopy as the aura of man, which is surely more reasonable than to suppose with Dr. Mackey that because the early Brn. met on the highest hills and in the lowest vales this symbol must refer to the over-arching vault of heaven.

THE ALTAR

The altar should be in the middle of the square nearest to the R. W. M., though this differs in different Obediences. In the Grand Lodge of England working there is generally no altar at all, or at the most only an appendage to the Master's pedestal; so that when the candidate is taking the O. he kneels before the pedestal of the R. W. M. In some Lodges the altar is a little east of the centre of the floor, and in others it stands in the middle of the floor.

On the altar, or close to it, or hanging above it in the middle of the eastern square, there is in Co-Masonic Lodges a small light burning, usually enclosed in ruby-coloured glass. This light symbolizes the reflection of Deity in matter, and it corresponds exactly to the light in Catholic churches which burns always before the Altar on which the Host is reserved.

Mackey, in his Lexicon of Freemasonry, speaks of the altar as: The place where the sacred offerings were presented to God. After the erection of the Tabernacle, altars were of two kinds, altars of sacrifice and altars of incense.

Fig. 2

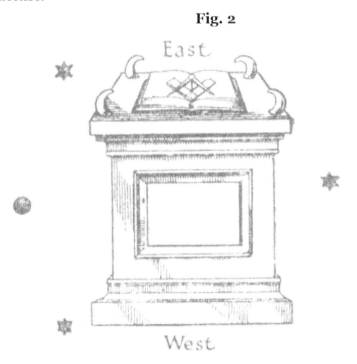

The altar of Masonry may be considered as the representative of both these forms. From hence the grateful incense of Brotherly Love, Relief and Truth, is ever rising to the Great I Am; while on it the unruly passions and the worldly appetites of the Brethren are laid as a fitting sacrifice to the genius of our Order. The proper form of a masonic altar is that of a cube, about three feet high, with four horns, one at each corner, and having spread open upon it the Holy Bible, Square, and Compasses, while around it are placed in a triangular form and proper position the three lesser lights.

Fig. 2 is taken from the same source. The stars represent the three lighted candles and the black dot the vacancy in the north, where there is no light. In our Co-Masonic Lodges we follow the English custom of having the three candles beside the seats of the three principal officers, but they are still in the same relative positions. In this, as in other matters, there is no orthodoxy in Masonry.

The symbol upon the eastern side of the altar is a circle bounded on the north and the south by two lines. In the centre there should be a point - the point within a circle round which a M.M. cannot err. The circle, as shown on the t ... b ..., is drawn the full size of the altar, so that it touches or almost touches the V.S.L. An explanation of this which is often given in Lodge lectures is that as the circle is bounded by two lines, which signify Moses and Solomon, and also by the V.S.L., anyone who keeps himself within that circle and follows the precepts of the V.S.L. as thoroughly as did Moses and Solomon will not err.

In ancient Egypt, however, long before the time of the Jews, it was already a symbol with many meanings. First of all, it was the symbol of the sun-god, Ra; secondly, it bore to the Egyptians the signification of the earth circling round the sun. That was with them a portion of the secret knowledge reserved for the Mysteries. There was a still older tradition, which held the circle to be the equator and the dot in the centre to be the pole-star, whose position changes because of the precession of the equinoxes, in which the Egyptians took great interest. The inclination of the chief passage of the great pyramid was determined by the position of the pole-star of the period. This symbol was used once more to indicate the all-seeing eye - an idea easily suggested by the dot in the middle of the circle.

Another interpretation of the symbol by the Egyptians was particularly beautiful, and all Brn. will find it well worth remembering whenever their eyes fall upon it. The three columns, representing wisdom, strength and beauty, were stated to stand round God's throne, which was the altar itself, which they took to signify love. Thus the circle describes the love of God, and the two lines which bound it are the lines of duty and destiny or, to put the idea in Oriental terms, of dharma and karma. It was said that while a M.M. kept himself within the circle of the divine love, and bounded his actions by duty and destiny, he could not err.

The same device also signifies the first manifestation of the Deity. It was held by the Egyptians there were three successive manifestations; the first aspect far above our reach, the second and third successively lower, and their conception of these three was very similar to that of the Three Persons of the Blessed Trinity in Christianity and the Trimurti among the Hindus; in fact, practically all philosophical religions have recognized the triple manifestation of the Deity. In *The Book of Dzyan* the same emblem, but without the two lines, was used to denote the same reality, the first Logos or Word; while in Christian mysticism it signifies the Christ within the bosom of the Father. It was also considered to be a reflection of the Blazing Star which should be in the centre of the Lodge ceiling, it being in this respect the same as the ever-burning ruby lamp. It symbolized His light that "burns ever in our midst" and "shineth even in our darkness". Some students of Masonry see the same symbol once more in many of the temples of the Druids and Scandinavians, which were formed of a circle of stones with one, generally taller than the rest, in the centre.

PEDESTALS AND COLUMNS

"Our Lodges are supported by three great pillars - wisdom, strength and beauty," says the Masonic ritual, "wisdom to contrive, strength to support and beauty to adorn; wisdom to conduct us in all our undertakings, strength to support us under all our difficulties, and beauty to adorn the inward man. The universe is the Temple of the Deity whom we serve; wisdom, strength, and beauty are about His throne as pillars of His works, for His wisdom is infinite, His strength is omnipotent, and His beauty shines through the whole of the creation in symmetry and order. The heavens He has stretched forth as a canopy; the earth He has planted as His footstool; He crowns His Temple with stars as with a diadem, and from His hands flow all power and glory. The sun and the moon are messengers of His will, and all His law is concord. The three great pillars supporting a Mason's L ... e are emblematical of these divine attributes."

Full-sized columns are rarely erected in any Lodges, but the W.S.W. and W.J.W. have miniature columns on their pedestals, and all three of the principal officers have usually larger columns beside them, upon which are supported their respective candles. In Craft literature various reasons are given for the presence of the three pedestals and for their arrangement. Some say that there are three because King Solomon had two other important people associated with him in the building of the temple; but the deeper fact is that the pillars on the t ... b ... and the columns near the pedestals of the three principal officers are intended to symbolize the three aspects of the divine life in manifestation, which have been spoken of by various religions as the Holy Trinity. In the earliest times inEgypt, as we have already explained, there were three kinds of Grand Lodges, with somewhat different methods of working, according as the R.W.M. represented wisdom, strength or beauty. In our modern days we have only one of these types, in which the Master's pedestal signifies wisdom, and the working is that of the Second Person of the Trinity, the Christ. In the now practically defunct Rite of Swedenborg the chair of the Master represented strength.

In the process of the development of our universe, the third member of the Trinity first exercised His portion of the divine power in preparing the world of matter; then the second Person put forth His energy, and that was the beginning of the evolution of conscious life. This is symbolized in the opening of the Lodge. At first the W.J.W.'s miniature column, which signifies the Third Person and the first outpouring of divine activity, is erect, but at the moment when the R.W.M. declares the Lodge open, that column is laid down and the W.S.W. raises his column to the vertical position. By the authority of the First Person, the Father, the Ruler of the world, the Second Person has now taken charge of the proceedings, and the work of evolution of the powers of consciousness is the order of the day in the open Lodge.

The three pillars, the columns and the pedestals, the candlesticks and candles, all mean the same thing. The column on the desk or pedestal of each of the principal officers of the Lodge is sculptured in a definite order of architecture which signifies his power or quality; his candlestick also is carved in the same design, and often it is depicted upon his candle as well. Our columns and candlesticks are now usually made of painted wood, but in reality they should be of three different kinds of stone; that of the R.W.M. should be of freestone, that of the W.S.W. of granite, and that of the W.J.W. of marble. These three kinds of stone are typical specimens of the three great classes of rocks freestone is aqueous or sedimentary; granite is igneous or plutonic, and marble is metamorphic.

If wooden columns are used, they should be painted to resemble these stones.

Plate IV. THE THREE COLUMS

(a) DORIC   (b) IONIC   (c) CORINTHIAN

ORDERS OF ARCHITECTURE

In looking at any column, there are two principal parts to be considered - the column itself, and at the top of it the entablature which helps it to support the roof. Each of these two parts is divided again into three. The column has its base, then a long thin shaft, then the capital. The parts of the entablature are first the architrave, that comes out above the capital, then the friezes which is a straight piece with ornaments, and above that the cornice. In almost all these points the different orders of architecture vary.

The three orders of architecture in ancient Greece were the Ionic, the Doric and the Corinthian which are now assigned to the R.W.M., the W.S.W. and the W.J.W. respectively. Afterwards two others were added of Italian origin - the Tuscan and the Composite, which we do not use in Masonry. The three columns are shown in Plate IV.

Of the three Greek columns the Doric is the simplest. Its shaft has twenty shallow flutings, and its height is eight times its diameter. It has no base, and the capital is solid and quite plain. In the entablature, which is not usually reproduced in the officers' pillars, its frieze is characterized by triglyphs, representing the ends of joists, and metopes, representing rafters, and its cornice exhibits mutules. This column is considered to be formed after the model of a muscular full-grown man; it shows strength and noble simplicity.

The Ionic column has twenty-four flutings and a length nine times its diameter. Its capital is adorned with two volutes, and its cornice with dentils. It is thought to be modelled with the grace of a beautiful woman, the volutes being suggested by the dressing of her hair.

The Corinthian Column is by far the most beautiful. Its flutings are not different from the Ionic, but its height is ten times its diameter, which gives a slender and very graceful appearance. The capital is ornamented with two rows of acanthus leaves and eight volutes, which sustain the abacus.

The following story is told with regard to the origin of the Corinthian column. A Greek poet and architect named Calimachus once visited a cemetery and saw there the grave of a child, on which an acanthus plant had grown in a manner that struck the poet as so pleasing and beautiful that he had it cut in stone, and it became the original of the form now seen on the capital of every Corinthian pillar. On the grave there was a circular box of toys which had been put there by the nurse of the child in order to please its spirit - for at that time the idea was prevalent that departed spirits were in the habit of visiting their places of burial or sepulture, and were in a position to enjoy the objects placed there for them, or the counterparts of those objects, which thus became their possessions on the other side of death.

On the top of the little box of toys the nurse had placed a flat tile to keep off the rain. It happened that she had put the box upon an acanthus root, and that the leaves had grown up and, when they reached the tile, had turned again to form a kind of fringe round it, with most beautiful effect. The acanthus plant grows wild all over Sicily and the south of Italy and Greece, and is everywhere charming.

The Tuscan column is the plainest of all; it has a perfectly plain base and top, the length of its shaft is only seven times its diameter, and it has no flutings. The composite column, on the other hand, is the most ornate of all, as it is an attempt to combine the beauties of the Ionic and the Corinthian. It has the same number of flutings and the same proportions as the latter, but combines with the acanthus ornament the volutes of the Ionic style.

The three columns are part of the Greek or classic style of architecture, which has always a flat or very slightly sloping roof, no arches, and many pillars arranged in rows, generally with a large shallow triangle, the pylon, at the front of the building. (See Plate V.)

Plate V. GREEK TEMPLE

In the religious architecture of Europe we find mainly the Gothic style. The guilds of Freemasons in the Middle Ages travelled over Europe in wandering bands, which were engaged in building churches. All the great Gothic building was cone, broadly speaking, about the same period, and at that time the famous cathedrals of Europe were erected by the Freemasons, who had the three orders. They were operative masons, but they had their practical secrets, and only they were able to do this kind of work. The Gothic was an entirely new method, departing altogether from the classic, and there is ample evidence to show that Freemasons were responsible for the change. The great cathedral of Cologne, for example, which has been five hundred years in course of erection and is not yet completed, was laid out by a man who signed himself with a sign known only by the M. M., and there are also documents to show that the early part of the building was done by Freemasons. It has the peculiar form of pointed arch, made by the intersection of two rising arches, which characterizes the Gothic style, differing both from the Norman and Roman styles with their rounded arches, and from the Saracenic or Byzantine with its serrated arches and round domes.

MEANING OF THE THREE COLUMNS

I am indebted for the following luminous suggestions to Bro. Ernest Wood. They are an interpretation of the three columns in the light of the principles embodied in his book, *The Seven Rays*, and I commend them to the careful study of the Brn.

In order to understand the full significance of the columns presided over by the three principal officers, we must recall the occult teaching of the great Divine Trinity of Father, Son and Holy Ghost, or Shiva, Vishnu and Brahma. In Their unity They are one Universal God in whom everything exists, whether it be animate or inanimate, for there is nothing but That. But in Their separate appearances, the Holy Ghost is the maker or builder of the outer world, and the Son is the life in all beings, the "light that lighteth every man that cometh into the world". Every material object in the world is part of the being of God the Holy Ghost in this large sense, and every life or consciousness is part of the consciousness of God the Son, who is the manifested Solar Logos. Behind these, invisible and beyond all imagining, is the ineffable glory and happiness of the Father.

Both the Holy Ghost and the Son are in turn triune; wisdom, strength and beauty are the three qualities of God the Holy Ghost, and they form the three supports of the objective world, as they also mark out its three divisions. These divisions are (1) the visible world of material objects, founded in beauty - God in things is seen as beauty; (2) the invisible energy with which the world is filled, and on which all things that are seen are built - this is the strength of God the Holy Ghost; (3) the universal mind, the world of ideas, the storehouse of archetypes, marking out the possibilities of material forms and relationships, which is seen in what the scientist calls the laws of nature - the wisdom of the Divine Architect, His settled plans. These are the three parts of any objective world; they constitute the Lodge, the building, in which life plays its part; and the three Pillars, Ionic, Doric and Corinthian, symbolize these three divisions of the world - the field of consciousness, as it has been called in the *Bhagavad Gita*.

All the living beings which people this world display the light of the divine life and consciousness in their varying degrees. They are all parts of God the Son, the Christ, the great sacrifice, the divine life crucified on the cross of matter. He also is a trinity, and this is seen in the three powers of consciousness appearing in man as the spiritual will, the intuitional love and the higher intelligence, which are the root of all human will, love and thought. Since the officers are the life in the Lodge, they represent these qualities in consciousness, which are called in Sanskrit philosophy Ichchha, Jnana and Kriya. The R.W.M. expresses the divine will of the Christ, directing the work to the perfecting of man; the W.S.W. represents the divine love of the Christ; and the W.J.W. the divine thought. These officers are to be known by their jewels, which represent will, love and thought respectively, not by the columns at which they preside.

Just as material energy is the strength in things, so is love the strength in consciousness; it is what has been called in Sanskrit terminology the buddhi in man, the wisdom that is direct knowledge of life, the energy of consciousness. It is the faculty in man with which he contacts and deals with life around him, while his thought is the faculty with which he deals with objective things. So when at the opening of the Lodge the W.J.W. lays down his pillar and the W.S.W. raises his, it symbolizes the fact that now we are interested in life, we are working upon man, upon consciousness, not upon material objects, as would be the case if we were building a material structure, and not the temple of man, his inner character, his immortal soul. The Great Architect is now building "a temple in the heavens, not made with hands".

Thus the columns represent the three qualities of the material Lodge, but the three principal officers express the three qualities of consciousness or life. Now the assistant officers must be explained. In his inner nature every man is a spiritual consciousness, threefold, as we have seen - but when we look at him in this world we see not the man himself but the body in which he lives, his material house, or rather, to use a more modern simile, his motor car in which he goes about to do the business of his life, to see what he wants to see and to work where he wants to work. That body, trained perhaps for a particular profession, brought up in the special culture of one of the nations, with its manners and habits of action, feeling and thought, constitutes his personality, the mask through which his voice can be heard in the world of outside appearances. This personality is fourfold - there is the physical body, then the etheric double or counterpart of that, then the emotional nature, then the lower mind - the last two constituting his own private storehouse and gallery of personal feelings and ideas. The S.D. stands for the lower mind, the J.D. for the emotional or astral nature; the I.G. for the etheric double, and the O.G. or T. for the physical body.* (*For a fuller study of these principles from this point of view, see Professor Wood's book, *The Seven Rays*.)

According to this interpretation the columns represent the three aspects of the outer world (the world of human tuition), but the three principal officers, who preside at their pedestals, stand for the three aspects of divine consciousness (the inner world of human intuition), as in the following diagram:

Diagram 1

God the Father		God the Son	Pillars of the Lodge	God the Holy Ghost
The Blazing Star				
The Sacred Fire	The Principal Officers	R. W. M. (Spiritual Will)		
		W. S. W. (Intuitional Love)		
		W.J.W. (Active Intelligence)		
The Reflection	The Assistant Officers	S. D. (Lower Mind)		WISDOM (Natural Law)
		J. D. (Desires and Emotions)		STRENGTH (Natural Energy)
		I. G. (Etheric Double) T. (Physical Body)		BEAUTY (God in Matter)

THE PILLARS OF THE PORCHWAY

Referring to King Solomon's temple, the English Craft ritual says: "There was nothing in connection with this magnificent structure more remarkable, or which more particularly struck the attention, than the two great pillars which were placed at the porch or entrance." The ritual goes on to explain that these two pillars were set up at the entrance of the temple to remind the children of Israel, on their way to and from divine worship, of the pillar of fire which gave light to the Israelites during their escape from bondage in Egypt, and the pillar of cloud which proved darkness to Pharaoh and his followers, when they attempted to overtake them.

Their original significance, however, dates much further back than this. It is claimed that these two columns originally represented the north and south pole-stars. They were at first the pillars of Horus and Set, but their names were afterwards changed to Tat or Ta-at, and Tattu, the former meaning "in strength" and the latter "to establish", the two together being considered as the emblem of stability. Tattu is the entrance to the region where the mortal soul is blended with the immortal spirit, and thereby established for ever, as I have already explained in Chapter I. It seems strange that so many authors should speak of the north and south pole stars, when the fact is that there is no star of any consequence at the south pole. The southern pole of the heavens is situated in an unusually barren tract of the sky, and the nearest star of any consequence is that at the foot of the Southern Cross, which is no less than twenty-seven degrees from the pole.

On the tops of the two columns in the very ancient symbolism there were at first four lines or cross sticks, which were symbols of heaven and earth, as in Fig. 3.

Figure 3

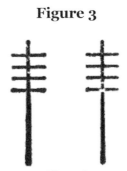

How the four quarters or the square, or rather the two squares, arose may be understood from Fig. 4.

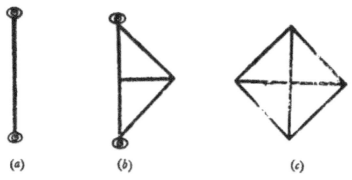

(a)   (b)   (c)

Figure 4

The first symbol shows the two eyes of north and south, with a connecting line. The second shows the line of Shu, where he makes a division at the equinox, and thus forms two triangles of Set and Horus; and the third figure completes the square of the four quarters. It is said that Tattu is thus the place established for ever, a heaven with its four quarters, as Tat represents the earth with its four quarters.

Figure 5

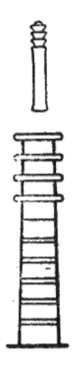

In the hieroglyphs the form has become like Fig. 5, while in the *Papyrus of Ani* it appears as in Fig. 6.

Dr. Mackey has made a special study of these two pillars in their later Jewish form. He speaks of them as memorials of God's repeated promises of support to His people of Israel, since Jachin is derived from Jah, which means "Jehovah", and *achin*, "to establish", and signifies "God will establish His house in Israel," while Boaz is compounded of *b*, which means "in" and *oaz*, "strength", the whole signifying "in strength shall it be established". Mackey thinks that the pillars should be within the porch (which in reality they were not), at its very entrance; and on each side of the gate. It will be seen how exactly the meanings given here correspond with those of the Egyptian names of the same pillars.

We find various descriptions of these columns given in the Christian Scriptures. The references are 1 Kings, vii, 15; 2 Kings, xxv, 17; 2 Chron. iii, 15 and iv, 12; Jer. lii, 21 and Ezek. xl, 49.

Figure 6

A description is also given by the Jewish historian Josephus, and another may be found in Mackey's *Lexicon of Freemasonry*. These accounts differ in various respects, and the details given are so confused that Masonic writers are by no means in agreement as to any but the chief features. I therefore thought it best to take the trouble to make a clairvoyant investigation, the result of which is given in Plates VI and VII. The first of these is what is called a scale-drawing, showing the proportions of the pillar exactly as it was, but as it never could have been seen by any human being, because of its size. The second is an enlarged drawing, of the same character, of the capital (or, as it is called in the

Bible, the chapiter) to show the detail of its somewhat complicated workmanship. There is also a small ground-plan (Fig. 7) of the temple, to show the position of the pillars in relation to the porch. It will be seen that they were not within the porch, but just outside it. This ground-plan has been drawn to scale according to the biblical measurements, but it should be noted that in it no account is taken of any other doors than that of the porchway, or of the curious little side-chapels which King Solomon added; nor is any attempt made to indicate the courts which surrounded the temple.

Figure 7

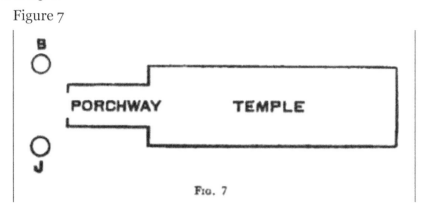

Fig. 7

These pillars are described in the Bible as of brass, but their appearance is much more that of what we today call bronze. The height of the pillar itself is given in all the accounts but one as eighteen cubits, and the chapter which swells out above it is said to have been five cubits in height, but as it overlapped the top to the extent of half a cubit the total height was 22 1/2 cubits. As the cubit is usually calculated to have been eighteen inches, this gives us the total height of the pillar and its capital as 33 feet 9 inches. Its circumference is given as twelve cubits or eighteen feet, which would make its diameter just under six feet. The pillars were hollow, and the thickness of the metal of which they were composed is usually supposed to have been three inches, though it has sometimes been given as four. At the back of each pillar, so that they were not seen at all from the front, were three small doors, one above the other, so that part of the pillar may be thought of as divided into safes, in which archives, books of the Law and other documents were kept.

The chapiters which fit on to the top of the pillars like caps are the most interesting part of these remarkable castings. The ornamentation of these capitals will best be understood from the illustration. The whole chapiter swells upwards in a somewhat urn-like form, with a flat circular disc resting upon it.

Plate VI. A PILLAR OF THE PORCHWAY

The upward curve of the urn is continued through the disc, and makes a projection above the disc which is a segment of a sphere, though this was of course not visible to anyone looking up from the foot of the pillar. It would be more correct to say that the form suggested is not actually a sphere but rather an oblate spheroid, and in the original stone pillar which occupied a similar place in the Egyptian temple, the symbology of which was copied by the Tyrian artificer, this somewhat unusual form was undoubtedly intentional, and was adopted in order to give an idea of the true shape of the earth, which was perfectly well known in ancient Egypt. As will be seen in a later chapter, the Egyptians were quite familiar with the exact measurements of the earth, but in the indication of it in the spheroid of the pillar the polar depression is naturally greatly exaggerated, as otherwise the difference could hardly have been visible. It is known that these pillars were intended to represent the terrestrial and celestial spheres respectively; and in some modern attempts to reproduce them they are crowned with these two globes. In the originals, however, there were no such globes, as the rounded chapiters sufficiently represented them.

It will be seen from the illustration that the surface of the chapiter below the disc is covered with a network, and that the lower ends of the network coalesce into a kind of fringe, from which depend a number of little balls. The Bible account tells us quite accurately that these balls were intended to represent pomegranates, and that there were two hundred of these pomegranates upon each pillar. Superimposed upon the network is a rather curious decoration of chains, hanging in festoons, and there are seven rows of these festoons one below the other. Each loop of chain consists of seven links, and in each case the central link of the chain is much the largest and heaviest, and the links diminish in size and weight as they rise towards the ends of the loop. Along the edge of the disc runs a line of lilies, and from this four chains of the same flowers are represented as hanging straight down the chapter on the north, east, south and west respectively. These flower-chains, however, do not hang loose in the air, but cling closely to the outline of the chapter. Between them two palm-leaves are crossed through the middle link of the central chain in each space.

Entirely apart from this scheme of decoration a very beautifully executed band of flowers is introduced to hide the junction of the chapter with the pillar. This consists of a triple row of lilies; the central row, which exactly covers the edge of the chapter, is composed of fully opened flowers facing outwards from the pillar, with leaves between them, while there is an upper row of tightly-closed buds standing up between the flowers of the middle row and giving an effect not unlike that of the points of a crown. The lilies of the third row hang gracefully downwards from the middle row upon curved stems, and face in various directions.

Plate VII. THE CHAPITER

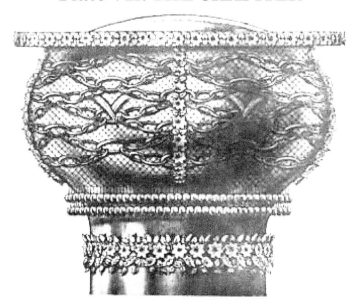

All this, we are told, was the work of H. A., a widow's son of Naphtali - a man described in the biblical account as a cunning worker in brass, who was sent down to Jerusalem by H., K. of T., especially in order to do this and other metal work for King Solomon. Undoubtedly this man was a true artist, for he took an almost inconceivable amount of trouble to carry out his design exactly as he wanted it. So far as the investigators were able to see, his work was based entirely upon a traditional account of the stone Egyptian pillars, which had been handed down from the time of Moses. It did not appear that he had any clear idea of the meaning of all these strange decorations, though Moses knew perfectly well the whole system of symbology which lay behind it.

It is to be understood that all this varied ornamentation was not arranged in *basso-relievo*, as would be expected in a casting; on the contrary it stood out boldly from the face of the pillar, many of the flowers being connected with it only by a comparatively thin stalk of considerable length. Some indication of the patience and care which the artist exhibited may be gathered from the fact that he carved in wood and in full size the entire triple band of lilies to go round the eighteen-foot circumference of the base of the chapiter, and then made his moulds round that wooden carving. Though the general idea of the threefold band of flowers was preserved, the whole thing was arranged in a very natural manner, no flower being an exact reproduction of its neighbour; it was not a mere repetition of a pattern, such as we might have in a modern wallpaper, but the whole conception was carried out as one great unit with the most loving and painstaking care.

Many experiments were tried before this ancient artificer was satisfied, and he adopted various ingenious methods to attain his object. He was anxious to make the whole chapiter and all its decorations as nearly as possible in one casting, and with the primitive appliances at his command this gave him an immensity of trouble. His lilies may perhaps be considered as somewhat conventional; at least they do not exactly correspond to any varieties with which I happen to be acquainted. They were on the whole more like the lotus than like an ordinary lily; but on the other hand the leaves were by no means lotus leaves.

To the ordinary worshipper in the temple all this rather complicated ornamentation was merely decorative, but to the initiate it was full of esoteric significance. First, these two pillars were an exemplification of the occult axiom, "As above, so below", for though they were absolutely alike in every particular it was always understood that they represented respectively the terrestrial and celestial worlds. On Tat, the left-hand pillar, each link of each chain symbolized what in our Oriental studies we call a branch-race, and the links as they descended became larger and thicker to indicate a deeper descent into matter, until the fourth was reached, when the life-force begins to draw inward and upward, and so its embodiment becomes less material.

Each loop of seven links therefore typified a sub-race, and the seven loops which extended round the pillar, making one festoon, correspond to one of the great root-races, such as the Lemurian, the Atlantean or the Aryan. The whole set of seven festoons hanging one below the other denoted one world-period, one occupation of this planet of ours.

Underneath the chain-work a beautifully executed system of fine network will be seen, and this was employed by the priests of old to elucidate yet another side of the marvellous mystery of evolution. When the Holy Spirit has brooded over the face of the waters of space, and has impregnated and vivified primordial matter, the activity of the Second Aspect of the Logos begins, and innumerable streams of His divine life pour down into the field prepared for them. In a thousand ways they interlace and combine, and so produce the bewildering multiplicity of the life which we see around us. From their interaction result the manifold fruits of evolution which we see exemplified in our pillars by the rows of pomegranates which depend from the fringe of the network, the pomegranates being chosen for this symbolism because each fruit contains a prodigious number of separate seeds, thus illustrating the amazing fecundity of nature and the vast variety of her types.

In Tat the lilies represented always the flower of humanity. Arranged in line round the edge of the disc they indicated the Great White Brotherhood the jewels in the crown of mankind, hovering above the human race and directing its evolution. The four pendant flower-chains symbolized the Holy Four who reside at Shamballa - the Spiritual King and His three pupil-assistants, the sole representatives on earth of the Lords of the Flame who came down long ago from Venus to hasten the evolution of mankind. The crossed palm-leaves between them typified the four Devarajas, the principal agents through whom the decrees of the Sons of the Fire-Mist are carried out.

The three bands of lilies which are arranged to hide the junction of the chapiter with the pillar were taken to represent the initiates of the three stages of the Egyptian Mysteries. The buds of the upper row, pointing upwards, typified the initiates of the Mysteries of Isis, who were full of aspiration, reaching upwards and in that way raising the general average of human thought. The flowers of the middle row, opened and facing outwards, were the initiates of Serapis, showing forth by their lives the glory, dignity and power of humanity as it should be. The third row of drooping lilies represented the initiates of the Mysteries of Osiris, reaching down into the world in order to devote themselves to the helping and enlightenment of humanity.

These three grads of initiates seem to correspond in a general way to three other divisions or grades of the occult life which I have described at length in *The Masters and the Path*. There are first those on the probationary path, who are aspiring to enter the Path proper, and are doing everything in their power to purify themselves, to develop their character, and to serve humanity with unselfish love under the guidance of the Masters. Then come those who have been initiated into the Great White Brotherhood, and have thus entered on the Path proper; their lives are dedicated entirely to the service of humanity; in them the bud of human life has opened into flower, and their consciousness has risen into the buddhic principle, which has been described as the truly human expression of man. Thirdly come the Arhats, those who have taken the fourth great Initiation; they are not compelled to reincarnate; if they do so it is quite voluntary; they dip down into human life on this plane simply in order to help.

On Tattu, the right-hand pillar, we take up the tale of evolution where we left it on the other. A single link here betokens one world-period, and therefore includes the whole set of seven festoons on Tat. To use once more the technical terms of Theosophical teaching, the loop of seven links on Tattu stands for what we call a Round, the completed festoon of seven loops is meant to suggest one Chain-period, and the full group of seven festoons equals one Planetary Scheme. The two pillars taken together correspond exactly to the table of evolution and the diagram which I give in the sixth section of *The Inner Life*, and almost the whole of the information contained in that section was taught by the Egyptian priests to their neophytes, and illustrated by means of this elaborate system of chapter decoration. It would be out of place to repeat here the whole of the explanation included in that book, but I would refer to it those students who wish to pursue further this most interesting subject. As there are several editions of the book I am unfortunately unable to give an exact page reference, but the diagram will easily be found.

In Tattu the crown of flowers round the edge of the disc seems to have been taken to symbolize the hosts of the Dhyan Chohans, including perhaps the Planetary Logoi. The four chains of lilies flowing down from that crown bore to the Egyptians a signification connected with the Tetraktys, or perhaps with a reflection or expression of that Mystery, while the triple band of lilies round the lower edge of the chapiter was taken as signifying the action in matter of the three Aspects of the Logos - the buds denoting the action of the Holy Spirit, the Arm of the Lord outstretched in activity, and always pushing upward and onward within the spirit of man, while the middle row was taken as showing the strength of the Father ever shining forth as the sun in his glory far beyond the clouds and mists of earth, and the lowest row betokened the action of the Second Aspect, God the Son, bending down into incarnation and raising humanity from within.

The crossed palm-leaves here indicate the Lipika, the Lords of Karma, who work through the four Kings of the elements symbolized by similar leaves on Tat. They are unconnected with the rest of the design because they represent forces not confined to our planetary scheme, or even to our solar system; they administer a Law which rules the whole universe, which Angels and men alike obey.

The upper segment of the spheroid, beyond the disc, was left entirely bare of ornament, in order to indicate that beyond all that could be symbolized there was yet something more, out of manifestation, and therefore entirely inexpressible.

Another reason for the placing of these two pillars at the entrance of the temple was that the man who would enter the higher world of the Lodge from the common world of every-day life must pass between them; and from this point of view they typified the overcoming in his own lower nature of the turbulence of the personal emotions and the Waywardness of the personal mind. First, his strength for fighting the battle of life came from the emotions, the astral nature; then that pillar of our personal nature, the pillar of Set, had to be conquered by the power of the mind, the pillar of Horus, end conjoined with it in order to add to the strength the stability necessary for going forward to higher things. Only then is the man established in strength, having the power to execute and the wisdom to direct.

The pillars also represent once more the two great laws of progress, karma and dharma, the former providing the environment or material world, and the latter the direction of the self within; by the union or harmonious working of these two laws a man may attain the stability and strength required for the occult path, and map thus reach the circle within which a M.M. cannot err.

Also the pillars were used in the teaching of the priests to illustrate the great doctrine of the pairs of opposites - spirit and matter, good and evil, light and darkness, pleasure and pain, etc.

It is interesting to note that Kabbalistic writers understood these pillars somehow to have represented involution, the descent of the divine Life into lower worlds, though they may not have been familiar with all the details. A treatise named *The Gates of Light* is quoted by Bro. A. E. Waite in this connection as follows:

He who knows the mysteries of the two Pillars, which are Jachin and Boaz, shall understand after what manner the *Neshamoth*, or Minds, descend with the *Ruachoth*, or Spirits, and the *Nephasoth*, or Souls, through *El-chai* and Adonai by the influx of the said two Pillars.

And again: By these two Pillars and by *El-chai* (the living God) the Minds and Spirits and Souls descend, as by their passages or channels.*
(*New Encyclopaedia, II, 280.)

They form also the portal of the Mysteries by which the souls ascend to their divine Source; and it is only by passing through them that the sanctuary of man's true Godhead may be reached, that divine splendour which when aroused in the depths of the heart indeed establishes its dwelling-place in strength and stability.

In the French working two large pillars are placed inside the Lodge on either side of the door, in the West, and the W.S.W. and W.J.P. sit at triangular tables beside these. This arrangement is derived from the Chaldaean system.

Several writers have made persistent attempts to attach a phallic signification to these two pillars; I can only say that in the course of a prolonged investigation by means of the inner sight we found no trace of the attribution of any such meaning.

CHAPTER III.
THE FITTINGS OF THE LODGE

THE ORNAMENTS

"THE interior fittings of a Freemason's Lodge", says the Co-Masonic ritual, "comprise the ornaments, the furniture and the jewels. The ornaments are the mosaic pavement, symbolizing spirit and matter; the blazing star, ever reminding us of the presence of God in His universe, and the indented border, the Guardian Wall."

THE MOSAIC PAVEMENT

The three ornaments all belong to the middle of the Lodge. The mosaic pavement is the beautiful floor, which is composed of squares alternately black and white, and is explained in the Craft ritual as the diversity of objects which decorate and ornament creation, the animate as well as the inanimate parts thereof. Its alternate squares, however, symbolize not only the mingling of living and material things in the world, but even more the intermingling of spirit and matter, or life and matter, everywhere. The double triangles interlaced indicate the same great fact in nature.

Throughout nature there is no life without matter, and no matter without life. Until recent years many scientific people thought that the life side of creation extended only as far down as the vegetable kingdom, but nowadays it is being recognized that it is not possible to draw a line anywhere and say: "Above this things are living and conscious in various degrees, but below it there is only dead matter." The researches made by Professor Sir Jagadish Chandra Bose of Calcutta (recorded in his book Response in the Living and Non-Living) which have won him the highest scientific honours and respect, show that such a line simply does not exist, but that there is some degree of life in the tiniest grain of sand. Some of his conclusions have been stated in brief and effective form in Dr. Annie Besant's well-known work, *A Study in Consciousness*, in the following words:

Professor Bose has definitely proved that so-called "inorganic matter" is responsive to stimulus, and that the response is identical from metals, vegetables, animals, and - so far as experiment can be made - man.

He arranged apparatus to measure the stimulus applied, and to show in curves, traced on a revolving cylinder, the response from the body receiving the stimulus. He then compared the curves obtained in tin and in other metals with those obtained from muscle, and found that the curves from tin were identical with those from muscle, and that other metals gave curves of like nature but varied in the period of recovery.

Tetanus, both complete and incomplete, due to repeated shocks, was caused, and similar results accrued, in mineral as in muscle.

Fatigue was shown by metals, least of all by tin. Chemical re-agents, such as drugs, produced on metals similar results to those known to result with animals - exciting, depressing, and deadly.

A poison will kill a metal, inducing a condition of immobility, so that no response is obtainable. If the poisoned metal be taken in time, an antidote may save its life.

A stimulant will increase response, and as large and small doses of a drug have been found to kill and stimulate respectively, so have they been found to act on metals.

"Among such phenomena," asks Professor Bose, "how can we draw a line of demarcation and say: 'Here the physical process ends, and there the physiological begins'? No such barriers exist."

Psychic experience and trained clairvoyance add their testimony to this conclusion, and affirm that without a shadow of doubt the same kind of life can be seen pulsating in the body of a tiger or an oak tree or a fragment of mineral substance. As *The Secret Doctrine* expressed it:

With every day, the identity between the animal and physical man, between the plant and man, and even between the reptile and its nest, the rock, and man - is more and more clearly shown. The physical and chemical constituents of all being found to be identical, Chemical

Science may well say that there is no difference between the matter which composes the ox, and that which forms man. But the Occult doctrine is far more explicit. It says: Not only the chemical compounds are the same, but the same infinitesimal invisible Lives compose the atoms of the bodies of the mountain and the daisy, of man and the ant, of the elephant and of the tree which shelters it from the sun. Each particle-whether you call it organic or inorganic - is a Life.* (*The Secret Doctrine, I, 281.)

In looking, then, at our chequered pavement, those of us who understand the full significance of it are constantly reminded of the omnipresence of life.

In ancient Egypt the sanctity of the mosaic pavement was guarded with the most jealous care, and it was never invaded except by the candidate and the officers at the proper times, by the I.P.M. in the pursuance of his duties, the S.D. at the obtaining of light from the sacred fire, and the Thurifer when he censed the altar.

The exceeding importance of squaring the Lodge accurately is another aspect of the same idea. The currents of force are rushing along and across that pavement in lines like the warp and woof of a piece of cloth, and also round the edges of it, and anyone who has to cross it, or even come near it, should be careful to move with the force and not against it. Hence the imperative necessity of always keeping to one direction. In modern days less care seems to be taken of the mosaic pavement; I have even seen a case in which the attendance-book, which all have to sign, was placed on a table in the middle of it. With us in Egypt that pavement occupied almost the whole of the floor of the Lodge; now it is often only a small enclosure in the middle of it.

THE INDENTED BORDER

All round the mosaic pavement runs the tesselated border. In older Masonry it is said that it was made of threads twining in and out, but now it is a machicolated border, a sort of dog-tooth arrangement. In the early eighteenth century, we are told, the symbols of the Order were marked out in chalk upon the floor, and this diagram was then encircled with a wavy cord, ornamented with tassels, and was therefore called "the indented tassel", later corrupted into the "tesselated border". The French call it "la houpe dentelée", and describe it as "a cord forming true lover's knots, which surrounds the tracing board". The tesselated border refers us, says the masculine ritual, to the beautiful border formed round the sun by the planets in their various revolutions. The Co-Masonic ritual makes it an emblem of the Guardian Wall protecting humanity, composed of Adepts or men who have attained the perfection of human evolution in past centuries and millennia. They stand around humanity in the spiritual worlds, it is said in a Buddhist scripture, to save mankind from further and far greater misery and sorrow.

There is a similar dual interpretation also for the four tassels which appear in the corners of the border. In masculine Masonry they are usually considered to mean temperance, fortitude, prudence and justice; their significance is always interpreted as ethical. But they stand also for four great orders of devas connected with the elements earth, water, air and fire, and their great Rulers, the four Devarajas, agents of the law of karma, which is always balancing and adjusting the affairs of man, and seeing that there is no injustice between living creatures in God's universe, just as there is no maladjustment in the relations of material substances and bodies. At the initiation of candidates in Co-Masonic Lodges these four Rulers of the elements are invoked, and the consequences of that are very real and beneficial, little as many members of the fraternity may be aware of the fact.

THE BLAZING STAR

The Blazing Star is properly six-pointed, and is made of glass, set in the middle of the ceiling and illuminated from inside by artificial light. Below it there should be another and movable star on the floor. The Blazing Star is the sign of the Deity, and to make that more evident, in the middle of it is usually inscribed the letter G, for God. In the old Jewish form of Masonry they had instead of that letter their sacred word YHVH, standing for Jehovah. In Co-Masonic Lodges the usual form of this figure is a serpent curled round with its tail in its mouth, a symbol of eternity. This was the original form, but the head of the serpent was altered so as to form the letter G. The Sacred Fire below the star is a reflection of it; in some Lodges, as for example at Adyar, in India, it hangs just underneath the ceiling on a pulley arrangement, and is lowered that light may be taken from it and carried to the candles. The Blazing Star also represents the sun, the dispenser of innumerable blessings to mankind and the world in general; but as the sun is the symbol of God there is no difference between these two interpretations. In many Lodges the Blazing Star is made five-pointed, and it formerly had wavering points or rays; this is usual in the English and American Obediences.

The spiritual verity expressed in the Blazing Star and its reflection in the Sacred Fire indicates that God's reflection is ever in our midst. The statement that man was made in the image of God is familiar to all; there is a reflection of God in man more than a reflection. The image of God in man is an expression or continuation of God Himself, for God is the light which carries the image, and insomuch as a man can receive that light in himself and reflect it he is a part of it, one with the Divine. As Emerson beautifully expressed it in his essay on the Over-Soul: "There is no bar or wall in the soul where God the cause ceases and man the effect begins."

Several different kinds of stars are to be seen in the Masonic Lodge, and it is well to consider the special significance of each of them, for there is nothing in the Lodge that is mere ornament, without meaning - on the contrary, even the simplest thing is there for a purpose and has great significance. The six-pointed star is, as we have seen, an emblem of the unity of spirit and matter, of God in manifestation in His universe. The five-pointed star is placed in the east on the wall over the head of the R.W.M. and is called the Star in the East, and also the Star of Initiation. It is the symbol of the perfect man, God manifesting through man, not through the universe as a whole. Man is a five-fold being - physical, emotional, mental, intuitional and spiritual; and when all these parts of his nature are perfectly developed as far as that is possible in a human state of existence, he becomes the perfect man, the Adept, master of himself and the five worlds or planes in which he has his being. Such a man has fulfilled the instruction: "Be ye perfect, even as your Father in heaven is perfect."

On the t ... b ... there is the seven-pointed star above the ladder reaching up into the heavens. It is a symbol of the seven great lines along which all life is moving slowly upwards to completer union with the divine, of the seven ways in which man may realize perfection, and the seven rays or emanations of God through which He has filled the whole universe with the light of His life. This star also typifies the Christian thought of the seven great Archangels, the Seven Spirits who stand before the throne of God. It is likewise another symbol for the perfected man or Adept, because while he is master of the five worlds, he is also the wielder of seven powers; he has developed his nature to human perfection on all seven rays, in all seven of the lines of activity of the divine life.

THE FURNITURE

The furniture of the Lodge is also threefold, and consists of the V. S. L., the square and the compasses. Without them the Lodge cannot legally be held. The Lodge is described as just, perfect and regular: it is just because the V. S. L. is open in it; it is perfect because it contains seven M.M.s or more; it is regular because it holds a warrant or charter from a Supreme Council, Grand Lodge, or other supreme body having an unbroken line of Masonic authority. It is to be understood, of course, that the Volumes of the Sacred Lore are not only the Bible of the Christians, but the sacred books of other religions as well, for the members of a Lodge may and often do belong to various religions. In a Lodge meeting on one occasion in Bombay there were among the Brn. present Christians, Hindus, Buddhists, Parsis, Jews, Sikhs, Muhammadans, and Jains. It is the custom there to place on the altar the sacred books of all who are likely to attend that Lodge. The Rev. J. T. Lawrence, the well-known author of many Masonic handbooks, tells us that he himself has initiated Jews, Muhammadans, Hindus and Parsis, and at least one Buddhist. He writes:

According to a pronouncement of Grand Lodge, the Bible need not be in the Lodge at all. The Volume of the Sacred Law, we have been told, is that which contains the sacred law of the individual concerned. That is to say, it may be the (Quran, the Zendavesta, the Shasters, the Rig-Veda, or any other volume. In the Grand Lodge of all Scottish Freemasonry in India a (Quran-bearer, a Zendavesta-bearer, and the like, are numbered among the officers. (*Sidelights on Freemasonry*, p. 47-50.)

Freemasonry has always been liberal in its views. The Grand Lodge of England has declined to limit or define the belief in God which is expected from every candidate; in the charge concerning God and Religion in the Book of Constitutions of 1815 it is said: "Let a man's religion or mode of worship be what it may, he is not excluded from the Order, provided he believes in the glorious Architect of heaven and earth and practise the sacred duties of morality." It will thus be seen that the ideals of Masonry are very high, and its views extraordinarily tolerant, and that its power for good in the world is unquestionably enormous.

In Co-Masonry the term "lore" is employed as describing all these scriptures, since in the use of them we are in pursuit of wisdom. The term "law" is used in many other Lodges, but even then it is explained in the ritual that the object of the Volume of the Sacred Law is to illumine our minds. So in the three articles of furniture we have the V.S.L. to enlighten the mind, the square to regulate our actions, and the compasses to keep us within due bounds in our relations with all, and especially with our Brn. in Freemasonry. Yet at the same time all these objects have much larger meanings.

With the Egyptians the compasses were a triangle and the square was a geometrical square - the ordinary figure with four equal sides and all its angles right angles. In modern days we use the tool that a working Mason calls a square, by means of which he tests the two adjacent sides of any flat stone to find out whether they are at right angles to each other. In Freemasonry when the candidate is now asked, "What is a square?" he replies: "It is an angle of ninety degrees or the fourth part of a circle." This is obviously not a correct description of a square, but only of one corner of a square.

The square which lies on the V.S.L. has quite a different genesis, and a different reason for its existence, from the implement which is worn by the R.W.M. It was originally a mathematical square, but it has lost its full shape, and is now represented only by one corner of the square. It is usually considered identical with the carpenter's or mason's tool of that name, which is worn by the R.W.M. as the symbol of his office, but the two ideas are in reality quite distinct.

In Egypt the triangle represented the triad of spiritual will, intuitional love and higher intelligence in man; while the square typified the lower quaternary, that is, his body with its visible and etheric divisions, his emotional nature, and his lower mind. Thus the triangle stool for the individuality or soul, and the square; fur the personality, the two together constituting septenary man.

The three articles of furniture were also regarded as intended to help men on their way; the V.S.L. drew attention to the value of tradition, the triangle spoke of the importance of inspiration, and the square emphasized the high use of facts, with also in the background the idea of the value of common sense. The tradition was handed down by the forefathers, the inspiration came from the higher self, and the facts were to be studied and used with common sense.

THE MOVABLE JEWELS

The three movable jewels are the square, the level and the plumb-rule. They are worn, depending from their collars, by the three principal officers, and are then called their jewels of office. They are movable because they are transferred by Master and Wardens to their successors on the day of installation of new officers. The collar was also worn in ancient Egypt, but it was much more nearly circular, like a necklace, instead of being pointed and hanging low on the breast, as it is now worn.

The square is usually considered to represent morality, the level equality, and the plumb-rule uprightness or justice. It will be seen that in this case the term "square" is applied exclusively to the tool, and not to the geometrical figure. In his *Masonic Encyclopaedia*, Kenning mentions that the square was often seen in churches as an emblem of the old operative builders, and that upon an early metal square found near Limerick, in Ireland, the following words and the date 1517 are inscribed:

I strive to live with love and care

Upon the level, by the square.

This seems to show that our speculative interpretations were already known at the early date mentioned.

There is also a translation from an ancient Persian inscription, which runs:

Square thyself for use; a stone that may

Fit in the wall is not left in the way.

The R. W. M. has as his jewel the square, which indicates the Third Outpouring of divine force, from the First Logos, the First Person of the Trinity, and has therefore the same significance as the gavel, his instrument of government. The symbolism of the gavel is very profound; to explain it I must draw attention to what is probably the oldest symbol in the world. (Fig. 8a).

Figure 8

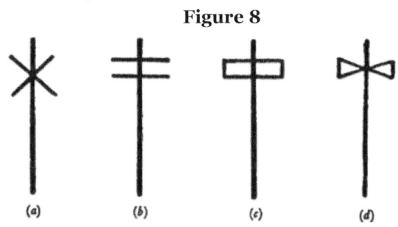

(a)   (b)   (c)   (d)

This long line with two crossed bars upon it has for uncounted thousands of years been the special sign of the Supreme Being. The pygmy race is probably the most primitive at present existing, but even they have that symbol for their chief. Older people will remember the excitement that was caused when the famous explorer Stanley journeyed into the centre of Africa to find Dr. Livingstone, and came back to us with the story of the pygmies living in the forests there. His new s way a confirmation of that which a French explorer, Du Chaillu, had brought some quarter of a century before, but it had not been generally accepted until Stanley's evidence arrived.

That pygmy race is a relic of the old Lemurians, and represents them more purely than any other people. The Lemurians were at one time a gigantic people, but in process of dying out they diminished in size. The African bushmen are also remnants of the same race, but with very mixed blood, and the same thing is true of those who are usually called the Australian aboriginals, except that in their case there is a very alight admixture of Aryan blood.

At one time the pygmies were spread over a great deal more of Africa than at present, and some of them were the first people to enter Egypt when the marshes were partially drying up after the great flood that followed the sinking of the island of Poseidonis some nine thousand five hundred years before Christ. They were driven out a little later by the Nilotic negroes, but that more advanced race was finally dispossessed (and, I think, to some extent absorbed) by the true Egyptians when they returned to their country. As I have explained in Chapter I, the wise men of Egypt had foreseen that there would be a great flood, and the Aryan portion of the Egyptian population had left the country and gone over to Arabia, where it was mountainous. When the returned a long time after the flood they found the Nilotic negroes in possession of their country, and to some slight extent they blended with them; that is the explanation of the traces of negro blood which are found in the ancient Egyptians.

These Nilotic negroes also used the same symbol, but they altered it somewhat; instead of having the two sticks crossed (Fig. 8 a), they laid them across the vertical rod one above the other (Fig. 8 b), thereby making the double cross which is still used by the Greek Church, having come to it via the Coptic Church. But in the meantime another development of this symbol had taken place. If we draw lines joining each of the two ends (Fig. 8 c & d), we get the double axe - the double-headed battle-axe, which appeared when hafting was invented. That was the sign of the chief or king in many parts of the world. Among the Chaldeans, for example, it was the token of Ramu, which was their name for the Supreme God, and one of His titles was the God of the Age. The same symbol was

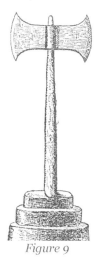

Figure 9

also found among the Aztecs, which shows their connection with Egypt. They represented their chieftain by this symbol of the age, which was their sign for God, because the chief was looked upon as God's representative. There are still tribes in Central Africa among which that double axe has a hut to itself, as a great chief would have.

Quite recently extensive archaeological researches have been made in the island of Crete, and among other things discovered there was this symbol of the double axe, which there also stood for the Deity.[3] In the outer courts of the temples of the great kingdom of Knossos there were many statues, but when one penetrated to

---

[3] Fig. 9 is reproduced (with permission) from an illustration in *The Palace of Minos in Knossos*, by Sir Arthur Evans.

the Holy of Holies there was no statue, but the double age was there set up as a symbol of the Supreme, and was called the Labrys. That is the origin of the word labyrinth; for the first labyrinth was constructed in order that this sacred symbol might be put in the middle of it, and the way to it was confused in order to symbolize the difficulty of the path which leads to the Highest. The stories of the Minotaur and Theseus and Ariadne came much later than this. Until these recent discoveries the Greek word "labyrinth" was marked as a foreign word of unknown derivation.

The gavel of the Master of the Lodge has descended from that, and it is held by the Master because in his humble way, in the symbolism of the Lodge, he is representing the Deity. It is a sign of government, and is held by him in exactly the same way as it was long ago by the first of the Pharaohs. It has now become modified in shape, and often takes the form of the mason's stone-hammer. The name gavel came from the word "gable", so that name belongs to an object of this later shape, rather than to the old double-axe.

In Egypt the double axe was also the sign for Aroueris, the first name given to the risen Horus, and Horus was called the Chief of the Hammer because this sign was sometimes drawn as a hammer. One of the old Egyptian gavels is still in existence, and there may be others also which have not been identified for what they are. That one is in the possession of the H.O.A.T.F., who uses it today in His own Lodge. It is the gavel which was used by Rameses the Great in Egypt - a most lovely implement of green jade inlaid with gold. With it the H.O.A.T.F. also has a cloak which was used by Rameses when acting as Master of his Lodge; I do not know its material, but it somewhat resembles the feathered cloaks which used to be worn in Hawaii.

The square of the I.M. is equally an instrument of government, as is indicated in its use as the seat of Osiris in the Judgment Hall, mentioned in Chapter I (Plate II-b) From it Osiris governs or judges the souls of men who are brought before him, and decides as to whether they are sufficiently perfect to pass onward. From this we have our modern idea of acting on the square; that is to say, with perfect justice to our neighbour.

The figure is in this case the working mason's square, an angle of ninety degrees, used for testing the sides of a stone to see that they are at right angles to each other, and that therefore the wall built of them will stand perpendicular, safe and strong. The difference between the two kinds of squares will now be clearly seen. The quadrilateral is intended when we speak of the compasses as dominating the square, but this right angle is signified when we refer to the tool wherewith the Master measures and decides. Although the R.W.M. has this symbol of the square, he is in fact the Son governing and judging on behalf of the Father, who remains in the background, since our Lodges are of the Christ or Sun-God type.

In Egypt they had a symbol of very great significance, called the Arrow of Ra, which includes both the square of the R.W.M. and his gavel of office. (Plate VIII)

Plate VIII.
THE ARROW OF RA

In our plate the different parts are separate, but sometimes they are joined together, and then one gets the effect of an arrow, whence it is named the Arrow of Ra, the Sun-God, who was also called Horus of the Double Horizon, the Son of Osiris and Isis, and yet a reincarnation of Osiris, God in evolution. The lower portion of the drawing refers to His descent into matter, the inverted square signifying descent, and the angle beneath symbolizing the cavern of matter into which He went down. The upper square then indicates that He ascended or rose again. The symbol in the centre - that of the double axe - is that of the Most High God; so the complete glyph is thus a kind of symbolic creed, which for those who drew it affirmed their faith in the descent of the Deity into matter and His final triumphant ascension from it: "descended He; ascended He". If we were to interpret it along lines of Christian symbology we might call it the emblem of the crucified and triumphant Christ; but it is also a token of the whole method of evolution.

This device appears in many places. It is to be seen in the museum of the Louvre in Paris, engraved upon a Chaldaean intaglio made of green jasper. It is also to be found on the walls of some very old churches in Devonshire and Cornwall in England, where it must have been engraved by the wandering Freemasons who built those churches, for the orthodox Christians could have known nothing of it.

While we are considering the symbols of the R.W.M. we may note also the three levels which appear upon his apron in place of the three rosettes. These are not true levels, but figures formed of a perpendicular line standing upon a horizontal - an inverted T, thus ⊥. This has the same significance as the W.S.W.'s column standing erect while the W.J.W.'s is recumbent in the open Lodge; it indicates that the life of the Second Logos, the Christ, is flowing. It is not that the life of the Third Logos, which is represented by the horizontal line, or by the W.J.W.'s column, has ceased to flow (it is flowing always while an external world exists) but that the Second Aspect of the Divine is also outpouring His life, and causing the evolution of living forms. Thus this emblem refers to the two outpourings, and shows that the Master presides over all three representations.

This figure, called the Tau, has another very important meaning, for the upright line signifies the masculine element, and the horizontal line the feminine, in the Deity - thus slowing that God manifests as Mother as well as Father, as we are told in *The Stanzas of Dzyan.** (**The Secret Doctrine*, vol. I, p. 59 *et passim*.) I shall refer to this again later when writing of the H.R.A. In ancient Egypt it took to a large extent the place of the cross and, conjoined with the circle or oval, it became the ankh, the symbol of everlasting life.

The jewel of the I. P. M. resembles that of the Master in that it contains the square, but it has certain important additions. The jewel of the I.P.M. in England was formerly a square on a quadrant, but it is now the forty-seventh proposition of Euclid's Book I, engraved on a silver plate suspended within a square. In the United States it is a pair of compasses extended to sixty degrees on the fourth part of a circle, with a sun in the centre. The proposition is of course well known, and a practical application of it is widely used by builders, in laying out walls at right angles to each other and in other work, in the form of a triangle having its sides in the ratio 3 : 4 : 5, the first two sides of which are invariably at right angles. Plutarch says that a triangle of this kind was frequently employed by the Egyptian priests, who regarded it as a symbol of the universal Trinity, Osiris and Isis being the two sides at right angles to each other, and Horus their product, the hypotenuse. The extent to which this measure was used by the Egyptians can be judged from the following extracts from the *Exposition du Systeme Metrique des Anciens Egyptiens* of M. Jomard, as given in Dr. Mackey's *Lexicon*:

If we inscribe within a circle a triangle, whose perpendicular shall be 300 parts, whose base shall be 400 parts, and whose hypotenuse shall be 500 parts, which, of course, bear the same proportion to each other as 3, 4, and 5; then if we let a perpendicular fall from the angle of the perpendicular and base to the hypotenuse, and extend it through the hypotenuse to the circumference of the circle, this chord or line will be equal to 480 parts, and the two segments of the hypotenuse, on each side of it, will be found equal, respectively, to 180 and 320. From the point where this chord intersects the hypotenuse, let another line fall perpendicularly to the shortest side of the triangle, and this line will be equal to 144 parts, while the shorter segment, formed by its junction with the perpendicular side of the triangle, will be equal to 108 parts. Hence, we may derive the following measures from the diagram: 500, 480, 400, 320, 180, 144, and 108; and all these without the slightest fraction. Supposing, then, the 500 to be cubits, we have the measure of the base of the great pyramid of Memphis. In the 400 cubits of the base of the triangle we have the exact length of the Egyptian stadium. The 320 gives us the exact number of Egyptian cubits contained in the Hebrew and Babylonian stadium. The stadium of Ptolemy is represented by the 480 cubits, or length of the line falling from the right angle to the circumference of the circle, through the hypotenuse. The number 180, which expresses the smaller segment of the hypotenuse, being doubled, will give 360 cubits, which will be the stadium of Cleomedes. By doubling the 144, the result will be 288 cubits, or the length of the stadium of Archimedes; and by doubling the 108, we produce 216 cubits, or the precise value of the lesser Egyptian stadium. In this manner, we obtain from this triangle all the measures of length that were in use among the Egyptians.

For the demonstration of the proposition in general, that in a right-angled triangle the sum of the squares on the two shorter sides is equal to the square on the hypotenuse, the modern world is indebted to Pythagoras. It is interesting that as the I. P. M. stands in the Lodge as a watcher to see that all is in order, and test everything by his judgment, so does an architect test the rectangularity of a structure by the triangle of ratio 3 : 4 : 5. It is he who also declares that "His light is ever in our midst", pronouncing his final authority upon the presence of the Divine, and opening the V.S.L.

The W.S.W.'s jewel is the level, an emblem of the equality and harmony which he must endeavour to preserve among the Brn. in the Lodge; but, as we have seen, this is also a symbol of the second member of the Trinity, the universal Christ-principle, the life-force in evolution. The two ideas, are not, however, inconsistent, for in Christ all men are brothers, since all lives are part of the one great Life in which we have our being. The most perfect equality should exist in the Lodge, just as in the sight of God, who treats all equally, with the same judgment and according to the same laws. An additional interpretation of this symbol is that it indicates that only those buildings which are erected on a good level can stand firm and strong.

Figure 10

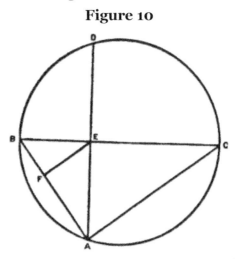

The W.J.W. has the plumb-rule as his jewel. It is taken as an emblem of the rectitude which should mark the conduct of the Brn. during the time of refreshment, when they are outside the Lodge. Such conduct at all times leads to a life that is full of grace and beauty.

The remaining officers also wear jewels of office. Those of the Orator, Secretary, Treasurer and D.C. are respectively a book, crossed pens, crossed keys and crossed wands, of which the meaning is obvious. In Co-Masonry, the S.D. and J.D. have each a dove as their jewel, signifying their quality as messengers; but in some other Lodges they have a square and compasses, with a sun in the centre for the S.D. and a moon for the J.D. The square and compasses are intended to indicate their qualities of circumspection and justice, for theirs are the duties of seeing to the security of the Lodge and the introduction of visitors. A lyre, a purse, crossed swords, and a single sword, are once more obvious as the jewels of the Organist, the Almoner, the I.G., and the T. respectively. The jewel of the Stewards is the cornucopia. They take their appointment from the W.J.W., provide the necessary refreshments, collect dues and subscriptions, and make themselves generally useful. It is said that the horn of plenty should remind them that it is their duty to see that the tables are properly furnished, and that every Bro. is suitably provided for.

THE IMMOVABLE JEWELS

The t ... b ... and the rough and perfect ashlars are called the immovable jewels, because they lie open and ever present in the Lodge, so that they may reflect the divine nature, and serve at all times for the Masons to moralize upon. In some Masonic books, however, especially those published in America, the square, the level and the plumb-rule are called the immovable jewels, because they are always in the same place in the Lodge, and the t ... b ... and the rough and smooth ashlars are spoken of as the movable jewels, because they can be moved about.

In the description of the t ... b ... which is given in some rituals we are told that it is for the Master to lay his plans upon. It is, however, obvious that it is not precisely suitable for that purpose, because it is already very fully occupied with the plan or drawing of an ideal Lodge. What is intended is simply that the R.W.M., with the assistance of the other Brn. assembled, should bring the Lodge down here as closely as possible into harmony and accurate relation with the ideal Lodge. It means that as T.G.A.O.T.U. has laid His plans up above, so should we down here make ours as nearly as may be in harmony with His and in imitation of them. To put it in other terms, the t ... b ... was intended to mean the plan in the thought of the Logos, which the Greeks called the "Intelligible World". They said that all things came down out of that into the world which we know, that everything is planned out beforehand, and that the world existed in the divine thought before it materialized. In the Lodges of two centuries ago, the t ... b ... was drawn afresh on the floor with chalk for each meeting, instead of being printed; and it was considered part of a good R.W.M.'s knowledge that he should be able to draw it quickly and quite perfectly without having to look at a copy.

In the diagram of the t ... b ... we see the altar, and on it the V.S.L. From that a ladder goes up to the seven-pointed star, which represents the Monad in man, in whom the seven types of life or consciousness are all to be perfect to the limits of human possibility. That star represents also the Logos, the supreme consciousness of our solar system, God's consciousness, which is already perfected in a degree altogether beyond human comprehension.

The ladder has many steps, which indicate the virtues by means of which we may ascend to the perfection symbolized by the star. In Egypt those steps were taken to express the initiations leading upwards; but of course these are only two interchangeable methods of expressing the same thing. If we take them to mean initiations, they represent definite steps taken, but if we regard them as indicating the virtues, they are the qualifications for initiation. In all cases the idea of degrees leading up to a condition of perfection is quite definitely recognized. Or it may be considered in another way, as Bro. Wilmshurst takes it in his wonderful book *Masonic Initiation*, in which he writes:

It is a symbol of the Universe, and of its succession of step-like planes reaching from the heights to the depths. It is written elsewhere that the Father's house has many mansions; many levels and resting-places for His creatures in their different conditions and degrees of progress. It is these levels, these planes and sub-planes, that are denoted by the rungs and staves of the ladder. And of these there are, for us in our present state of evolutionary unfoldment, three principal ones; the physical plane, the plane of desire and emotion, and the mental plane, or that of the abstract intelligence which links up to the still higher planes of the spirit. These three levels of the world are reproduced in man. The first corresponds with his material physique, his sense-body; the second with his desire and emotional nature, which is a mixed element resulting from the interaction of his physical senses and his ultra-physical mind; the third with his mentality, which is still further removed from his physical nature, and forms the link between the latter and his spiritual being. ...

Thus the Universe and man himself are constructed ladder-wise, in an orderly organized sequence of steps; the one universal substance composing the differentiated parts of the Universe "descends" from a state of the utmost ethereality by successive steps of increasing densification, until gross materialization is reached; and thence "ascends" through a similarly ordered gradation of planes to its original place, but enriched by the experience gained by its activities during the process.

It was this cosmic process which was the subject of the dream or vision of Jacob. ... What was "dreamed" or beheld by him with supersensual vision is equally perceptible today by any one whose inner eyes have been opened. Every real Initiate is one who has attained an expansion of consciousness and faculty enabling him to behold the ethereal worlds revealed to the Hebrew Patriarch as easily as the uninitiated man beholds the phenomenal world with its outer eyes. The Initiate is able to see the angels of God ascending and descending; that is, he can directly behold the great stairway of the Universe, and watch the intricate but orderly mechanism of involution, differentiation, evolution and resynthesis constituting the Life-process. He can witness the descent of human essences or souls through planes of increasing density and decreasing vibratory rate, gathering round them as they come veils of matter from each, until finally this lowest level of complete materialization is reached, where the great struggle for supremacy between the inner and the outer man, between the spirit and the flesh, between the real self and the unreal selves in veils built round it, has to be fought out on the chequer-work floor of our present existence among the black and white opposites of good and evil, light and darkness, prosperity and adversity; and he can watch the upward return of those who conquer in the strife and, attaining their regeneration and casting off or transmuting the "worldly possessions" acquired during their descent, ascend to their Source, pure and unpolluted from the stains of this imperfect world.* (*Op. cit. pp. 64-66.)

On the ladder appear three emblems, a cross, an anchor, and a cup with a hand stretched out to reach it. The explanation of the t ... b ... in the ritual speaks of these as the three principal virtues, faith, hope and charity. Strictly speaking, the standard symbol for charity is a heart, and this does actually appear on some t ... b ... s instead of the cup; but the cup is the more ancient symbol, and really means much more to us.

Another and a very beautiful interpretation of the cross upon the ladder is given to us by Bro. Wilmshurst, who takes it to represent all the aspirants who are engaged in mounting that ladder. He says:

Each carries his cross, his own cruciform body, as he ascends; the material vesture whose tendencies are ever at cross purposes with the desire of the spirit, and militate against the ascent. Thus weighted, each must climb, and climb alone; yet reaching out - as the secret tradition teaches, and the arms of the tilted cross signify - one hand to invisible helpers above, and the other to assist the ascent of feebler brethren below. For, as the sides and separate rungs of the ladder constitute a unity, so all life and all lives are fundamentally one, and none lives to himself alone.* (*Op. cit. p. 69.)

These three symbols also refer once more to the three outpourings of the divine life, which have their correspondence in the development of the self in man. First he has to realize the world of material things, then that of consciousness or life, and finally he must rise to the real self. Since Egyptian times both the cross and the anchor have been modified, but the cup has not. The cross was originally what is now called the Greek cross, with equal arms. That has always been the token of the first outpouring of divine life through the Third Aspect of God, or the third member of the Trinity, called among the Christians God the Holy Ghost, and sometimes the Life-Giver, who brooded over the waters of space.

A further point in the symbology is that the cross contains within itself the square, the level and the plumb-line combined; and we find in the *Epistle to the Ephesians* written by St Ignatius (who according to tradition was the little child whom Christ once took and set in the midst of His disciples as a type of those who should inherit the kingdom of heaven), this remarkable Masonic passage:

Ye are stones of a Temple, which were prepared beforehand for a building of God the Father, being raised to the heights by the working-tool of Jesus Christ, which is the cross, and using for a rope the Holy Spirit, your faith being a windlass, and love the way leading up to God.

Sometimes the rose is impressed upon that equal-armed cross, and then we have the Rose Croix, the great emblem of the Rosicrucians, which figures largely in the Eighteenth Degree. The Maltese cross is another form of it, with the arms widening or spreading out, conveying the idea that the force that is pouring out is constantly increasing. Again, we find it with flames shooting out from the ends of the cross; and when it is in active revolution, with the flames trailing at right angles to the arms of the cross, we have the well-known form called the swastika.

In these days the cross on the ladder is usually drawn in the Latin form, which makes it a sign of the Second Outpouring, from the Second Person of the Trinity, and it is usually considered as the cross of Christ, though crosses of many forms were used as symbols thousands of years before Christ incarnated in Palestine. The First Outpouring, typified by the Greek cross, prepares the world for the reception of life; it brings into being the material elements, but not bodies formed by their combination. We might have oxygen and hydrogen produced by this outpouring, but not their combination, water; for combination of the elements into bodies of ever-increasing complexity of organized structure and function is the work of the Second Outpouring of the divine life or power.

The Second Outpouring is indicated by the anchor, for that was originally in Egypt a little pendulum swinging over a scale, curved to coincide with the arc of its motion. It is not difficult to see how that might be changed into an anchor, especially among people who were thinking of the cross and anchor as representing faith and hope. Such a modification may easily have come about without deliberate intention; and when it had been determined that the third virtue should be charity, we can understand why the cup was sometimes changed into a heart. The cup may stand also as suggesting charity, as being the cup of life from which the overflow is charity; but many people would feel the heart to be an easier symbol for that virtue.

Those who have read Greek philosophy or the Gnostic systems will remember that the *krater* or cup plays a prominent part in them. It was the vessel into which the wine of the divine life was poured. In Christian thought it is the Holy Grail filled with the precious blood of Christ; the chalice used at the institution of the Holy Eucharist, the cup which Joseph of Arimathea is supposed to have held to catch the sacred blood of Jesus as He hung upon the cross. All these things are, however, an allegory. The real meaning of the symbol is that the cup is the causal body of man, and the wine is the life from God that flashes into it in the Third Outpouring from the First Logos, at the moment of individualization, which makes the animal into a human being, not perfected yet, of course, but capable of perfection.

So the three symbols represent the respective gifts of the divine life, or three great emanations of the Logos. In Egyptian times the Greek term Logos did not yet exist, and they spoke of Osiris and Horus, but the teaching was the same, for there is only one fundamental truth about these things. The t ... b ... thus shows that the man who intelligently comprehends the scheme of the evolution of life in the world can deliberately co-operate with the divine plan, until he becomes perfectly evolved as man and reaches the seven-pointed star; and that then he is ready to pass on into still higher conditions, which are indicated on the t ... b ... by the clouds, the sun, the moon and the stars above. In fact, true philosophy discerns the plan drawn by T.G.A. on the Tracing Board of Time for the building of the Universe.

The remaining jewels, the rough and smooth ashlars, are seen in the t ... b ... near the pillars which represent the columns of the W.J.W. and W.S.W. respectively. The smooth ashlar is generally suspended from a pulley, and held by the lewis, (See fig. 11.) an implement consisting of wedge-shaped pieces of steel which are fitted into a dovetailed mortise in the stone to be hoisted. This instrument was so named, by the architect who invented it, in honour of the French King Louis XIV. One who is the son or daughter of a Mason is called a lewis (because he is supposed to support his parents in their old age), and it is generally held that he may be initiated into Masonry when only eighteen years old. Though some assert that this can be done only by special dispensation, the custom is to regard it as a right.

Figure 11

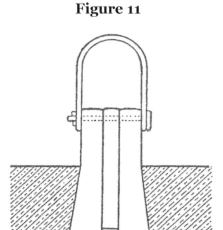

The rough ashlar indicates the untrained mind of the candidate. He is supposed to be in a state of darkness and ignorance, but gradually through Masonic work and knowledge his mind will be polished, and it may then be tested by the square, the plumb-rule and the level, and will be found accurate. The smooth ashlar represents the condition which should be attained by the F.C. In the light of evolution and reincarnation we may regard the rough ashlar as the symbol of the young soul. Through much experience and effort life after life he must polish his nature and develop his powers. The three degrees in Masonry represent three stages in that process. The business of the E.A. is to take himself in hand morally and conquer the physical body, so that its impulses will not stand in the way of his rapid progress or evolution. The E.A. of Egypt used to remain seven years in the First Degree, because he had to fit himself thoroughly for the illumination which could come only to one who had his emotions under control and sufficiently purified to reflect and serve the higher self. That being done, the smooth ashlar was to be perfected until it was ready to be used as a living stone in the temple of T.G.A.O.T.U., fit to form part of the heavenly Man of the future.

CHAPTER IV.
PRELIMINARY CEREMONIES

THE CO-MASONIC RITUAL

IN commenting upon the ceremonies of Freemasonry I shall take those of Co-Masonry as the basis of my disquisition, because they have been arranged largely with a view to their effect on planes other than the physical. The workings there described were prepared with the aid of several of the best existing rituals and in consultation with experienced Brn. They will be found to embody some of the best points of these rituals, in addition to many valuable features peculiar to our own workings. It has been found eminently desirable to give to the Brn. in the columns a larger share in the working of the Lodge, so certain verses of the V. S. L. and some well-known Masonic hymns have been inserted for their use.

The Supreme Council of Universal Co-Masonry has with the utmost liberality and the widest tolerance allowed those who owe their allegiance to it to choose between several variants of the Ritual. Some Lodges prefer the simplest form, which is practically identical with that used by the masculine Craft; others find a slightly more elaborate working more inspiring and helpful, because it expresses somewhat more fully the work upon inner planes which is to them the main object of the ceremony. It is this latter working which I am about to try to expound; but I wish to make it perfectly clear that the interpretation which I place upon it is my own private opinion only, and that the Supreme Council under which I have the honour to serve must not in any way be considered as endorsing that opinion because it permits the use of the Ritual.

It must not be supposed that the shorter Masonic ritual of the masculine Craft is ineffective; all that we claim is that the objects of the various ceremonies are more fully and more expeditiously achieved when their real intention and signification are thoroughly understood.

THE PROCESSION

Everywhere on the surface of the earth there are great magnetic currents passing both ways between the poles of the earth and the equator, and others coming at right angles to them round the earth. The Co-Masonic procession of entry into the Lodge makes use of these currents, forming of the space which we circumambulate a distinct eddy or specially magnetized portion of space.

As the Brn. march round the floor, singing, they should be thinking of the words of the introcessional hymn and canticle, and taking care that the procession is well done and in good order; but in addition they should be deliberately directing their thoughts to the magnetization of the mosaic pavement and the space above it. In ancient Egypt it was considered to be the duty of the R.W.M. to direct the currents and form the eddy in them, so as to magnetize very strongly the floor round which he passed. It is for this purpose that the officers and distinguished visitors pass clear round the Lodge, and even go over some of the ground twice; for they do not go straight to their places on first approaching them as do the E.A.s, the F.C.s and the M.M.s, but continue so as to complete the circumambulation, as described in *The Ritual of Universal Co-Masonry* (5th Edition).

With us also it is the Master of the Lodge who is responsible for the magnetization of the double square, but the Brn. ought all to help in that work. The object is to charge that space heavily with the highest possible influence, and to erect a wall round it in order that the influence may be kept in place. The part played by the thought-form is much like that of a condenser. It matters not how much steam may be generated, it is useless for work unless it is enclosed and kept under pressure. In this scheme we accumulate and use the force which otherwise would scatter itself freely over the surrounding neighbourhood.

As has been explained in Chapter III, when the floor has thus been set apart and prepared, no one passes across it except the candidates who are taken there for the purpose of initiation and are intentionally submitted to the influence of its magnetism, the Thurifer when he is censing the altar, and the I.P.M. when he goes down from the dais to perform the duty of opening the V.S.L. or of altering the position of the s ... and c ... as we change from one degree to another. One other exception is made when the S.D. during the ceremony of lighting the candles comes to the altar to receive the sacred fire from the I.P.M. The I.P.M. lights a taper at the sacred fire, and with it kindles the small candle standing in an ornamental brass vessel, which the S.D., as Lucifer, carries to the R.W.M. and the W.W.s.

The floor has now rushing across it magnetic currents or lines of force like the warp and woof of a piece of cloth, and this forms the foundation upon which we build the great thought-form which is one of the objects of our Masonic meeting. In view of the enormous value of the thought-form made on the floor of the Lodge, we can see how important it is that none should disturb or confuse the currents by walking in the wrong direction, or by bringing into the Lodge thoughts of ordinary business- the cares and worries and conflicts of the world of daily life. We go to the Lodge to do a definite piece of work for humanity, and we must devote our entire attention to it during the whole time of the meeting.

The singing of the introcessional canticles is intended to help us to harmonize our minds. The words of the canticles tell us of the basis upon which all edifices are built, T.G.A.O.T.U., who is Himself the foundation and structure of all things, because there is nothing that is not part of Him. Every member, as he goes round in the procession, should be dedicating himself and all his thought and strength to the great work about to be undertaken. These words that we sing have a strong Masonic association, for this metrical version of the hundredth psalm has been used at the opening of Lodge Canongate Kilwinning ever since its foundation in 1723. There is one word in that version to which I want to make special reference in passing. In the first verse, where we sing "Him serve with mirth", some uncomprehending hymnologist has changed the word "mirth" to "fear", which is entirely inaccurate and utterly indefensible. In the Bible we are asked to praise the Lord with gladness and come before His presence with a song, and we must be careful to preserve the correct spirit and rendering. The other canticle: "I was glad when they said unto me: we will go into the house of the Lord", consists of texts taken from the V.S.L., put together so as to form a beautiful and appropriate invocation.

All this dedicated thought forms the basis of the splendid edifice which the Lodge is about to build, the true temple of which the earthly one is an outer symbol, a temple of finer matter through which perfectly real work can be done and enormous volumes of spiritual influence can be distributed. This temple is also an image of the vortex which T.G.A.O.T.U. made when He was about to form His solar system. He began by limiting Himself, by marking out the limitations of His system, within which He set up a vast etheric vortex, the remains of which we find today in the system of revolving planets condensed from the original nebula, as it cooled and descended into denser physical matter.

In Co-Masonic Lodges the procession has at its head a Thurifer swinging a censer, giving off the smoke from aromatic gums specially compounded with other substances for the purpose. After him comes the T. with his sword, and behind him the D.C. That little group is especially entrusted with the business of purifying the Lodge. The D.C. is supposed to be the directing brain in this work, and the T. with his sword is the hand used to drive out of the mental and emotional atmosphere all thought that is not wanted there.

Behind this purifying wedge come all the ordinary members, arranged in reversed order of precedence. At the end of the procession come the officers and those of higher degree, and eventually the R.W.M., who has to complete the work of all those who have gone before him, using the devotion which the other people have supplied, and building the walls of the *cella* as far as possible with the material available. The form that we are building is that of the old Greek temple with the columns outside it, and inside the inner shrine called the *cella*, which was enclosed and dark, the only opening being its entrance. In the Lodge the members stand outside around that, like the columns of an old temple, such as that shown in our illustration (Plate V).

THE APRON

Every Mason at a Lodge meeting must wear the distinctive badge which is called an apron, and it is only when doing so that he is, in Masonic parlance, "properly clothed". He may wear additional decorations, such as collars or jewels, indicating the special office which he holds, or the degree which he has taken, but unless he wears at least the apron he cannot be admitted to the Lodge - the only exception being in the case of a candidate for initiation, who, not being yet a Bro., has no right to wear that distinguishing badge. There are certain higher degrees in which the apron is not worn, but its place is taken by other insignia. That is only because the need for it is past. There are some Lodges in which people put on and take off their aprons in the temple, but that should never be countenanced.

The necessity that Masons should be properly clothed brings with it an interesting suggestion of the ancient Mysteries, and also explains why the essential part of the Masonic clothing, to be worn by all with the exceptions above mentioned, is the apron. Our modern apron has departed somewhat from the form used in ancient Egypt; no doubt it was modified at the time when it was found necessary to merge the speculative and operative Freemasons, in the days of persecution by the Church. The ancient Egyptian apron (See Plate I, and Fig. 12.) was triangular, with the apex upward, and its ornamentation differed in several respects from that used at the present time. But the most important change is in the thought that now prevails, that the apron itself is everything, and that the band which passes round the body exists merely to secure it and retain it in place.

Figure 12

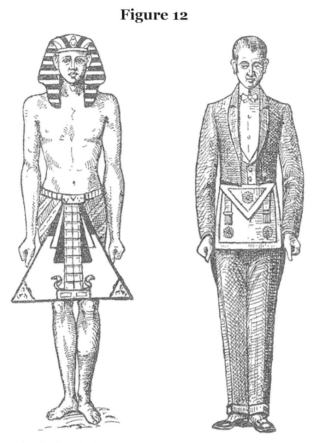

In old days the belt of the apron was the most important practical feature, and it was far more than a mere symbol. This belt was a highly magnetized circle, intended to enclose within itself a disc of etheric matter, separating the upper part of the body from the lower, so that the tremendous forces which it was the object of the Masonic ceremonial to set in motion might be entirely shut off from the lower part of the man's body.

In *The Meaning of Masonry, p.21,* Bro. Wilmshurst writes:

Masonry is a sacramental system, possessing, like all sacraments, au outward and visible side consisting of its ceremonial, its doctrine and its symbols which we can see and hear, and an inward, intellectual and spiritual side, which is concealed behind: the ceremonial, the doctrine and the symbols, and which is available only to the Mason who has learned to use his spiritual imagination and who can appreciate the reality that lies behind the veil of outward symbol.

He reminds us how, in the case of the E.A., the point of the apron is turned up, making it therefore a five-pointed figure, symbolical of the fivefold man. The triangle made by the uplifted flap, he explains, is then above the square, and it symbolizes the fact that the soul is hovering over the lower body at that stage, but yet can hardly be said to be working through it. Later on that flap is turned down, showing that the soul is within the body and acting through it. He tells us also how the lambskin is first of all a symbol of purity, but also typifies the blankness of the undeveloped soul, or of what in Theosophy is called the causal body. In that, as some of us know, in the course of development a great quantity of glorious colour shows as new vibrations are awakened in it. Some account of that will be found, illustrated with coloured plates, in *Man, Visible and Invisible.*

Bro. Wilmshurst further explains that the pale sky-blue colour of the rosettes on the F.C. apron and the blue lining and edging and silver tassels of the M.M.'s apron indicate that at that stage the blue of the sky begins to break through the whiteness that innocence, however beautiful it may be, is being replaced by knowledge to some extent, and as the higher degrees are reached more of colour and beauty appears. He especially mentions that there are two lines of influence, or spiritual force, which come down from above, each ending in seven silver lines - a kind of tassel - indicating the seven colours of the spectrum. These are really symbolical of the seven great divisions or varieties or temperaments of life. In American Masonry, according to Mackey's *Encyclopaedia* (Article: *Apron*) the apron is the same in all the three degrees of Blue Masonry, being made of white lambskin with a narrow edging of blue ribbon. Co-Masonry follows the usage prevailing in the Grand Lodge of England, save that instead of sky-blue for the edging and rosettes, an edging of deeper blue with a narrow border of crimson is prescribed, and the rosettes are made of similar material. The tassels are gilded instead of silvered, and their seven lines symbolize the seven rays of life and the seven grades of matter. Our illustrations give an idea of the M.M. aprons as worn in Egypt and at the present day. (Fig. 12.)

THE CEREMONY OF CENSING

When all have taken their places the ceremony of censing begins. The Thurifer advances to the pedestal of the R.W.M., who places upon the charcoal in the censer some incense which he has previously magnetized, or better still, he magnetizes the incense as it is melting in the censer, for that is the condition in which it is most responsive to his power. As the ceremony is not known in some Lodges I reprint it here from the Co-Masonic ritual:

During the ceremony appropriate music is played, the Brn. remaining standing. When all are in their places, the Thurifer advances to the pedestal of the R.W.M., who places upon the charcoal in the censer some incense which he has previously consecrated. The Thurifer steps back and bows to the R.W.M., who returns the bow. He then censes the R.W.M., with three triple swings *** *** *** the chains being held short and the censer extended at the level of the eyes, but slightly lowered after the first and second sets of triple swings. The censer is then grasped firmly by the chains in the right hand, and swung with full chain (if space permits) in the form of a V, three long dignified strokes to the right of the pedestal, then three to the left. Then, with the arm extended in front, the censer is swung in seven graduated circles, each circle above the other, so that by the time the seventh and smallest circle is made, the arm is raised to its full height. The Thurifer bows again to the R.W.M., and then passes directly to the altar, which he encircles, beginning at the E., swinging the censer at short chain with a circular motion. He then returns to the R.W.M.'s pedestal, bows and squares the Lodge to the W.J.W.'s pedestal, where the ceremony which took place at the previous pedestal is repeated, save that the W.J.W. receives five swings of the censer, one triple and two single *** * *. A pause is observed between single swings, just as between triple swings. He next passes to the W.S.W.'s pedestal, censing him in identical fashion, save that he receives seven swings, two triple and one single *** *** *. The Thurifer now turns to the J.D., bows to him, and after the bow has been returned, censes him with three single swings * * *, after which they bow as before, and the Thurifer squares the Lodge to the S.D., who is censed in a similar manner, but with four swings, one triple and one single *** *. The Thurifer now censes the distinguished visitors according to their rank, beginning with those of highest dignity (nine swings for 33°, seven for 30°, five for 18° and visiting P.M.s.-the swings to be divided as above), bows as he passes the R.W.M.'s pedestal and censes the P.M.s (the I.P.M. receives seven swings). He then takes up his position before the Master's pedestal, having returned directly thereto; then, having bowed to him, he turns and faces the Brn., bows to them collectively, and (himself remaining stationary) censer them successively, beginning with those on his left hand, and ending with those on his right. This is accomplished by a number of short swings, aimed down the S., column and up the N. in rapid succession. The Brn. stand with the hands joined before the breast and the palms laid together, and bow successively as the gaze of the Thurifer meets theirs. This ceremonial should be carefully carried out, each Bro. bowing a moment later than his predecessor. The above-mentioned position of the hands should be adopted by all officers while they are being censed. The Thurifer squares the Lodge and passes to the position of the I.G., whom he censes with two single swings * *; then he hands the censer to him. The I.G. censes the T. with a single swing *, and then hands the censer to him. The whole ceremony should be carried out as briskly as is consistent with dignity; there should be no unnecessary delay. As the Thurifer censes the different pedestals the Brn. should unite in thought upon the three principles which they represent R. W.M. - Wisdom; W.S.W. - Strength; W.J.W. - Beauty. This should also be done while the candles are being lighted at each pedestal. When the altar is reached the thought should be on the Unity of Brotherhood.

The censing of the pedestals in this manner produces in front of each of them a highly magnetized cone, or beehive-shaped form, in which the candidate stands when he comes before any of the pedestals. It is erected for that purpose, and can be stretched when several candidates come together, but it becomes a little tenuous if the number is large. The censing of the officials is intended to prepare them for the work which they have to do. The varied number of swings is given not only to honour the person, but to strengthen him for his work, and it does so by setting up a line of communication with the forces of the inner planes. The higher the man is in degree, the more does he himself give in proportion to what is received. The Master gives most of all, but the columns receive more than they give; yet each one should try as the Thurifer turns to him to give as much as he possibly can.

This use of incense is perfectly scientific. All occult students are aware that, as was said in the last chapter, there is no such thing as really dead matter, but that everything in nature possesses and radiates out its own vibration or combination of vibrations. Every chemical element has thus its own set of influences, which are useful in certain directions and useless or even hostile in others. It is in this way quite possible, for example, to mingle certain gums which, when burnt as incense, will strongly stimulate the purer and higher emotions; but one could just as easily make another mixture whose vibrations would promote the most undesirable feelings. This is a matter about which some people are sceptical, because humanity is at present passing through a stage in its evolution during which its development is almost exclusively that of the lower mind, which is fiercely intolerant of anything which it has not specially studied. We all know how difficult it has been until quite lately to gain any recognition for non-physical phenomena, such as those of telepathy or clairvoyance, or indeed anything outside the most materialistic science.

Now the time has come when men are beginning to see that life is full of invisible influences, whose value can be recognized by sensitive people. The effect of incense is an instance of this class of phenomena, as is also the result of the use of talismans and of certain precious stones, each of which vibrates at its own rate and has its own value. Such things are not usually of importance so great that we need give much time to their consideration, but they all have their effects, and are therefore not to be entirely neglected by wise people.

The incense used in the Lodge tends to purify that part of man's nature which is sometimes called the astral body, as it is made of gums which give off an intensely cleansing vibration. In this respect its effect is analogous to the sprinkling of a disinfectant, which will spread about in the air and destroy undesirable germs, though in this case the operation is on higher levels and in finer matter. It has also the effect of attracting denizens of the inner worlds whose presence is helpful to our working, and of driving away those which are unsuitable.

Two of the most important constituents of such incense as is useful for our work are benzoin and olibanum. The benzoin is a vigorous purifier, and tends to drive away all coarse or sensuous feelings and thoughts. The olibanum has nothing to do with that, but it creates a devotional and restful atmosphere, and tends to stimulate those vibrations in the astral body which make people responsive to higher things. Attar of roses is also useful, and adds greatly to the effect produced.

If the incense is intelligently magnetized its strength is increased enormously; for example, by putting into olibanum the definite force of the will in the direction of calmness and devotion, its influence may be increased by perhaps a hundredfold. That is why the incense in church is always taken up to the celebrant to be blessed, and why in the Lodge it is brought to the R.W.M. in order that he may magnetize it with whatever special quality he thinks will be helpful for the work of the day. The sprinkling of holy water in a church is another way of producing a similar effect, but incense has the advantage that it rises into the air, and wherever a single particle goes the purification and blessing is borne with it.

It is desirable on all occasions, and especially in Lodge, in the interests of the work, that the Brn. should have in their minds but a few definite and strong vibrations of emotion and thought; but instead of that they sometimes have forty or fifty small vortices of emotional and mental activity all whirling at once, each representing some small worry or care or desire. It is difficult for a person to do good work while these are present, and almost impossible for him to make real progress in the evolution of consciousness. If he is trying to attain a better emotional and mental condition, the incense will offer him a strengthening current of vibration which will help very much in combing out the tangle and producing calm and steadiness.

We sometimes find that there is much prejudice against the use of incense, because it is supposed to be connected exclusively with the ceremonies of the Roman Church, for it is only there and in some of the higher Anglican churches that Western people ever see it. Those who have travelled in the East, or are interested in the study of other faiths, know that practically all the religions of the world use incense in one form or another. It appears in the temples of the Hindus, the Zoroastrians, the Jains, and in the Shinto of China and Japan. It was used in Greece, in Rome, in Persia, and in the ceremonies of Mithra. All these people, including the Roman Catholics, avail themselves of it because they know it to be a useful thing; why then should not we?

For a time in England there was a very strong puritan wave, shortly after the Reformation, which led to the murder of King Charles, to the Commonwealth and to Cromwell's rule. True, there was a reaction at the time of the Restoration, but the puritan feeling seems to have been of the most intense kind, and traces of it still remain in England, some of them showing themselves in the most amazing and unreasoning prejudice.

That feeling has sometimes entered Masonic circles, and efforts have been made to induce the Grand Lodge to limit the definition of the Great Architect, so as to exclude the possible association of Masonry with non-Protestant beliefs. But the Grand Lodge has liberally refused to create any such limitations. Under the Grand Lodge of England incense is prescribed for the ceremony of consecrating a Lodge* (*See *The Chaplain's and Organist's Work*, by the Rev, J. T. Lawrence.) and the Consecrating Officer and the Wardens are censed, though no definite number of swings appears to be laid down. Incense is also used in the

Consecration of a Chapter of the Holy Royal Arch, under the Supreme Grand Chapter of England, and in the ceremonial of many of the higher degrees. Thus its introduction into Co-Masonic Lodges is in no way an innovation, but is in full accordance with Masonic usage.

The number of swings given to each of the non-official Brn. indicates his particular rank in the Order, for the degrees of the Ancient and Accepted Scottish Rite are taken into account in Co-Masonry. Each thus receives the influence he needs, that he may be strengthened for the work which his rank qualifies him to do. Each Bro., as he is censed, bows out of respect, and as a token that he dedicates all the force that he has to T.G.A.O.T.U.

LIGHTING THE CANDLES

The S.D. is the Lucifer, who bears the light to his fellow-men. The light having been given to him from the Sacred Fire by the I.P.M., he carries it to the R.W.M., who by means of a small taper lights from it the tall candle standing on his right, and then puts out his taper with an extinguisher. He must not blow it out, because that would suggest the pollution of the sacred fire by the breath, which is unclean. It is for the same reason that the Parsis, who are sometimes called fire-worshippers, because they regard that element as the greatest symbol and expression of the divine, will on no account pollute it with refuse. The R.W.M. says: "May the light of wisdom illumine our work" (here he lights his candle); "His wisdom is infinite." The S.D. then carries the light to the W.S. and J.W.s, who light their candles and speak appropriately of the strength and the beauty of T.G.A.O.T.U.

In this ceremony we are reminded once more of the three Aspects of T.G.A.O.T.U., and here they are symbolized as coming forth from the unconditioned into conditioned form in the order of wisdom, strength and beauty, in preparation for the opening of the Lodge, the commencement of the work of the building of the temple. When the work begins, as we shall see in the next chapter, the process is reversed, but here we have only the preparation, the coming forth of the wisdom to plan, the strength to execute, and then the beauty to adorn.

The use of fire in ecclesiastical or Masonic ceremonies is but little understood. The lighting of a candle with religious intention is analogous to a prayer, and always invokes a downpouring of force from on high. Thus the three principal officers, in uttering these phrases as they light their candles, are not only announcing in symbol that they represent certain Aspects of the divine, but are actually opening the way to a definite link with those Aspects, which is made in response to their request. The electric lights which are used instead of candles in some Lodges do not produce the same effect; they give light, but not fire, and therefore fail of their full result. Electric light is, however, permissible for the Blazing Star and the Star of Initiation, where the action and the symbolism are solely that of the light.

What I have said before about the assistance that should be given to the officers by the Brn. applies here most emphatically. When the R.W.M. says: "May His wisdom illumine our work," all should join with him in a strong effort to call down the divine wisdom, so that through him it may pour out upon the Brn. So also when the W.S.W. says: "May the light of strength sustain our work," all should think earnestly of the divine strength, and send up an aspiration that it may flow through him; and once more a similar effort is to be made when the W.J.W. says: "May the light of beauty make manifest our work," and the I.P.M. declares: "His light dwelleth ever in our midst."

We must not attach to these thoughts the old, and I think false, idea of prayer - that we need to beseech the attention of T.G.A.O.T.U. We know that He is always sending down His force; it is our business to open the channel. His symbol down here is the sun, which is always pouring out light and life and glory without being asked to shine. In the utterance of these words, therefore, we are only seeking to make ourselves and the Lodge channels for His service.

During all these processes the thought of the Brn. is important, but most of all when the altar is censed should they think of the divine love. It falls to the R.W.M. to direct the whole work and to each of the officers to bear his part, but the full success of the scheme depends upon the recollectedness and unselfishness of every Bro. in the Lodge. Without that there is no real life in the work. It is to be feared that in many Masonic Lodges, though their work is deeply coloured by the great ideal of charity, there is an entire failure to radiate the spiritual influence. They perform the ritual accurately and beautifully, but they have not realized how much depends upon the thought given to it, and the comprehension of all that it means and implies. The blessing of the Great Architect is invoked not so much by the mere formula of words and acts, as by the spirit that underlies the work of the Lodge.

CHAPTER V.
THE OPENING OF THE LODGE
THE BRETHREN ASSIST

WHEN the ceremony of lighting the candles is completed, the Brn. take their seats, and the R.W.M. asks them to spend a few moments in aspiration to T.G.A.O.T.U., earnestly resolving that the work to be done that evening shall be well and thoroughly done, and that each member shall never forget that he is doing it in His name and to His glory.

The R.W.M. then gives a single k ... k and calls upon the Brn. to assist him in opening the Lodge. Some may ask why he needs their assistance in so simple an act as declaring the Lodge open; but the fact is that it is by no means so simple as this. The opening of a Masonic Lodge is in itself an exceedingly beautiful and interesting ceremony, and the success of the evening's work depends upon its being properly and thoroughly done. The work before us is no light matter, for it is nothing less than a concerted effort to carry out the duty that is laid upon us, as those who possess the Light, to spread that Light abroad through the world, and actually to become fellow-labourers with T.G.A.O.T.U. in His great plan for the evolution of our Brn.

He pours spiritual strength into the world just as the sun pours out its light; but as there are many dark places in the world which the sunlight cannot directly reach, so are there many souls in the world who are unable to receive and assimilate this divine force. As man by means of mirrors can reflect the sunlight into a cave or cellar, so also can man reflect the spiritual light upon those darkened souls, and perchance present it to them so that they may be able to receive it and profit by it. All light in the world is but transmuted sunlight; if we burn coal and make gas, or if we burn oil in a lamp, the energy is none the less converted solar energy.

The Great Architect sends forth His power at all levels, but most of all on the higher planes. But the majority of men are not yet sufficiently developed on those higher planes to be directly affected by this force. If, however, those men who are already somewhat developed at those levels will lay themselves open to receive that force, and slow down its vibrations by passing them through their own subtle bodies, it can then be poured out upon the world at large in an assimilable form. And this is a great part of the work that is being done by all those who wish to co-operate with Him.

I have explained in *The Masters mad the Path* how one who approaches a Master of the Wisdom with a view to becoming His pupil and working under Him for the good of mankind, is first drawn into a wonderfully intimate association with that Master, so that he may become a perfect channel for the distribution of spiritual forces. Precisely the same thing on a much smaller scale is being done by every human being who wishes well to his fellow-man. Being developed somewhat above the average, he is able to receive and to profit by some at least of these forces, and he assuredly pours them out again on lower levels in good-will and kindly feeling. The ceremonies of all great religions aim at producing such results on a larger scale by some sort of common action. In *The Science of the Sacraments* I have explained the mechanism of this common action as far as the great Christian services are concerned; and the ceremonies of Freemasonry attain a similar object, though in a different way.

The Christian service begins by building a great thought-form to act as a kind of storage-battery or condenser for this force, in order that as it is gradually generated it may be stored up for use instead of being allowed to dissipate itself uselessly in the ambient air; and we in Freemasonry have to take the same precaution. In both cases we invoke the aid of non-human entities - the inhabitants of those subtler planes, who are thoroughly accustomed to deal with and control the forces belonging to their respective levels; but there is a certain difference between the methods adopted in the Christian religion, and in the old Egyptian Mystery-faith from which Masonry is derived.

In Christianity we invoke great Angels who are far above us in spiritual unfoldment, and place ourselves to a considerable extent in their hands, supplying them with the material of love and devotion and aspiration which the service calls forth from us, and leaving them largely to do the form-building and the distribution.

In Freemasonry also we invoke angelic aid, but those upon whom we call are nearer to our own level in development and intelligence, and each of them brings with him a number of subordinates who carry out his directions. All around us there is a vast unseen evolution, which may be thought of as parallel to our own.[4] And just as our line of progress passes through the vegetable kingdom, the animal kingdom and the human kingdom, and then carries us on to the superhuman developments of

---

[4] See plate, "The Evolution of Life" in *The Hidden Side of Things*, vol. i, p. 116 (1st edition)

Adeptship, so does that parallel evolution run through the various elemental kingdoms, the kingdom of the nature-spirits, and then the kingdom of Devas or Angels. There are many levels of intelligence and holiness in this great angelic kingdom; and while it stretches upwards to heights far above those at present attainable by human beings, it has also members who are hardly at a higher level than our own.*

(*In the course of involution the Second great Outpouring of divine Life descends from the Second Logos into the matter already vivified by the Third Logos. Very slowly and gradually this resistless life pours down through the various planes, spending in each of them a period equal in duration to one entire incarnation of a planetary chain - a period which, if measured as we measure time, would cover many millions of years. As a whole, this life-wave is spoken of as monadic essence when clothed only in the atomic matter of the various planes at different stages of its descent. When it energizes the matter of the higher mental plane, it is known as the First Elemental Kingdom. When it descends to the lower or rupa levels of the same plane it is the Second Elemental Kingdom, and on the astral plane it is the Third Elemental Kingdom. Even when this monadic essence first comes before us, in the earliest of the elemental Kingdoms, it is already not one monad, but very many - not one great life-stream but many parallel streams, each possessing characteristics of its own. The monadic essence ensouls the matter of the sub-planes below it on each plane or division of a plane, and thus forms the Elemental Kingdoms. It is the same life that goes on into the mineral kingdom, and then begins to ascend, and proceeds through the vegetable and animal kingdoms until, upon its junction with rays from the life of the First Logos, human beings are formed. See Man, Visible and Invisible, Chapter vi.)

Those, however, are only the lowest members of the angelic kingdom; next below them in development come the highest of the nature-spirits, in the same way as the highest members of the animal kingdom come only just below the lowest human beings; and indeed in many cases the kingdoms overlap, for the most intelligent of the animal kingdom are frequently superior in many respects to the most degraded of human beings. In the Church service we invoke the great Archangels - beings very far above ourselves - though they also have their cohorts of assistants at a level much below their own; in Freemasonry we call rather upon beings at our own stage or slightly above it, and they bring with them assistants from the kingdom of the nature-spirits and even of the elementals.

In both cases the work is initiated by someone who is specially qualified and set apart to do it; in the Church the priest; in Freemasonry the R.W.M. Still, the assistance of the brethren present is always a matter of importance and significance. In ecclesiastical circles they often speak of the priesthood of the laity. Certain things the priest is commissioned to do, and only he can do them. But he requires the help and co-operation of the laity in order that he may work at the highest degree of effectiveness. It is exactly the same with the Master of a Masonic Lodge; he also has certain work to do, and unless there are other P.M.s. present, he is the only man who can do it; but it will be done better and more easily if the Brn. understand and co-operate.

I remember well that when first I was elected R.W.M. of my Mother Lodge, I had to do all the magnetization in the opening procession myself; I had to march round the Lodge, making an eddy in the flowing forces, building the preliminary thought-form and filling it with a strong current of magnetism. Presently I explained matters to some of the older members of the Lodge and told them how they could help in this work, and when they got into the habit of doing so I found that it made my own labours very much less.

But remember that what the H.O.A.T.F. wants is not a sort of bored acquiescence, but cordial co-operation. He wants the members really to be thinking vividly all the time and keeping their minds on what they are doing. If we hear the same thing over and over again, there is a certain tendency for it to become a matter of course, so that people give only half of their attention to it. That is not the way to get the best results; we must fig our minds strongly upon what we are saying and what we are doing. Only the officers have to give the responses at the opening of the Lodge, but every member ought to know these responses by heart. When we come to the temple, we come for a definite purpose-not to get, but to give; and the amount that we are able to give in the way of spiritual force and help depends largely upon the intentness with which we fix our thought upon what we are doing, and the amount of definite understanding that we bring to it. It means a considerable mental effort, no doubt; but it is very well worth while to make it.

When the R.W.M. asks for the assistance of the Brn. he also means that they should specially prepare themselves to co-operate in the work of the evening, and this important preliminary is achieved by his next questions.

TYLING THE LODGE

The Brn. being upstanding, the R.W.M. begins the proceedings by asking from the W.J.W. (carefully addressing him by name, and not using the title of his office) the characteristic question which is the keynote of every Masonic meeting: "What is the first care of every Freemason?" and receives the traditional reply: "To see the Lodge close tyled." He continues: "Direct that that duty be done." The W.J.W. passes on the command to the I.G., who goes to see that the T. is at his post, and reports that he is, this report being at once passed on to the R.W.M.

What is the symbolism here? The first requisite when we are about to do a great piece of work is to concentrate upon it, and in order to do that we must be free from interruption; so the fortress of Mansoul (to adopt John Bunyan's picturesque terminology) needs a strong wall all round outside, and our entrance must be well guarded. Therefore the Spirit calls to the intelligence, which is its link with the lower worlds; the intelligence asks the etheric double, who in turn signals the dense physical body to know how things look from the outside, and receives the satisfactory reply that all the defences are in order, so that the Spirit is reassured on the important point that the Lodge may labour in safety.

Each one of us has to tyle his own Lodge on various levels, and this must be done with great care and wisdom. Through thousands of years of past evolution each man has been learning to build a strong shell for himself, so that within it he may grow into a powerful centre, capable of radiating spiritual force upon his fellows. Inevitably in the earlier stages of that growth he becomes a self-centred being, thinking and caring only for his own interests - tyling his Lodge indeed, but shutting out from it much that is noble and beautiful. Only by degrees does he learn that power is given to him for use in the service of others, and that while he must so tyle his Lodge as always to maintain the strong centre of consciousness which he has been at such pains to create (because without that centre he would be useless in the work of the world) he must at the same time watch ceaselessly to see that the force generated in that centre is employed only in the helping of mankind and in the furtherance of the designs of T.G.A.U.T.U. The man does not lose his individuality and initiative, but he learns to use them rightly.

The man must learn to tyle the Lodge of his mental body; but this must be done with discretion and indeed with exceeding great care. We often find the physical world uncomfortably crowded, especially if our lot imposes upon us the necessity of living or working in one of the great cities. But we must remember that the astral and mental worlds are also crowded - very much more so than the physical, although not quite in the same way. Those finer worlds have far greater extension than the physical, and also in them bodies freely interpenetrate one another. So the crowding is not of the same nature; but nevertheless, we need to shield ourselves even more strictly on those higher levels than down here.

It is not only that on the mental plane there are many millions of people. It is also full of centres of thought on all kinds of subjects, which have been established mostly by men like ourselves. We who are students are earnestly trying to raise ourselves somewhat above the thought of the average man; therefore a very large proportion of all this insurgent thought which is so constantly pressing upon us is at a lower level than our own, and we require constantly to guard ourselves against its influence. There is such a vast ocean of thought upon all sorts of utterly unimportant subjects that, unless we rigidly exclude it, we shall find ourselves unable to concentrate upon the higher subjects about which we really wish to think. Therefore in that respect we must tyle the Lodge of the mental body and must exercise great care to whom and to what we open its doors.

There are also other respects in which care is necessary on the mental plane. For example, there are many who are cursed with an argumentative nature. Such men throw open the doors of their mental fortress and rush eagerly out to battle on the slightest provocation, or on none at all - quite forgetting that they thereby leave the fortress undefended, so that any thought-forces which may happen to be in their neighbourhood can enter in and possess it. While they are wasting their strength in wrangling over points of no importance, the whole tone of their mental bodies is being steadily deteriorated by the influences which are flowing into it. Such a man should learn to tyle his mental body, so that only those thoughts may enter it which he as an ego really approves.

The Lodge of the astral body must be tyled also, for it is even more difficult to resist the surging of emotions than the pressure of thoughts. The majority of emotions in the world are ill-directed, being motived by selfishness in some one among its many protean forms - jealousy, envy, pride, anger, or intolerance. To keep our own feelings pure and high, to retain the philosophical calm which is as necessary for right feeling as it is for right thinking, we must sternly tyle the Lodge against all this vast ocean of unnecessary excitement. Yet on the other hand we must take great care that we never fail in true sympathy. Our ears must ever be open to the appeals of suffering, even though we close them resolutely against the meaningless babble of those who pursue only their own ends. In this, as in so many other ways, the middle path of occultism is narrow as the edge of a razor, as we are told in the old Indian books; and we must watch ceaselessly lest on the one hand we are wrecked upon the Scylla of indifference or overwhelmed on the other in the confusion of Charybdis.

Even as regards our physical bodies there is the same reason for strict tyling of the Lodge. We do not despise or shun our fellow-creatures, though we do shun some of their undesirable haunts. No one who knows anything of the inner side of things will voluntarily approach such a centre of ghastly influence as a prize-ring, a butcher's shop or a drinking saloon; anyone who has even to pass by such places in the course of his daily avocations should make a strong shell round himself that he may not draw into himself even the least trace of their psychic infection.

Again, there are many people who are unconscious vampires; without being in the least aware of it, they draw out vitality from those who are near them, so that if one sits and talks to such an one for a little while, one feels utterly exhausted and incapable of useful work. If such a person were helped by the strength which he draws from his healthier friends, one might at last regard it as an act of charity to allow him to deplete one; but the fact is that these unfortunate people are themselves incapable of retaining what they take, so that they gain nothing from the transaction, while their hapless victims lose health and strength. In approaching such cases, we shall do well to tyle the Lodge of our physical bodies by making a strong etheric shell round them, even while we radiate all love and kindly feeling upon the unfortunate vampire.

The constantly repeated charge to see that the Lodge is close tyled should bring to our minds a succession of useful warnings; and whenever we hear it we should remember to ask ourselves: "Is my heart full of the divine love, and have I kept it close tyled against all evil and foolish thought since last I heard these mystic words?"

So when this question comes now, just before the opening of the Lodge, it serves to remind us of the instant necessity of bringing ourselves into the right frame of mind for the wonderful piece of work which we are going to do.

The Egyptians taught that this phrase had yet another meaning, though one which scarcely concerns us. They understood the necessity of tyling the world as a whole. Our earth is surrounded by a gaseous atmosphere in which the lightest matter tends to find its way to the top. Hydrogen is the lightest, and what little of it there is in a free state gradually rises to the top of the atmosphere, and some of it escapes and becomes lost in space. That is one of the reasons why the older planets always have less hydrogen than the younger - it leaks away to a certain extent as the planet rushes along through space. That reduces the amount of water on the globe. Thus we find that Mars, which is older than the earth in proportion to its size, and is in a later period of its life, has slightly more land than water on its surface, while Jupiter and Saturn which are younger, not in actual age, but in proportion to their size, are almost entirely liquid. There is a great being called the Spirit of the Earth, who uses the earth as his physical body; he has made his own arrangements to prevent the too rapid escape of his hydrogen, and takes constant care to tyle his Lodge; but we of course have nothing to do with that.

In thinking of all these symbolical meanings, we must not forget the actual tyling of the Lodge in which we sit. There are several reasons for our extreme care in this matter. We want to keep the Lodge shut not merely to preserve our mysteries from the outer gaze, but because only so may we keep its influence pure and undisturbed. The thought-form that is about to be built is a thing very delicately balanced and carefully graduated, and is composed not only of the etheric substances of our material plane, but also of the still finer matter of the emotional and mental worlds. This thought-form is constructed for a definite purpose, and if outsiders, whose minds are working along different lines, were present, they would quite unintentionally cause a good deal of friction and destroy the balance and efficacy of the form. It is not that we consider ourselves to be superior to those other people, but that we are training ourselves to think along certain definite lines, and they as a rule arc not.

We must also keep prominently in our minds the obligation to preserve absolute secrecy in the outer world about our Masonic meetings and all that takes place at them. There unquestionably is a certain danger of inadvertence in these matters. None are likely even for a moment to contemplate the betrayal of any Masonic secret, nor to exhibit any lack of caution with regard to the w ... s and s ... s which we have solemnly sworn never to reveal, but in other matters there is sometimes incaution; for example, on one occasion I heard some Brn. discussing in a tramcar the excellent manner in which a certain J.D. performed his work in the Lodge. This is, of course, no betrayal of any of the secrets, but it contains an element of distinct danger, for it is so easily possible when speaking of the ceremony to make some reference from which an intelligent and inquisitive bystander might deduce more than he ought to know.

THE E.A. S ... N

After it has been seen that the Lodge is close tyled, the next thing to be done is to see that all is right within - that all present are Freemasons.

As a matter of fact we are already sure of that, for the members of a Lodge are well known to each other, and any stranger presenting himself is always carefully proved before he is admitted. But this is the formal proof appointed in the ritual, to make assurance doubly sure; so the R.W.M. calls his Lodge to order, and all adopt a certain attitude of attention with a s ... p and s ... n, both of which are highly symbolical, and have remained unchanged for a very long period. It should be distinctly understood that a man who joins Freemasonry does thereby take a step forward in evolution, and the fact that his identification as a Freemason begins with that s ... p is a constant reminder and acknowledgment of that.

The l ... f ..., because it is nearest to the heart, symbolizes the intuition, while the r ... f ... is supposed to represent intellectual faculty. The meaning of the s ... p is therefore obviously that in occult matters intuition always takes precedence over mere reasoning processes. The position adopted is intended to show that reason must always spring from the centre of right feeling.

Having thus indicated the method of our advancement, we proceed in Co-Masonry to give the Dieu-garde, a contraction of the French "Dieu vous garde," which means "God keep you," though in English it has been corrupted into due-guard. In addition to the thoughts suggested by the s ... p, this shows us that we learn but to bless, for this position is that which the candidate adopted at the moment when he took his O. It indicates that the E.A., being himself but a beginner, has as yet neither the right nor the power to give any blessing but that which is prescribed in the V.S.L.; he may use only the words which are taught to him, for he is not yet in the position to be either a direct channel or a reservoir of the higher force.

Then follows a gesture which is at the same time a salutation to God and a declaration of power. The rest of the s ... is commonly interpreted as a reminder of the p ... y attached to any violation of the E.A.O.; and it is certain that the idea of that p ... y has been associated with it from an early period in history, as may be seen by reference to the works of Dr. Albert Churchward. There is, however, yet another more occult meaning for that s ... than the explanation usually given. Students of the inner side of man's constitution and of Oriental occultism are aware that there are seven great force-centres (called in Sanskrit chakras) in the human body, and that in the course of occult progress all of them have to be opened, developed and made effective.

There are many methods of psychic development, some of which commence with the opening of one centre and some with another; but in the scheme advocated in ancient Egypt and continued in Freemasonry the centre indicated by that s ... is taken first. So when the Freemason makes that movement he not only designates the opening up of that centre as the special work, from the occult point of view, of this degree, but he also commands the aid of the powers in nature connected with and controlled through that centre in whatever work he is about to undertake. The gestures and words taught in Freemasonry are not chosen at random; each has a definite meaning and a definite power in the world of the unseen, quite apart from its signification on the physical plane. Lodges in Europe usually know nothing whatever of all this; perhaps there may be some in Oriental countries which are better instructed.

The force-centres exist as points of connection at which energy flows from one vehicle or body of a man to another. Anyone who possesses a slight degree of clairvoyance may easily see them in the etheric double, where they show themselves as saucer-like depressions or vortices in its surface. When quite undeveloped they appear as small circles about two inches in diameter, glowing dully in the ordinary man; but when awakened and vivified they appear as blazing, coruscating saucers, much increased in size. We sometimes speak of them as roughly corresponding to certain physical organs; in reality they show themselves at the surface of the etheric double, which projects slightly beyond the outline of the dense body. If we imagine ourselves to be looking straight down into the bell of a flower of the convolvulus type, we shall get some idea of the general appearance of a chakra. The stalk of the flower in each case springs from a point in the spine, so another view might show the spine as a central stem, from which flowers shoot forth at intervals, showing the opening of their bells at the surface of the etheric body.

The seven centres with which we are at present concerned are indicated in the accompanying illustration. (Plate IX.) It will be seen that they are situated at: (1) the base of the spine; (2) the spleen; (3) the navel or solar plexus; (4) the heart; (5) the throat; (6) the space between the eyebrows; and (7) the top of the head. I have described them fully in *The Inner Life*; and I have also published a monograph on them, called *The Chakras*, with unique coloured illustrations.

There are several force-centres besides these, and there are schools of magic that use them; but the dangers connected with them are so serious that we should consider their awakening as the greatest misfortune. It is precisely in order to avoid the arousing of those lower centres that so much importance was attached in Egypt to the belt or girdle of the apron, and the etheric web which stretched across it.

Plate IX. THE CHAKRAS

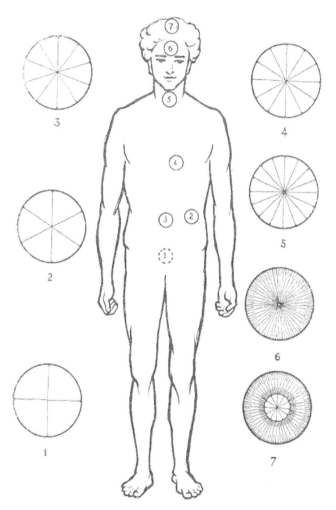

When at all in action, these centres show signs of rapid rotation, and into each of their open mouths, at right angles to the surface of the body, there rushes a force from the higher world - one of those which T.G.A.O.T.U. is constantly pouring out through His system. That force is sevenfold in its nature, and all its forms operate in each of these centres, although one of them in each case greatly predominates over the others. Without this inrush of energy the physical body could not exist. Therefore the centres are in operation in every one, although in the undeveloped person they are usually in comparatively sluggish motion, just forming the necessary vortex for the force, and no more. On the other hand, they may be glowing and pulsating with living light, so that an enormously greater amount of force passes through them, with the result that there are additional faculties and possibilities open to the man.

This divine energy which rushes into each centre from without sets up at right angles to itself, that is to say, in the surface of the etheric double, secondary forces in undulatory circular motion, just as a bar magnet thrust into an induction coil produces a current of electricity which flows round the coil at right angles to the axis or direction of the magnet. The primary force itself, having entered the vortex, radiates from it again at right angles, but in straight lines, as though the centre of the vortex were the hub of a wheel, and the radiations of the primary force its spokes. The number of these spokes differs in the different force-centres, and determines the number of waves or petals which each of them exhibits. Because of this these force-centres have often been poetically described in Oriental books as resembling flowers.

Each of the secondary forces which sweep round the saucer-like depression has its own characteristic wave-length, just as has light of a certain colour; but instead of moving in a straight line as light does, it moves along relatively large undulations of various sizes, each of which is some multiple of the smaller wave-lengths within it. The number of undulations is determined by the number of spokes in the wheel, and the secondary force weaves itself under and over the radiating currents of the primary force, just as basket work might be woven round the spokes of a carriage wheel. The wavelengths are infinitesimal, and probably thousands of them are included within one of the undulations. As the forces rush round in the vortex, these oscillations of different sizes, crossing one another in this basketwork fashion, produce the flower-like form to which I have referred. It is, perhaps, still more like the appearance of certain saucers or shallow vases of wavy iridescent glass, such as are made in Venice. All of these undulations or petals have that shimmering iridescent effect, like mother-of-pearl, yet each of them has usually its own predominant colour.

In the vivification of the particular centre with which this degree of E.A. is principally concerned, three factors are important. When the centre in the emotional body which corresponds to this is awakened, it gives to the man the power of hearing in the subtle world at that level -

that is, it causes a development of that sense which, in what is usually called the astral world, produces on our consciousness the effect which on the physical plane we call hearing. So, if the etheric centre were fully working, the E.A. would be clairaudient as far as the etheric and astral planes. Its slow and partial unfoldment gradually tends to dissipate prejudice in the man, to open his mind to suggestions and, generally speaking, to widen and liberalize his thought.

Secondly, the development of the brain largely depends upon the opening up of this centre, because it plays an important part in the division and distribution of one of the main streams of vitality which course through the human body. I have already explained the detail of this action in *The Chakras* and *The Hidden Side of Things*, to which I must refer any reader who desires further information on the subject of vital circulation.

Thirdly, another important action of this centre deserves our notice, as the especial object of the first Degree is the conquest of the passions of the physical body and the development of morality. Among the various kinds of vitality is an orange-red ray, which contains also a certain amount of dark purple. In the normal man this ray energizes the desires of the flesh, and also seems to enter the blood and keep up the heat of the body; but if a man persistently refuses to yield to his lower nature, this ray can by long and determined effort be deflected upwards to the brain, where all three of its constituents undergo a remarkable modification. The orange is raised into pure yellow, and produces a decided intensification of the powers of the intellect; the dark red becomes crimson and gradually increases the power of unselfish affection; while the dark purple is transmuted into a lovely pale violet, and quickens the spiritual part of man's nature. The man who achieves this transmutation will find that lower desires no longer trouble him; and it is with that consummation in view that the development of the centre in which those modifications and transmutations are achieved is so strongly emphasized in the preliminary stages of Freemasonry.

The unfoldment of this centre is closely associated with the power of paying attention, as well as with the opening of higher forms of hearing. In all occult systems of training great importance was attached to this in the case of the neophyte. In the school of Pythagoras the pupils were kept for several years in the order called Akoustikoi or Hearers; in the mysteries of Mithra the lowest order was that of the Ravens - a name which signifies that they were allowed only to repeat that which they had heard, precisely as a raven or a parrot does; for in all these ancient systems students were strictly forbidden to launch out upon the perilous waters of originality until they were thoroughly grounded in the established principles of philosophy. The s ... also evokes or calls to the assistance of the man who uses it a particular class of non-human intelligences of the subtle world.

In view of the great influence of this s ... of power, all will see the necessity that it should be preserved with the greatest care and secrecy. If it is made wrongly, not in exact form and at the proper place, the effect will be lost. In these matters we are working what is commonly called magic; and that is a dangerous thing to play with and should be taken up only with the greatest seriousness of purpose and precision in work.

If a member should make this s ... carelessly and without thinking what ho is doing, he opens himself up to influences of which he is unaware, for which be is unprepared; and things may happen which should not happen. It is this idea which is at the basis of the grossly exaggerated and misleading statement that a man who takes the Holy Sacrament in the Church, while permitting his mind to be full of evil, really eats and drinks damnation to himself. The man who receives the Holy Communion becomes a very high centre of radiating force, and is also made receptive to the highest degree; let him be sure therefore to eliminate evil thoughts, lest such thoughts may draw into him other influences like unto themselves. It is the same with the Masonic s .... He who performs it as a salutation to another opens up his heart towards that person, and that is good; but all should be on guard lest they carelessly open themselves to unpleasant influences which might otherwise have passed them by.

When made thus at the opening of our Lodge, this s ... reminds us that we must put ourselves in a receptive attitude, so that we may obtain the greatest possible benefit from the influx of spiritual force which we are about to invoke.

THE OFFICERS

Having thus done our best to prepare our selves for the work of the evening (a) by the purifying of the Lodge-room by means of the censing, (b) by closing our hearts and minds against all distracting thoughts and feelings, and (c) by putting ourselves in a receptive attitude, we now proceed to set in motion the marvellously arranged Masonic machinery by which we can invoke the assistance of non-human beings in our altruistic labours. The method by which this is done is exceedingly ingenious and most skilfully concealed. Man is a complex being, and the rough division into body and soul is not sufficient for scientific working. For the purposes of his evolution he exists upon five of the seven planes of nature, and has sheaths or bodies built of the matter of the lower of those planes, and principles or constituents within himself which correspond to the higher. This will be made clearer by Fig. 13, and its accompanying diagram.

Therefore for our work we need forces of all these different levels, and each officer of a Masonic Lodge has, besides his duties on the physical plane, the function of representing one of these levels, and acting as a focus for its special energies. The arrangement made by the Founders of Freemasonry is that the enumeration of the officials and the recitation of their positions and duties shall act as an evocation of the devas or Angels belonging to and working on those respective levels. The fact that thousands of R.W.M.s have asked the appointed questions without the faintest idea of producing an effect in unseen worlds has not deprived them of angelic assistance which, if they had known of it, would have astounded them beyond expression, and probably even terrified them.

So the spirit turns again to the intelligence, and calls on it to formulate the great divisions; intelligence responds and names the three lines through which the force flows, thereby attracting the attention of the Angels of those lines. To symbolize that, the R.W.M. asks how many principal officers there are in the Lodge, and receives the answer that there are three. These are the R.W.M., the W.S.W., and the W.J.W., who represent the divine or spiritual trinity which appears in the Deity, and also in man, who is made in the image of that Deity. These three principles in man are familiar to many students of Theosophical psychology under the names of atma, buddhi and manas, which may be rendered into English as the spiritual will, the intuitional love and the higher intelligence.

Then the R.W.M. asks how many assistant officers there are, and is told that these are likewise three, not including the O.G. or. T. These represent the personal constitution of man or his lower self-composed of the lower mind, which the S.D. represents, the emotional nature, personified by the J.D., and the etheric double of the physical body, for which the I.G. stands. The T. represents the dense part of the physical body.

The porchway of the Lodge is the entrance to the inner world which is invisible to ordinary sight. Therefore the T., who typifies the denser part of the physical body, is the only officer of the Lodge who stands outside it, visible to the sight of the profane. All the other six principles of the human constitution are beyond physical sight, which deals with only one grade of the matter of the world, and that the lowest and densest. Those principles exist on distinct planes of nature, of ascending degrees of subtlety or fineness of matter.

Fig. 13 and the diagram connected with it show the seven principles in man, the planes of nature on which they exist, and the corresponding officers in the Masonic Lodge.

Figure 13

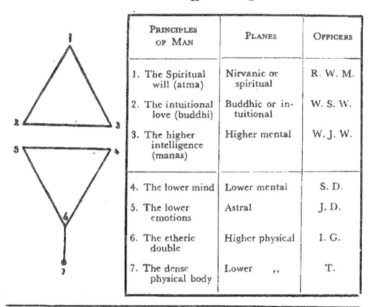

Principles of Man	Planes	Officers
1. The Spiritual will (atma)	Nirvanic or spiritual	R. W. M.
2. The intuitional love (buddhi)	Buddhic or intuitional	W. S. W.
3. The higher intelligence (manas)	Higher mental	W. J. W.
4. The lower mind	Lower mental	S. D.
5. The lower emotions	Astral	J. D.
6. The etheric double	Higher physical	I. G.
7. The dense physical body	Lower ,,	T.

COMBINED TERMS	
	Principles
The Ego	1, 2 and 3
The Personality	4, 5, 6 and 7
The Psychic Duad	4 and 5
The Physical Duad	6 and 7

THE DUTIES

The list of situations and duties is then rehearsed. It is commonly supposed that the object of this enumeration is to make sure that the facts are thoroughly known to all the Brn., and that all the officials are duly present. It has in reality another and far more important function, as I have explained.

The upper triangle, containing the first, second and third principles, represents the ego or higher self in man, commonly called the soul, who in the course of his long pilgrimage or evolution towards human perfection, takes many incarnations, each of which is called a personality. The lower triangle is a reflection of that higher one in the matter of the lower planes, and it forms with the dense physical body the lower quaternary, which constitutes the personality, and lasts through one incarnation. The evolution of man is really the development of the ego or higher self, but in most people at the present stage of human progress that ego may be described as still in his infancy; he has not yet fully awakened to the positive and purposeful life of a man on his own planes, nor has he realized what can be learnt through incarnation in the lower planes. In course of time and many incarnations the three higher principles gradually unfold themselves, and the man realizes more and more of the divinity which is truly his. Though the principal object of Freemasonry is the collection and distribution of spiritual force for others, it is also deeply concerned with the welfare and progress of the Brn., so its ritual and its teaching clearly indicate the path which man should tread, and offer him the most valuable help as he passes along it.

Several interesting points of symbolism are brought out in the apparently curious answers which are given with respect to the duties attached to the various offices. The physical body should protect the lodge of a man's soul from the dangers of the outer world, from temptations or evil influences. The T. is ordered to keep out all cowans and intruders to Freemasonry, and when we recollect that the word "cowan" is simply the Greek *kuon*, a dog, and that from time immemorial the dog has been used as a symbol of violent animal passions, we shall readily comprehend what the work and office of the T. are intended to typify.

The etheric double, in the person of the I. G., also joins to defend the Lodge, and is especially under the command of the higher mind or intelligence, the W.J.W., who is concerned with testing all who seek to enter; which shows that it is the duty of the intelligence to discriminate, and to decide what thought or emotion shall receive lodgment within the temple of man. The R.W.M. communicates with the T. only through the W.J.W. and the I.G., which signifies that spirit does not act directly on dense matter, but through his intelligence impresses himself upon etheric matter; though when he has once sent out his enquiry, the mind may instruct the etheric double to report directly to the R.W.M. on the particular subject. To typify this, in many Lodges it is the custom that the W.J.W., in passing on his command, should say, "Bro. I.G., you will see who seeks admission, and report to the R.W.M."

The reflection of the upper triangle in the lower takes place point for point, and there is therefore a sympathetic relation between principles 2 and 5, as well as between 3 and 4, and between 1 and 6. It is with the aid of the emotions, by their purification and development, that the man unfolds principle 2, the intuitional love, so that it is brought into activity in his life. And it is with the aid of the mind that he casts off the five fetters to further progress (namely, the delusion that his personal self is the real self, doubt about the reality of spiritual things, superstition, and unreasoning likes and dislikes) and so enables the spiritual will to express itself in his life. About these stages, and the great Initiations that accompany them, I have written in full in The Masters and the Path. They are mentioned here to show why it is that the J.D. acts between the W.S.W. and the W.J.W. and the S.D. acts between the R.W.M. and the W.S.W. They explain also why it is that the W.J.W. takes charge of the E.A.s, and the W.S.W. of the F.C.s, while the M.M.s may be considered to be under the immediate charge of the R.W.M. As the open Lodge is a place where the Brn. are symbolically undergoing the advanced course of evolution before mentioned, the officers who represent the principles in man must show those principles acting in relation to one another as they do in man in the course of that evolution.

The Third Aspect of the Divine Being is typified by the W.J.W. when he directs the passage from the labour of evolution to the refreshment of periodic rest; while it is the Second Aspect which is symbolized by the W.S.W. when he closes the Lodge at the R.W.M.'s command, because when the Second Aspect of Deity withdraws from the forms that He has made, everything is resolved into its primal elements and the universe as such ceases to exist, and so the Lodge of the solar system is for the time closed. This is what is called among the Hindus the end of the *manvantara* and the beginning of the *pralaya*.

It is not implied that the officials who happen to hold the positions representing the principles in man in any given Lodge are necessarily able to function upon the planes to which they correspond; but it is to be understood that not only the nature-spirits, but also the strange half-conscious creatures which we have called elementals, existing on the downward arc of evolution on each of these levels, will and do respond to the invocation which is employed in this closely condensed formula of opening. The enumeration of the officials in answer to the earlier questions of the R.W.M. is in the nature of a call to attention - a call which reverberates through these different kingdoms of nature - and lets devas, nature-spirits and elementals know that an opportunity is about to be offered to them. For that, remember, is the way in which these creatures at all levels look upon such a call. It is one of the chief methods of their evolution to be used in work such as this, and they therefore greatly rejoice to respond.

That general enumeration by the W.s is quickly followed by the specific questions addressed to each of the officers; and of these the first enquiry as to their situation in the Lodge sets the machinery in motion, acts as a call to a deva of the particular type required, who immediately presents himself and acts as a captain of the nature-spirits and elementals who next gather round. The second question and answer in each case, as to the special duty of the officers in question, brings round him these myrmidons of his, and he influences them to arrange themselves as required. For example, when the J.D. is mentioned a thrill shoots out through the astral levels, and when he is asked what is his situation in the Lodge, a deva, having for his lowest vehicle a body of astral matter (what is called in Buddhism a *kamadeva*), at once steps forward and takes up his position above the head of the J.D. At the same time the attention of a number of nature-spirits wearing bodies of astral matter is aroused, and also a great mass of the elemental essence belonging to the third of the great elemental kingdoms is awakened into activity. Then when the question as to the duties is asked, the deva captain draws round him those astral myrmidons, and arranges them as he needs them, and at the same time seizes upon the floating mass of elemental essence and welds it into thought-forms such as he requires to carry out the work that has to be done.

In exactly the same way the S.D. is represented by a deva captain whose lowest vehicle is built of the matter of the lower sub-planes of the mental plane (a *rupadeva*), and lie employs nature-spirits and elemental essence at his own level. It will be noticed that in each case not only the actual situation and duty of the official are defined, but also his relation to other officials, his part in the work as a whole. The deva captains corresponding to the three principal officers are all what are called in the East *arupadevas*, and they possess the consciousness and wield the forces of the planes which they respectively represent. It is not easy for us to understand the working of forces at such levels, as they act upon the corresponding principles in man, and those principles are only slightly developed as yet in the majority of human beings.

By the time, therefore, that the last of the list of questions and answers has been exchanged, the whole Lodge is pulsating with elemental life, all of which is filled with the most intense eagerness to launch itself upon the work in hand, whatever that may be. The elementals and nature-spirits of the different levels vary greatly in development and intelligence, some being fully defined and exceedingly active, whereas others are comparatively vague and cloud-like. But a very striking appearance is presented by the Lodge when these various groups of beings are gathered together, each group showing its distinctive colour and floating over the head of the official who is its physical plane representative - all this taking place while the Lodge is still in semi-darkness, lit only by the three candles and the sacred fire. It is to this condition that the R.W.M. refers (whether he knows it or not) when he says: "Our Lodge being thus duly formed."

In the case of the lower officers, at any rate, it requires but a slight development of clairvoyance to see these creatures floating in their appointed places, each group making a sort of luminous sphere or cloud. (See Plate X.) This cloud is violet-grey in the case of the I. G., crimson for the J.D. and yellow for the S.D. It is not so easy to define the hues of the three principal officers, for each of them seems to carry something of all possible colours; but it may perhaps be said that a golden hue predominates in the W.J.W.'s sphere, and a strong electric blue in that of the W.S.W. The R.W.M's light-globe is the brightest of all, glowing equally with rose, gold, blue and green, each of which flashes out into prominence at certain points of the ceremony. It is through these deva representatives of the various officers that the building of the thought-form and the outpouring of the force is really done; but on the physical plane the officer of the Lodge should also participate in the work to the extent of his power. If he reaches upward to his deva representative, and allows the force to flow freely through him, blending his will with it as it flows, his higher principles will become one with that deva; and he will not only be an excellent channel for the divine force, but will himself be greatly helped and strengthened in the doing of the work.

THE OPENING

The deva-representative of the R.W.M. is a highly developed and very capable seventh-ray Angel, and the moment that he arrives with his cohort of assistant-angels and elementals he takes full charge of the whole of the proceedings. The captains of all the other little groups spring to attention, and everything is at once made ready for the supreme moment of the opening of the Lodge. The R.W.M., having declared that his Lodge is duly formed and that he stands there as its head and representative, turns to express his gratitude to T.G.A.O.T.U. for this, and then offers up an earnest wish that the work of the evening, having thus begun in order, may be continued in harmony and closed in peace. To this his whole Lodge replies with a ringing response, like the cheer of an army: "So mote it be." "Mote" is an old Anglo-Saxon form of "may", and this expression is the Masonic "Amen". But just as "Amen" is often interpreted "so may it be", so is this splendid Masonic expression often degraded to the level of a mere assent or pious wish. And again, just as "Amen" is not a wish but an assertion - the most sacred oath of ancient Egypt, which none would ever dare to break – "By Amen it shall be so" - so is this Masonic exclamation to be taken as the strongest affirmation – "so *shall* it be". Not: "We pray or we hope that it may be so", but "We shall make it so". This is shown by the emphatic outstretching of the right hand at the level of the shoulder, this being a well-known sign of power and command.

Immediately after this the R.W.M., acting in the name of T.G.A.O.T.U., declares the Lodge duly open, and all the lights are turned fully on. It is not only the physical light which leaps forth at this moment, for as the R.W.M. says the opening words his deva-representative also lifts his staff, and all the seven groups of assistant spirits, which until now have been seen even by clairvoyant sight as merely luminous clouds, flash out into their full brilliancy and their natural beauty of colour. At once also each group is connected by a line of living light with the physical official over which it hovers, and through this line its force is poured down upon him whenever he is called upon to take part in the ceremony. The deva representative usually remains floating above the regular situation of the official, but as the latter moves about the Lodge in the course of his work the line of light never leaves him for a moment, though it becomes more vivid during his activity.

Just before the Lodge is opened, the I.P.M. is escorted by the two D.s with crossed wands to the altar, where he kneels and awaits the exact moment of opening. As the R.W.M. utters the word "open" the I.P.M. opens the V.S.L., and arranges upon its pages the s ... and the c ... thus displaying what we esteem the three great emblematical lights in Freemasonry simultaneously with the physical illumination. It is the I.P.M. who thus brings the symbolical light to the Lodge, just as it was he who gave the physical light from the sacred fire to the S. D., because he represents the Silent Watcher, the influence which sees that everything is correctly done and stands ready always to supply anything that is needed. He has reached the Light in its fullest sense; he has done his work and is therefore in a position to help others. It should be specially noted that he should open the sacred volume at random, not searching for any particular passage; it is the whole book that is given to us to illumine our minds, not only this verse or that. It will be found most convenient to open it somewhere about the middle.

To show that the sacred volume is here being used as a symbol, the I.P.M, solemnly recites the ancient formula quoted by St John the Evangelist at the beginning of his Gospel: "In the beginning was the Word, and the Word was with God, and the Word was God." We all know that the Greek translated in this text as "word" is in the original "Logos"; and so the opening of the V.S.L. typifies the manifestation of the Logos at the beginning of a solar system, while the c … s and the s … show further that He manifests Himself as spirit and matter; for there is nothing which is not God. To indicate that the Second Person or Aspect of the Logos is about to descend into His universe, the column of the W.S.W. is now erected, and that of the W.J.W. is laid down. The brooding of the Holy Spirit over the waters of chaos is now no longer the only divine activity; the groundwork is laid, and the active life of the system is to begin. The tracing-board which indicates the plan of its activity is now exposed, and the nature of that activity is indicated by the fact that we commence it with a hymn of praise to T.G.A.O.T.U., during the singing of which the Brn. should pour out all the love and devotion of which they are capable.

In those Lodges which use a portrait of the H.O.A.T.F. it is just before the singing of this hymn that that portrait is unveiled, all the Brn. turning towards it and saluting. In instant response to this salutation the great Adept projects a thought-form which is an exact image of Himself; just as at a higher level the Lord Christ projects that thought-form which is called the Angel of the Presence at every celebration of the Holy Eucharist. So fully is this thought-form a part of the H.O.A.T.F. that the Lodge has the benefit of His presence and His blessing just as though He stood there in physical form. The Deva representative of the R.W.M. bows low before the Head of his Ray, and leaves the direction of affairs in His hands. It will be seen that those of us who know of the existence of this great Adept, and of His keen interest in our work, have a great advantage; but it must not be forgotten that every regularly constituted Masonic

Lodge is in charge of a Seventh Ray Angel, however little the Brn. may know about the matter.

I have explained how at the moment of the opening of the Lodge all the assistant angels, nature-spirits and elemental creatures and their deva captains flash out into brilliancy, and stand round ready to spring forward at the word of command. To say that they are ready is far from expressing the fact; they are overflowing with eagerness, like dogs straining at a leash. And now comes the moment for which they have been waiting, for immediately after the return of the I.P.M. to his seat and the display of the tracing-board by the S.D. comes the opening hymn, with the first note of which the super-physical entities burst into tumultuous yet ordered activity. The hymn itself, or rather the devotion and enthusiasm with which we sing it, provides them with the material for their building, and immediately they are all working away at its erection, each at his own level, and with the materials belonging to that level with which the Brn. supply him.

In the opening procession the R.W.M. and his officers have already constructed the lower part of the *cella*, or interior chamber of the temple, shutting in the whole of the mosaic pavement and charging it heavily with magnetism. These creatures pounce upon that first of all and rapidly make its walls both thicker and higher, the greater ones reinforcing its magnetism by filling it with the splendid power of their respective levels. Again with lightning-like rapidity they spread a ceiling over the whole of the Lodge, and from that ceiling, beginning at the edges, just within the walls of the physical Lodge, they drop supporting columns from above downwards like the roots of a banyan-tree, one of them surrounding each of the non-official Brn. It will thus be seen that our thought-form is very nearly a reproduction of a Greek temple-the rows of columns which support its tremendously heavy roof being outside the central chamber, which is the only part of the temple fully enclosed. The accompanying picture may help to make this clear, and we give at the same time in Plate V a drawing of an existing Greek temple for the sake of comparison. The mere outline of the temple is always finished during the singing of the opening hymn, but in certain circumstances friezes and other decorations may be added later on under the direction of the controlling Angel.

It will thus be seen why the unofficial Brn. who sit at the sides of the Lodge are sometimes spoken of as the columns; and some light is also thrown on an ancient text which runs: "Him that overcometh will I make a pillar in the temple of my God, and he shall go no more out." Incidentally, we see how necessary it is that the Brn. should put their hearts and souls into the words that they sing or say, for upon their efforts in this direction depends the amount of material provided for our super-physical fellow-workers, and consequently the massiveness and richness of the thought-form which they build. All through the ceremony that follows, whatever it may be, the deva representatives of the three principal officers continue to pour into the *cella* their beneficent influence; and though its strongest force is reserved for those who enter upon the mosaic pavement as candidates, it also somehow filters through the roof and down the columns upon all who are present.

THE E.A. K ... s

At the moment of opening the Lodge the R.W.M. also gives the E.A. K ... s.

K ... s in Freemasonry have a double significance and a very definite use. The latter is based on the fact that they are a recognized method of communication with certain orders of earth-spirits whose attention is attracted by them, whose eager service is at once at the disposal of those who are duly qualified to summon them, though they will take no notice of a call from one who has not been properly introduced to them by initiation into the E.A. degree. Their main use in the ceremony is to create an atmosphere - the atmosphere appropriate to the degree which is being worked; and in that special work they become extraordinarily proficient, answering instantly to the call of the k ... s with military promptness and precision, so that even when the Lodge is being raised or lowered by the short method they are able to produce the required changes as quickly as the commands can be issued.

This generation of the proper atmosphere is one of the most important special features of Freemasonry, indispensable to really efficient working. Any one who is at all sensitive to such influences may feel the change which takes place when we pass from one degree to another, but only those who have opened the sight of the soul can see the variations of colour, or watch the busy workers who are so energetic in producing them. The Deva captains of the three principal officers take charge of this important part of the work - the W.J.W. of the servants of the First Degree, the W.S.W. of those of the Second, and the R.W.M. of those of the Third; but the earth-spirits themselves obey the call of the k ... s, appearing at the first round and unobtrusively returning to their normal haunts when another battery announces that their work is done.

The k ... s of the closing correspond to the "Ite, missa est" of the Catholic Church. It may be noted that similar creatures are fond of announcing their presence by k ... s at a spiritualistic seance.

The k ... s of the First Degree have also a moral significance, indicating that the E.A. has three planes in front of him to conquer, the physical body with its impulses coming from the past, the astral with its strong desires and emotions, and the mental with its curiosity and waywardness. With each of these every man in the course of his evolution has a twofold work to do first he must conquer it, govern its impulses and bring them into a state of obedience to the soul within, and secondly he must develop it as a positive, well-trained, useful instrument for his service.

The E.A. is supposed to have conquered the physical body before entering into Masonry - without that he could not be well and worthily recommended for admission - but he has still to develop it; and while he is doing that be is supposed to be gaining complete control of his astral nature; that is the special work of this degree as far as self-development is concerned, though of course the Mason is trying to perfect himself in every way all the time. The k ... s of the Second Degree indicate that the physical work is complete, and that the F.C. has still two planes to conquer. He is engaged in making his astral body into a perfect instrument for the expression of high emotion, and is at the same time learning to gain control of his mind. In this stage a Mason should be making every day some advances in Masonic knowledge, till presently the mind will no longer be wayward and fickle, but controlled. At this point he will pass on to the Third Degree, and then the k ... s indicate that he has but one plane to conquer, has but to perfect the mind as an instrument in the service of the higher self. This work will go on for as many years as are necessary before he passes through the Chair.

From the above it will be seen that there are four stages in Craft Masonry - three degrees and then a further attainment when the M.M. becomes an I.M. There is a similarity between these stages and those which have been prescribed in the Christian Church, although one is at a much higher level than the other. This is shown in the following diagram.

In the Church certain people are set apart as priests - but they have to pass through the earlier stages before reaching that position. First the man must be a subdeacon; his business then is to prepare himself for the great surgical operation which takes place at the diaconate, when he is definitely joined with the World-Teacher, in a way which has been fully explained in *The Science of the Sacraments*.

Diagram X

	MASONRY	THE CHURCH
1	E. A.	Subdeacon
2	F. C.	Deacon
3	M. M.	Priest
4	I. M.	Bishop

In the stage of the subdiaconate, which corresponds somewhat to the E.A., the man is supposed to learn to control himself perfectly. In the next grade, during the time of the diaconate, he has to learn; he is preparing himself for the work of the priesthood, just as the F.C. is preparing himself for the work of the M.M.

As I have said in speaking of the due-guard, the power of blessing of the E.A. is contained within the book from which he learns. He may use only the words of the book, and must not go beyond them. He is not himself yet a direct channel for the divine power, so he puts the book between his hands. But the F.C. puts one h ... on the b ... and raises the other in the f ... of a s ... He corresponds to the deacon, because he is a channel linked with the Christ, but only that which comes down and pours through him may he give. He is not yet himself filled with grace and power, but he is able to act as a channel. His holding of the l ... h ... in that way corresponds, though at a lower stage, with the bishop's holding his crosier in the left .hand. He is drawing down divine power through that highly magnetized staff, while he is pouring it out on the people with the other hand. It is the same gesture, though of course in the case of the bishop it is far more highly specialized.

Then the M.M. puts both his h ... on the b ... He is supposed when he has attained that high degree to be in a position of power, to be filled with the energy which has been poured into him in the symbolical death and rising again. Therefore he can give that energy; he may give a blessing to other people just as a priest does, and as the priest has authority to administer certain sacraments, so is the M.M. qualified to accept office in the Lodge.

Still, neither the M.M. nor the priest can convey his power or authority to anyone else. The bishop alone has power to ordain priests or to consecrate other bishops, and only the I.M. is able to initiate, pass and raise Masons, and to create other I.M.s. Both the bishop and the I.M. have also the power to give a fuller blessing than the priest or the M.M. can bestow. Thus there is a succession of I.M.s in Masonry, just as there is a succession of bishops in the Church.

In *The Science of the Sacraments* I have explained something of the inner meaning of the apostolic succession, the method designed by the Christ for handing down the spiritual powers of the Catholic Church. It will be seen that we have a similar succession in Masonry, extending back to the priests of the Mysteries of ancient Egypt, and beyond.

There is a further analogy between the degrees of Freemasonry and the orders of the Church, for just as the clergy of the Church are linked in various degrees of connection with the Head of the Church, the Lord Christ Himself, and with the reservoir of power which He has set apart for the celebration of the sacraments, so are the initiates of the various degrees in Freemasonry linked according to their rank with the H.O.A.T.F., and with the reservoir of power set apart for the work of the Craft. Every Freemason has a certain touch with Him; but the first great link directly with Him is given in the degree of I.M. (for it is practically a separate degree, although it is not called so), and closer links still are conferred in the higher degrees of the Ancient and Accepted Scottish Rite; so that the earnest Mason becomes a veritable outpost of His consciousness, a channel of His power and a minister of His will. Such Brn. act as His representatives in their Lodges and Chapters, and have the right to give His blessing according to their Masonic rank. It is a matter of deep regret that so few of our modern Brn. realize in the least the sacredness of their office, and the heavy responsibility laid upon them to use their power without thought of self in the service of the world.

There are, however, considerable differences between the methods of transmission in these two great sacramental systems. It is recognized in Catholic theology, and confirmed by occult investigation, that the spiritual powers given at ordination are invariably conferred, provided only that the bishop be in the line of the apostolic succession, that he have the intention to confer Holy Orders and that the recipient have the intention to receive them, and that the laying on of hands take place according to the ancient tradition. The particular beliefs of the bishop and the candidate do not affect the validity of the sacrament in the slightest degree, nor will it be withheld if they are out of communion with any particular branch of the Church, or even if they are persons of questionable moral worth. The Lord Christ out of His great love for His Church is willing to overlook the human frailties of the minister, so that His flock may be fed.

But the transmission of power in Masonry seems to be by no means so unalterably fixed, probably because of the fact that Masonry is a secret Order and is not therefore in direct relation with the outer world; the whole scheme of transmittal is much more elastic than that of the Church. Although it would appear that the succession both of I.M.s and Sovereign Grand Inspectors-General has been to a large extent handed down on the physical plane, it is by no means necessary that it should be so handed down, and the sacramental powers may be introduced or withheld as the H.O.A.T.F. sees fit. When a clandestine meeting is held, even though a duly qualified I.M. be present, the inner recognition is not given, and the powers are not conveyed. Two such cases of the withholding of inner recognition are within my personal experience. In the Church a priest can anywhere and by himself perform a sacrament, and a bishop can also pass on his power at his own discretion, but in Craft Masonry the unit is the Lodge, and the presence of a number of Brn. is essential to the validity of the rites, except when degrees are conferred by communication by one who has due authority. It is said that "three rule a Lodge, five hold a Lodge, and seven or more make it perfect".

In making this comparison between Masonic degrees and Church Orders, I am not for a moment asserting that the powers conferred upon the many in the degrees of freemasonry are in any sense equal to those bestowed upon a few carefully selected and prepared candidates in the Major Orders of the Church; I wish only to draw attention to a series of curious correspondences between the two systems, too numerous and remarkable to be due to mere coincidence. Masonry does give powers commensurate with those appertaining to the Church, but only in its very highest degrees, and to the very few.

CHAPTER VI.
INITIATION. THE CANDIDATE

WHEN any member of the general public wishes to become a Freemason, he usually applies to some friend whom he knows to be a member of the Craft. This friend will probably introduce him to the Secretary of the Lodge, who then supplies the applicant with certain papers. The candidate will then find that he is expected to give some particulars with regard to himself - his age, his occupation in life, his reason for wishing to join the Craft, etc. Also, in Co-Masonry the following notice will be handed to him:

The Candidate should clearly understand the obligations he takes upon himself in joining the Order. These obligations are of the most serious and solemn character, and he is expected to discharge them honourably.

A. The candidate undertakes to try to lead a noble and upright life, and to work at the improvement of his character.

B. He undertakes to attend regular meetings of the Lodge, unless prevented by cause sufficiently grave. These are usually held once or twice a month, except at holiday seasons. Sometimes Emergency Meetings are called for special work, but attendance at these is not obligatory. The true Mason, however, regards it not only as a solemn duty, but also as a great privilege to attend his Lodge, realizing that, though the Lodge exists to help its members, it has a far greater and wider function in shedding the spiritual influence of Masonry upon the world. By his regular attendance at the meetings he is definitely participating in that great work. His progress in the Order will depend upon the zeal and assiduity which he shows in this service.

C. He undertakes to remain in the Order and in his Mother-Lodge for at least three years. He is permitted, after Initiation, to visit other Lodges, and after he is a Master Mason to join other Lodges, if he so desires; but he must not leave the Mother-Lodge under the specified period. It is to the Mother-Lodge that he owes allegiance and the duty of loyal co-operation. Where there is more than one Lodge near his place of residence the Candidate should ask his introduces for information regarding the work of the several Lodges, so that he may be sure of entering the Lodge whose work and members are likely to be most congenial to him.

D. The Candidate is bound to true Masonic secrecy and caution concerning Freemasonry and the affairs of the Order, and this promise is to be regarded as binding for all time, even if he leaves the Order.

DIVISIONS OF THE CEREMONY

We now come to the consideration of the ceremony by which the candidate is admitted to Freemasonry, a ceremony which is commonly called his initiation. We must recognize from the beginning that this ceremony is no mere form; first because it produces definite inner effects, and secondly, because it contains a great deal of most valuable symbology, the understanding and application of which will be of great moment in the candidate's future life.

As I have stated earlier in the book, one chief object of freemasonry is to train its members for the work which they have to do in the world, and therefore to cultivate within them the qualities necessary for that work. The various degrees in Masonry are all stages in that training; and in each stage not only is certain definite education given, but also definite powers are conferred. It is to be feared that through ignorance of these facts many Masons make but little real progress; for unless the developments initiated in each degree by the ceremony of admission are duly understood and put into practice by the candidate, he is in no true sense prepared to pass on to a higher stage, or to take advantage of the opportunities which that in turn puts before him.

The outer ceremony confers certain powers and opens up certain possibilities; but it remains for the neophyte to develop them and make use of them. Some neophytes take the hints offered to them, and accordingly make progress; others understand little of the inner requirements, and so are only temporarily affected. The very word initiation is derived from initium, a beginning; and that is precisely what it is intended to be - the beginning of a new and higher life. But it is not enough to begin; one must also continue.

In the Buddhist teaching it is said that in each of the great steps which are the true Initiations there are four stages

(1) The Way, in which the neophyte is mastering the lessons of his new step, casting off (as they put it) the fetters which have previously bound him, finding himself at his new level, and learning how to use the powers conferred upon him.

(2) The Fruit, when he finds the results of his action in so doing showing themselves more and more.

(3) The Consummation - the period when, the results having culminated, he is able to fulfil satisfactorily the work belonging to the step, on which he now firmly stands.

(4) The Readiness, meaning the time when he is seen to be in a fit state to receive the next Initiation.

We see, therefore, that initiation involves something more than the mere outward ceremony - more even than the upliftment of the inner nature which accompanies that ceremony; all that is but the gateway at the entrance of a path along which we may proceed as quickly or as slowly as we will.

In considering this ceremony of initiation to the stage of the E.A. it will be useful to regard it from three aspects or points of view. (1) As an impressive ceremony of admission. (2) As a preparation for and an indication of the life which the man must lead and the work which he must do while in the degree to which it admits him. (3) As putting in a powerful and effective symbolical form the teaching which it is one of the purposes of this degree to impress upon him. When we examine the ceremony in detail I think we shall find that every incident in it falls under one or other of these three heads.

Thinking of the ritual from the point of view of a ceremony of admission into the Order, it seems naturally to divide itself into three parts. The central point of the ceremony, the climax of our effort, is the definite admission into the Order - the point at which a certain centre or chakra is opened, a certain potentiality of power given. All that precedes that in the ceremony is of the nature of preparation for that point; all that follows it is in the nature of explanation of what has been done, or of exhortation as to how the power can best be developed and used. All through the ceremony everything is arranged so that the candidate may receive the greatest possible benefit from the forces which are being outpoured; and that is the principal object of the very curious preparation upon which Masonry has always insisted, even before the candidate is allowed to enter the Lodge.

PREPARATION OF THE CANDIDATE

Before his admission he is divested of all m ... s and v ... s, is h ... d, and has his r ... a ..., l ... b ... and l ... k ... b ..., and his r ... h ... s ... d. All Masonic bodies agree in viewing the continuance of this conventional form of preparation as a matter of the greatest importance, and give as their reason for this the practice of ancient times. It was a rule among the

Jews, says a treatise connected with the Talmud, that "no man shall go into the Temple with his staff, nor with shoes on his feet, nor with his outer garment, nor with money tied up in his purse".

The very specific character of the preparation, which is different in each degree, points, however, not to a general rule of this kind, but to real knowledge of the occult physiology of the process of initiation on the part of those who originated the method which has been so faithfully preserved. Certain forces are sent through the candidate's body in a definite manner during the ceremony, and especially at the moment when he is created, received and constituted an E.A.F.

Certain parts of the Lodge have been very heavily charged with magnetic force, especially in order that the candidate may absorb as much as possible of this force. It will be remembered that in the process of censing the Lodge a beehive-shaped structure was erected in front of the pedestal of each of the principal officers; and the *cella* or enclosed central space, founded upon the mosaic pavement and including the altar, is the most highly magnetized of all. The first object of this curious method of preparation is to expose to this influence those various parts of the body which are especially used in the ceremony. Thus, the r ... a ... is made b ... because the candidate must use that, as soon as he is taught to extend it in the sign of power which accompanies the asseveration: "S ... m ... i ... b ..." It is also said to be a token of sincerity, to shove that the candidate has no weapon about him.

The l ... b ... is made b ... because upon it is received the touch of the point of the s ... on entering the Lodge. The masculine Craft adds as another reason that they are hereby assured that their candidate is not a woman in disguise. The l ... k ... is that upon which he kneels when he is received, so it also is made b ..., and the r ..., h ... is s ... d because that must touch the floor when he holds the r ... k ... in the form of a s ... The 1 ... k ... and the r ... h ... are his supports or points of contact with the floor at the moment of his admission. Another reason sometimes given for the r ... h ... being s ... d is that this is in accordance with the ancient Jewish custom when a man was taking upon himself an obligation or making an agreement. (See Ruth, iv, 7, 8.)

In ancient Egypt there was yet another reason for these preparations, for a weak current of physical electricity was sent through the candidate by means of a rod or sword with which he was touched at certain points. It is not practical here to say more about this part of the ceremony, except that it is concerned with the stimulation of an etheric current in the spine that is known to the Hindu occultists under the name of the *ida nadi*; it will be more fully described in explaining the ceremony of raising.

It is partly on the same account that at this first initiation the candidate is deprived of all m ... s, since they may very easily interfere with the flow of the currents. Very great importance has always been attached to this part of the preparation, and the strictest adherence to the rule is necessary. The vigilance of Co-Masonic officials in this respect should be even greater than is necessary in the Masculine Craft, because in the intricacies of a lady's costume it is more easily possible to overlook some breach of the regulation. Most kinds of hairpins must of course be rigorously excluded; the same caution applies to hooks and eyes and many types of buttons and garters. Our Indian Brn. need to exercise care with regard to the embroidery on dhoties and saris. We have sometimes encountered sentimental objections on the part of ladies to the removal of the wedding ring, and I think that similar difficulties sometimes exist in India with regard to bangles and other ornaments.

Direction on this point was asked from the H.O.A.T.F., and he said very definitely that modification of this rule should not be permitted, though He also said that in several cases in the past, where an official was ignorant of the stringency of the rule, He had Himself performed an act of healing which validated the initiation. Otherwise; He requires its strict fulfilment, and intimates that those who feel unable to comply with this requirement should not join the Co-Masonic Order. We had a case in which a man inadvertently went through the ceremony with a gold charm or medal sewn into the lining of one of his garments. This was not remembered until the conclusion of the ceremony, which of course had to be repeated from the beginning.

There was another instance in which by an unworthy subterfuge a feminine candidate succeeded in retaining a wedding ring until the conclusion of the ceremony and, when this was discovered, absolutely refused to have it removed that the initiation might be repeated. The question then arose as to the status of this candidate, who had irregularly received certain secrets. The decision of the H.O.A.T.F. was clear and uncompromising, that in spite of the ceremony of initiation she was not a Mason, and could not in any way be recognized as such. There have been cases in my Mother Lodge in which it has been found necessary to file through a tightly-fitting ring; but that can easily be done by a skilful operator, who is also able to restore the ring quite perfectly to its previous appearance. Obviously, care must also be taken with regard to spectacles and eyeglasses. We are given to understand that gold and silver in teeth are not objectionable, as they are a permanent part of the person.

Another suggestion which has been made as to the meaning of this stringent prohibition is that the wearing of m ... s would render the candidate ceremonially unclean, therefore his initiation would be null and void, so that it would be necessary to remove the m ... l and to repeat the ceremony. Some writers have supposed that this feeling that m ... s are to a certain extent impure probably dates from the close of the stone age. The same idea of conservatism dictated that only a stone knife might be used in the offering of sacrifices or in the rite of circumcision.

This part of the preparation is also supposed to refer to the fact that at the building of King Solomon's Temple there was not heard within its precincts the sound of any axe, hammer or tool of iron, as the stones were fully prepared in the quarries and were laid in their places by means of wooden mauls.

That the candidate should enter without any v ... s on his person is symbolic of the fact that he is going into a brotherhood in which money, titles, and other distinctions of the outer world do not count.

The rich man leaves his rank and state

Outside the Mason's door;

The poor man meets his true respect

Upon the chequered floor.

The Freemason is equal to a prince, but brother to a beggar, if he be worthy. In the Lodge this brotherhood is seen in the entire absence of any favouritism; everyone who becomes a M.M. may in due course rise to the position of Master of the Lodge.

There is also a personal side to the matter. He must be "poor"; that is to say, he must not be dependent upon external wealth and possessions, for they will not avail him in the progress of the evolution that he is now taking in hand. On the contrary, great possessions may be a hindrance to him, unless he is a man of such strong character that he is entirely their master, and can take them up and put them down at will, and can see them come and go without elation or sorrow. Strictly speaking, he who enters on the occult path owns nothing at all; though he may have to handle great wealth and large interests, he cannot feel them as his personal possessions, to be held for the delight or benefit of his separate self. He deals with them only as a steward on behalf of God in the service of man. He has in that sense given all that he had to the poor, and has thus at the same time become one of the poor himself.

The candidate is blindfolded for the obvious reason that he shall not see the Lodge or any of its decorations or arrangements till he has taken the solemn O. on no account to reveal them to any outsider. Until the O. is taken the candidate is at liberty to withdraw. There have been cases in which the candidate objected to the form of the O. offered to him, and declined to proceed further. In such rare instances he may honourably be permitted to withdraw, and he will be conducted from the Lodge still blindfolded, so that no question can arise of his disclosing anything that should be kept secret. As soon as that solemn O. has been taken, the very first step is to remove the handkerchief from his eyes. If at any time subsequent to that the candidate should wish to withdraw he is of course nevertheless bound by the oath of secrecy which he has taken.

The h ... g typifies the state of mental darkness of the candidate. The man in the street thinks that he sees and knows, but the candidate must now realize that that is not so. He begins to understand the words of an ancient sage, who said that when it is day with ordinary men it is night to the wise, but when it is night to ordinary men it is day to the wise. What looks to men in the world like light and knowledge, he sees to be ignorance and darkness; and where all is dark to them, he sees. It seems sad that so little of the true knowledge vital to the well-being and progress of the human soul is taught in our schools at the present day. Much time and energy are expended in trying to make a boy a good classical or mathematical scholar; far less attention seems to be devoted to making him a man of noble life, an honourable, unselfish, loyal and upright citizen. Therefore about many of the most important points in life we are truly left to walk in darkness; and it is precisely from that particular sort of darkness that Freemasonry delivers its candidates. Therefore they symbolically acknowledge the existence of the darkness, and are willing to go forward through it in search of Light.

Moreover, as is said in the Mystic Charge, it also symbolizes the blank unconsciousness which follows the passage through the gateway of death, ere the subtler part of the physical body has fallen away.

The candidate wears a c ... t ... about his neck, with the loose end hanging in front, and he is admitted to the Lodge upon the p ... of a naked s ... pressed to his left b ... These two things typify the fact that in life men have responsibilities and limitations, both of which must be taken into account by every wise man; there can be no turning back from the former, nor any impetuous rushing forward regardless of the latter. Here again we have a symbol of the two great laws of dharma and karma. Through dharma - the use of the powers that we have, in the duties of life that those powers make us fit to perform - there is growth or evolution from within. Through karma - the outer environment that comes to us as the result of the actions that we have done in past lives - come opportunities for progress and sometimes obstacles, which, however, when rightly faced, increase our inward strength. As Emerson put it, man learns in this world through tuition and intuition - both externally and internally he is being taught. On the occult path it is still more important that the aspirant shall proceed without impetuosity or reluctance, without rashness or fear. Just as one wishing to walk on a line must go neither too slowly nor too fast, so must the candidate proceed on the path which is narrow as the edge of a razor. "*Festina lente*" might well be taken as his motto.

It should be noted that the symbolism of the c ... t ... requires that whoever conducts the candidate in these earlier stages of the ceremony should in all cases lead him by it, as well as grasp him by the hand or elbow. It also, as well as the h ... k, has been described as symbolical of the bondage of ignorance under which the candidate remains until the light of Masonry shines upon him.

This emblem of the c ... t ... has also been considered to typify the psychic umbilical cord - the connecting thread of matter which joins the etheric double to the dense physical body when the former is temporarily partially withdrawn from the latter - the "silver cord" mentioned in a well-known biblical passage (Ecclesiastes, xii, 6.) as being definitely loosed at death. Bro. Wilmshurst in *The Masonic Initiation*, p. 85, tells us that "silver is the technical esoteric term for psychical substance, as gold is for spiritual, and iron or brass for physical". He suggests also that the c ... t ... is intended to hint to us that all the true and higher Initiations take place out of the physical body.

THE INNER PREPARATION

But little is said in the ritual about the other and even more important aspect of the necessary preparation of a candidate for initiation into Freemasonry - the inner and spiritual part of it. At a later stage, when the neophyte is about to pass on into a higher degree, he is asked: "Where were you first prepared to be made a Freemason?" and the beautiful and suggestive answer which is put into his mouth is: "In my heart." In one of the masculine rituals the R.W.M. reminds the candidate that internally he was prepared to be made a Mason in his heart by having a preconceived good opinion of the Order, a wish to be ranked among its members, and a desire for knowledge. Furthermore, in the first lecture the questioner asks: "What come you here to do?" and the answer is: "To learn to rule and subdue my passions, and to make further progress in Masonry."

Before the door is opened to his knock the candidate has to convince the I.G. that he is rightly prepared in his mind and heart, as well as in external form. He comes, announces the T., of his own free will and accord, humbly soliciting to be admitted to the mysteries and privileges of ancient Freemasonry, and hopes to obtain them by the help of God, and the t ... of g ... r ..., being free. No man can tread the occult path on the inspiration of another; he must feel within himself the impulse, a lack of satisfaction with the things that the world of ordinary life can give, an inner hunger for the things of the spirit, which among the Hindus is called *mumukshatva*. It is a path on which external things do not stand by to support the traveller, who has nothing but his own inner strength to sustain him and urge him on.

Though this is so, it is also happily true that when the man makes this effort for himself he does find a response from within, and so he is justified in saying that he hopes to obtain initiation by the help of God as well as by the t ... of g ... r ...

He solicits humbly because he is looking upwards to the light; his attitude is the exact opposite of that of the man of pride, who is content to look downwards, enjoying the comparison of his own greatness with the littleness of inferior persons and things that come within his supercilious vision. Humility is the possession of the man of ideals, who is never self-satisfied, because he regards always that which is above. It is thus the key to the gateway of the upward path. The humble man will not think that he achieves his triumph by his own proud prowess alone, but, realizing that all strength is the divine strength, he will recognize that, like the heroes of old, he is but employing the powers with which he has been endowed from on high - just as Arjuna in the battle of Kurukshetra used the celestial weapons presented to him by Shiva during his pilgrimage in the Himalayas - just as Perseus, in the fearful adventure which he undertook against the Gorgon, used the helmet lent to him by Pluto, the shield or mirror of Pallas Athene and the wings of Mercury - just as King Arthur received the mystic sword Excalibur from the Lady of the Lake. And even Christ said: "I do nothing of myself, but as my Father hath taught me, and he that sent me is with me."

The t ... of g ... r ..., it is said, has already been heard in his favour in the Lodge. This phrase has a double sense. It may undoubtedly be taken as referring to the testimony to the candidate which has already been given by his proposer and seconder. But it has also another and more esoteric meaning, which has been beautifully expressed by Bro. Wilmshurst in Masonic Initiation as follows:

This does not mean of good reputation. It means that on being tested by the initiating authorities he must be found spiritually responsive to the ideals aimed at and "ring true", giving back a good sound or report like a coin that is tapped to determine its genuineness. In the wonderful Egyptian rituals in *The Book of the Dead*, one of the Titles always found accorded to the Initiate was "true of voice". This is the same thing as our reference to possessing the "tongue of good report". It does not mean that he was incapable of falsity and hypocrisy, which goes without saying, but that his very voice revealed his inherent spirituality and his own speech reflected and was coloured by the divine Word behind it. The vocal and heart nervous centres - the guttural and the pectoral, as we say - are intimately related physiologically. Purity or impurity of heart modifies the tonal quality and moral power of one's speech. The voice of the real Initiate or saint is always marked by a charm, a music, an impressiveness, and a sincerity absent in other men; for he is "true of voice"; he possesses the "tongue of good report". (Op. cit., p. 31).

Every man pronounces his own true name. Just as he has his own odour materially, by which a bloodhound can track him, so has he his sound spiritually; and those who can hear that sound of his in the inner worlds know where he stands on the ladder of evolution, and what he can and cannot do. The distinctive sound which every man has is often spoken of as his chord. Each of his vehicles contains vibrations of all sorts of different rates, and these blend together so as to make for each vehicle a certain complex sound - the average sound of the whole vehicle, somewhat analogous to the composite photographs which we sometimes see, in which a number of faces are superimposed upon the same plate. Such composite notes are produced by each of the vehicles - etheric, astral and mental - and these taken together make up the distinctive chord of the man, by which those who can hear it can always identify him. This is sometimes called the occult name of the personality; the true name which is first heard at his Initiation as an Adept is that belonging to other and far higher vehicles. Much ancient magic took its power from the knowledge of such names. Thus it is his own knock, his own report, made with the t ..., of the inner self, that opens for the man the way into the true Lodge.

The stipulation that the candidate must be a free man takes us back in thought to those ancient days in which a large majority of men were not free, in which vast hosts of people lived in the condition of serfs or slaves. We need not think of that great class as being necessarily ill-treated or degraded. Many of them were men of other races, whose fate it had been to be taken prisoners in battle; they were consequently quite often of just as good birth as their captors. In ancient Egypt at any rate this fact was fully recognized, and it was by no means infrequent for a slave to marry into the family of his master, when of course he became at once a free man. It was, however, the immemorial tradition in times of old that only one who held the status of a free man could be admitted into a Masonic Lodge. The definition now given of the man who is a fit and proper person to be made a Mason is that he shall be just, upright and free, of mature age, sound judgment and strict morals; and this enumeration of qualities gives us some idea of the inner preparation necessary before the Masonic initiation.

To this qualification also there is a symbolical meaning, for the man who is aspiring towards the light ought even already at least to have begun to free himself from the domination of circumstances, which so hopelessly enslave the ordinary man of the world. He ought at least to have some glimmering of the truth that these very circumstances which so limit and oppress him may themselves be used by the strong soul as steppingstones to a wider and more glorious life.

All these preliminaries being finished, the R.W.M. issues the command that the candidate shall be admitted in due course. The I.G. receives him between the two p ... s and touches his 1 ... b ... with the p ..., of the p ..., asking him whether he feels anything. Receiving an affirmative reply he then gives the candidate the solemn warning that the remembrance of this action should always operate as a reminder if he should ever be in danger of forgetting his O. to guard the s ... s of Freemasonry.

Just inside the door of the Lodge stand the S. and J.D.s with crossed w ... s, representing thereby the triangular door of the ancient Egyption Lodge, and also the first of the symbolical portals through which the candidate has to pass. As he stands within that portal the candidate is directed to bow his head as a further token of the humility which should mark the aspirant. From the emblematical point of view the Lodge typifies the higher world into which man passes when he leaves this physical plane, so that this first portal represents the gate of death, and in relation to this the bowing of the head signifies that submission to the divine will with which the man should enter upon this new field of life, calm, and ready to receive without agitation whatever may come.

The I.G., having performed his office, has nothing further to do with the candidate. This we may take as indicating the fact that the man should withdraw entirely from his etheric double as soon as may be after entering the portal of death. He is now taken in hand by the J.D., who signifies the astral body in which the newly deceased has to live for a time.

The candidate now kneels at the left of the S.W. while the R.W.M. invokes the blessing of the Ministers of T.G.A.O.T.U. and that of the Most Worthy and Venerable Master of the Wisdom, who is the H.O.A.T.F. throughout the world. Once more a true name is sounded, and the great Master and others stand ready to help the candidate to attain to wisdom in himself, to display the beauty of divine humanity in his outward form and actions, and to co-operate with the Supreme Will in evolution, so preserving perfect harmony between the inner life and the outer form.

By this invocation the R.W.M. acknowledges that our temple is but a lodge at the gate, an entrance to the driveway of a greater Temple, the hidden Lodge of which the M.O.T.W. has charge. In the cyclic progress of civilization the seven rays or types of life take pre-eminence in turn. During the middle ages devotion, the sixth type, was predominant, but now the seventh type, which includes many forms of ceremonial, is coming into force, so that everywhere interest in it is on the increase, and the time is ripe for a large extension of Masonry, and for the more perfect working and understanding of its ritual.

When a man joined the Lesser Mysteries in Greece or Egypt, it was considered that the first and most important teaching to be given to him was the truth about conditions after death, since they felt that a man might die at any moment, and should therefore be in possession of that knowledge. We continue that practice to the present day, and as a prominent part of that teaching we take the candidate on the three symbolical journeys.

THE THREE SYMBOLICAL JOURNEYS

There are three portals, or doorways, through which the candidate must pass. They are invisible to physical eyes, but are nevertheless perfectly real, because they are made by thought. The first one, as has already been explained, is an emblem of death, the passing out of the physical world into the next stage of life in the lowest part of the astral plane. The candidate enters without sight into that world, but feels the touch of a friend, who takes hold of his hand or arm and guides him on his journey. This friend is the J.D. who, it will be remembered, represents the astral or emotional principle in the human constitution. The I.G. presides over the first portal on behalf of the R.W.M., of whom he is an expression on the physical plane.

In the first circuit of the Lodge, or the first symbolical journey, the candidate finds himself surrounded by horrible noises, including the clanking of chains and the clashing of swords, which are intended to tell him of the din and confusion of the lowest sub-plane of the astral world, where are gathered after death those who are in bondage to sensual pleasures, or filled with fear, hatred, malice or revenge. Afterwards the W.J.W. explains that this journey is a faint copy of the trials through which the candidate had to go in the ancient Mysteries, when he was led through gloomy caverns, symbolizing the underworld, amid tumultuous sounds, in darkness, surrounded by perils which he could pot understand. It is not probable that the average decent person who presents himself for admission to the Masonic fraternity will have after death any consciousness at all of passing through this lowest region, but if it should happen so, he will be prepared to go through the experience calmly and without fear.

As the candidate approaches the W.J.W.'s pedestal he arrives at the second portal, and is there introduced to the elementals of earth and water, who are related to the region through which he has just symbolically come, which may be thought of as consisting of the solid and liquid sub-planes of the astral world. First he turns to the north and makes a suitable offering to the earth-elementals, and then to the south to make his offering to the elementals of the water. They are not the same creatures as those who were engaged in building the temple, but they stand quite definitely under their captain, who in turn obeys the W.J.W. as the guardian of the second portal. These elementals, which are of the kind sometimes called nature-spirits, gather round, and recognize thenceforth the man who has been presented to them. After this ceremony, should the man find himself in any kind of non-physical danger, or in the presence of a malignant influence, he can draw round him a bodyguard of these beings, on account of the brotherhood with them that has now been established.

Plate X is an attempt to show the appearance of this portal. The W.J.W. is seen seated at his pedestal, which is as it were within the thickness of the wall of the second portal. Over his head floats the sphere of his Deva-representative, who is surrounded by his band of assistants. At the right hand side of the portal the earth elementals are grouped, and on the left side those of the water - tricksy sprites, ready to play with great gusto their part of resisting intrusion upon their domain until the candidate is properly presented to them, and demonstrates his friendly intentions by a formal offering.

Plate X. THE SECOND PORTAL

For the purpose of clearness we omit from this illustration all that is not necessary for our object; the candidate and the J.D. who is leading him are not shown, nor are the Brn. in the columns. Only the W.S.W. appears in the distance, seen faintly through the second portal. The third portal is of course close to his pedestal; but as it is exactly similar in shape to the second, though differing in colour, no attempt is made to represent it.

It is the quality of discrimination between the higher and the lower, between the real and the unreal, which has enabled the candidate to pass scatheless through these regions of the astral world. The J.D., seeking passage for his charge, tells the elementals that he is a blinded child of mortality, seeking immortality. Passing through their regions in the course of his pilgrimage to the higher planes, the candidate is prepared to give up all that belongs to them - all that matter which appertains to these levels, earth to earth and water to water. In this region after death must linger all those who cling to the low grade of emotional existence that embodies itself in this order of matter; only when they have become purified through suffering, and are ready to give up their low emotions, can they shake off this matter from their astral bodies, and pass to higher parts of the astral plane. The candidate will not linger here, for discrimination has taught him that there are better things. He must henceforth be recognized as one of the brothers of light and immortality, not in a state of darkness so far as this level is concerned.

The second symbolical journey is similar to the first, except that the noise is gentle instead of harsh. The candidate is still in the astral world, but in the middle part of it, which is much finer and subtler than that through which he has come. This is the place of the common human emotions; the former was rather that of blind passion. The desires that attach ordinary men to the matter of these middle regions are by no means reprehensible, but on the other hand they are not uplifting. All the pleasures of the body that are not coarse or gross build their tenements here, for the abiding of the souls of the dead until they have tired of these things, and are ready to pass onwards. I have given an account of these regions and the people living in them in *The Astral Plane* and *The Other Side of Death*, and The First Lieutenant Sovereign Grand Commander of the Co-Masonic Order, the Very Illustrious Bro. Annie Besant has also dealt with them at length in *The Ancient Wisdom*.

The candidate arrives at the third portal, near the pedestal of the W.S.W., who is its guardian. There, facing east, he is introduced to the elementals of the air, who guard the right side of the portal, and facing west, to the elementals of the fire, who guard its left side.

Desirelessness is the quality which can pass him through the allurements of this region, so that once more he gives to the elementals what he carries that belongs to them, and passes on, their friend, to whom they will be ever ready to lend their treasures, because they know him as a Brother of Light who will not keep them for himself, but will use them well and return them in due season.

Of this journey it is explained by the W.S.W. that in the ancient Mysteries, as the candidate left the gloomy caverns behind him, he passed into a quiet region, symbolizing the higher sub-planes of the underworld, whereinto the rougher, harsher sounds did not penetrate, though still there was some disharmony amid the souls.

It is not inappropriate that life in the astral plane after death should be thought of as a journey, or a series of journeys. The "dead" person does go through a series of well-marked changes, as his astral body becomes more and more purified by the elimination of its denser grades of matter. During life the man's emotions have been acting like magnets, drawing into the astral body coarse astral matter of the lower regions when they have been base, and fine matter of the higher levels when they have been lofty. After death the man has to sojourn on each of these levels in turn until he has eliminated its grade of matter from his astral body. The Mason who knows this meaning of the symbolical journeys will be prepared after death to use his will so as to vanquish his lower emotions, free himself quickly of the heavier matter, and pass rapidly onward into the heaven-world.

The third symbolical journey is trodden in the perfect silence that typifies the highest part of the astral plane, on the very borders of the heaven-world. At the end of this the R.W.M. tells the candidate that the dead man whose experience he has been repeating had at this stage reached the threshold of the heavenly world, where perfect silence lulled the weary senses and calm peace enfolded him. The lower world lay below him; before him the joys of heaven; and in the interspace was silence. This was, and is, his experience in the true Mysteries; it was symbolized by utter silence in the mysteries of Egypt and Greece; in Freemasonry it is kept in memory in the silence of the third symbolical journey.

At this point the journeys end. No further elementals or portals are mentioned in the ceremony, though there are seven orders in all, and many ancient peoples have recognized them in their worship by bowing to the devas of the N., S., E. and W., the zenith, the nadir and the centre of all. The candidate is not going beyond that particular region of the astral plane on this occasion; he is merely being introduced to a world which he will have to visit many times before he can traverse it readily, and live and work there with perfect ease. In this stage of his career he symbolizes the pupil on the probationary path, and must practise the three qualities of discrimination, desirelessness and good-conduct or self-control, which will make him free of the emotional plane, as he was free of the physical plane before he entered the Lodge. Further information as to these requirements will be found in *At the Feet of the Master,* by J. Krishnamurti, *The Path of Discipleship*, by the V ∴ Ills ∴ Bro ∴ Annie Besant, and my own book *The Masters and the Path.*

Three kinds of dangers these qualities will help him to overcome - dangers from the outside world, dangers from his own lower nature, and dangers from within himself, that is, from his own virtues, if they be unbalanced. The s ... d at his b ... typified the first of these; later on he will find the s ... of his own lower nature in place of it, and later still the c ... s that typify the triangle of his higher self, whose very virtues may be exaggerated to become his undoing unless he is ever watchful to keep poise and calmness, and to walk on that Middle Way which the Lord Buddha has described as the path of safety.

In course of time the candidate, through the practice of these three qualifications, will be able to range the entire plane at will. For this activity discrimination will give him the mental power, desirelessness the emotional power, and good conduct the will-power; and in the highest part of the region no ceremony will ever be needed in order that he may pass through without hindrance, for everything there is instantly responsive and obedient to the enlightened human will. The Brothers of Light are easily recognized there.

This portion of the ritual is mainly derived from the symbolic or blue degrees of the Ancient and Accepted Scottish Rite, but does not appear in the working of the Grand Lodge of England. In the Scottish Rite ritual worked in Lodges under the auspices of the Supreme Council of France the three symbolical journeys exist, with noise and clashing of swords in the first, with a *"cliquetis d'armes blanches"* in the second, and perfect silence in the third, but there is no invocation of the elementals, although the journeys are compared to the ancient trials by earth, air, fire and water.

An interesting confirmation of the use of these trials or journeys is given in the transactions of the A.Q.C., in an account of his own initiation by Robert Guillemand, the man who killed Lord Nelson at Trafalgar by shooting him from a French ship. He was initiated during the siege of Strasburg, and tile account, which is dated 1807, says:

It took place accordingly, with all the splendour circumstances admitted, in a hut about 15 ft. in length and 6 in breadth, where there was no room to stand up, but which served as a Temple notwithstanding. After having made my journeys, which were not very long ones, undergone the trials by fire and water, and the usual tricks, received the signs, words, touches, and other forms, the adjutant, who was our orator, addressed me a very fine speech, in which he explained to me the sublimity of the character I had just obtained, creating me a child of the Light.

In masculine Masonry in England swords are not brought into the Lodge, and in the days when gentlemen used to wear swords, they left them outside; but with the Co-Masons they are used in Lodge as powerful instruments of love in the practical magic of the ritual.

THE O ...

The candidate is now standing in the north-west corner facing the east, and the W.S.W. presents him to the R.W.M. as one properly prepared to be made a Freemason. At this point he is given an opportunity to withdraw if he so chooses, but having declared his determination to go forward without fear or rashness, he is led to the altar, the place of Light, by the p ... s ... s. The first s ... is taken with the l ... f ... pointing forward, and the r ... f ... is brought up to it at right angles, h ... to h ... - a s ... about n ... i ... long. The 1 ... f ..., is first moved because it is nearest the heart, and should remind the candidate to let love have the primary authority in all his decisions. The second and third s ... are similar, but of t ..., and f ... i ... respectively. Three s ... s there must be, because the qualifications are three; the quality of love is sometimes counted as a fourth, but really it must permeate them all, and when it is strong it will carry the disciple up into the higher path of the next degree.

There are two reasons for the length of these three s ... s. Each one carries a man forward further than the preceding one. That is the way of evolution. Every step that is taken adds to a man's strength, so that his next step will be both stronger and longer. Always something is gained but nothing is lost, so that his speed increases on this path by arithmetical progression, and later on he may expect geometrical progression and even progression by squares, in his advance.

Again, nine, twelve and fifteen are in the proportions three, four and five, which reminds us of the Pythagorean theorem, which is of constant use to the human architect, and presumably in some greater way in the plans of the G.A. Himself. To the P.M. especially belongs the use of this great tool, but even now the E.A. should learn to reverence it and aspire to use it later on.

While the candidate k ... s at the a ... to take his O. some Brn. from the seats in the west of the Lodge usually stand round behind the candidate, forming a hollow square touching the corners of the altar, with their s ... pointing towards the candidate while the Master takes from him his O. While standing in this attitude each Bro. should fig his attention upon the candidate, and should endeavour to pour forth upon him with all his strength the blessing which, as a M.M., it is within his right and power to give.

Many candidates are surprised at the terrible solemnity of the O., which has come down to us from the Middle Ages. In those times the Masons were teaching facts about the inner life and the nature of man for knowing which the Church would have burnt them alive, and there was thus great need for secrecy, to an extent that excuses the strong language used in the O., especially when it is remembered that had one person revealed anything, it would have placed all the rest of the Lodge in danger of being judicially murdered.

The recitation of the O. being completed, the Brn. standing round bring their swords to the carry, that is, upright in the hand, with the elbow in the form of a s ..., and the Brn. in their seats in the east stretch out their r ... a ... horizontally in blessing, and swords and arms are both raised as all sing, "May the vow be kept". When these words are uttered every Bro. should wish with all his force that the candidate may have the strength to keep the vow which he has just taken.

The R.W.M. now creates, receives, and constitutes the candidate an E.A.F., with k ... s with the g ... upon the f ... s ... placed upon his s ... s and h ... in turn. Though the R.W.M. confers the degree, he is of course acting on behalf of the H.O.A.T.F., and is a channel for his power. Obviously also the three touches of the f ... s ... convey different aspects of that power, corresponding to the three Aspects of the blessed Trinity, the first conveying strength to the brain, the second love to the heart, and the third executive ability to the right arm. The general effect of this downpouring of force is to widen somewhat the channel of communication between the ego and the personality of the candidate - another example of the curious correspondence between the admission to this degree and the ordination of the sub-deacon.* (*See *The Science of the Sacraments*, p. 315.)

Now that the solemn O. of secrecy has been taken the h ... k is removed and the blessing of light is restored to the candidate. In commenting upon this Bro. J. S. M. Ward says:

Notice the word *restored*. Mystical re-birth marks the beginning of our journey towards the light, of our ascent towards God, but it is a restoration - a journey back to Him from whom we came. Exactly the same procedure is followed in the initiatory rites of the Turkish dervishes. Among them the incident is followed by a beautiful exposition of the mystical meaning of Light. It is the divine light, emblem of God Himself, and of divine inspiration. It is present not only in the sacred writings, but in every true believer's heart. The light of the sun itself is but a faint similitude of the divine light of God's love through which and in which we have our being.

THE E ...1 I ... s

On being restored to the blessing of light, the eye of the new A. falls upon the t ... g ... e ... l ... s in Freemasonry. The furniture of the Lodge here reappears under this new name, but as we have already discussed the matter in Chapter III, we need not repeat here the explanation of the symbology involved.

In the Co-Masonic ritual the R.W.M. now raises the newly-made brother to his feet and turns him round so that he sees for the first time the Brn. with their s ... s at the carry. He explains to him that he must not regard this martial display as a menace, but as a symbol of the protection with which Freemasonry henceforth surrounds him. The Brn. then return to their seats.

The neophyte is led to the north, facing the W.J.W., and stands there, within the *cella*, subject to the special force which plays in that region, while the R.W.M. stands in front of him and instructs him. First the Master draws the candidate's attention to the three great columns upon which a Lodge of Freemasonry symbolically rests - those of the R.W.M. and his two Wardens, symbolizing respectively wisdom, strength and beauty or harmony. These have already been explained in Chapter II. In the masculine ritual this explanation of the three columns is put somewhat differently, as they are there described as the three lesser lights, which are explained to be the sun, the moon and the Master of the Lodge. This connects up modern Masonry with much old symbology in which the moon and the sun largely figure.

THE S ... AND P ...

In this situation the R.W.M. also instructs the N. in the s ... s of this degree, a s ..., a g ... and a w ... The s ... in this degree is often supposed to be related to the p ... mentioned in the O., but the s ..., existed long before the p ..., which was invented to fit it. Among the Egyptians the same p ... existed, and even before them among the Nilotic negroes in Egypt, and probably in other places as well. It mattered enormously to an ancient Egyptian that his body should be cast into the waves, and that he should not be decently buried with the proper rites, which he believed would set him free from the physical body, to which otherwise he might be tied. In the ghost stories of Homer, in the Iliad and the Odyssey, in nearly all cases when unhappy ghosts returned they did so because they wanted their bodies to be buried with proper rites, in order that they might be set free. The same idea appears in Hindu thought, as, for example, in the Garuda Purana, in the story of the ghost of Sudeva, who was released by King Babhruvahana. This neglect of ceremonial would not matter to us in modern times, because we have not those ideas; but it is a literal fact that after death a man's own thought could keep him bound in that way until he knew or believed that his body had been properly interred. So this was a very ancient p ... In reality the s ... refers to a certain chakra and its working, as I have already explained. It is, of course, not permissible to describe the g ..., but it will not be difficult for a Freemason to understand that it implies the repression of the astral body, which is the first of the superphysical principles of man.

EXAMINATION AND INVESTITURE

The J.D. next takes the N. to the pedestals of the W.J.W. and the W.S.W. for examination of his knowledge of the s ... g ... and w ..., and he stands before each for a little while, during the series of questions and answers, within the beehive form which has been described in Chapter IV. While he is standing in that place, the force of the inner planes plays upon him with concentrated intensity, and strengthens him in the qualifications which he has to develop.

At the command of the R.W.M. the W.S.W. now invests the new Bro. with the distinguishing badge of a Freemason, the a ..., which has already been described in Chapter IV. Having thus invested the neophyte, the W.S.W. delivers a little homily, in which he refers to the great antiquity and dignity of this symbol, and the R.W.M. adds to this a remark on the importance of not entering the Lodge if one Bro. is at variance with another. On this point Bro. J.S.M. Ward makes the following very suggestive remarks:

At first sight this may seem a somewhat unnecessary charge. Normally well-conducted gentlemen are not likely to start an unseemly wrangle in Lodge, even if they are at enmity; and should two men so far forget the common decency of life as to do so, the R.W.M. has ample power to deal with the situation. The real significance of the injunction is that it implies that the mere presence of two brethren who are at variance will disturb the harmonious atmosphere of the meeting. This is a purely spiritual atmosphere, and the belief that such disturbance would occur without any open disagreement is correct. In short, such differences disturb the spiritual atmosphere, preventing concentration, and can be detected by sensitive individuals. Every Lodge has an atmosphere of its own, and any sensitive man who comes to it can detect it. I have myself noticed the different atmospheres of various Lodges, and also variations in that of my own. Too much regard therefore cannot be paid to this rule, and if it is ignored the Lodge will certainly suffer. (The E. A. Handbook, pp. 78, 79.)

After this advice has been given, the new A, is directed to his seat in the north-east part of the Lodge, that being the point of the compass where the Egyptians believed that the sun began his journey when he was first created.

THE WORKING TOOLS

The interpretation given to the working tools of the E.A. in ordinary Craft Masonry is explained to the new Bro. by the W.J.W. at his initiation. This officer does it because he is in charge of the chamber where the E.A.s work.

In masculine Craft Masonry the t ... f ... i ... g ... is described as indicating a measure of time, to remind him that the hours of his day are to be spent not in mere carelessness or selfishness, but partly in meditation and study, and partly in labour, refreshment and sleep; in Co-Masonry we add "but all in the service of humanity". It is also explained that this symbol indicates that accuracy and precision are essential for the proper conduct of our lives.

The E.A. is further taught that the c ... g ..., reminds us that skill without exertion is of little avail, and that labour is the lot of man. It also represents the force of conscience, which should keep down all vain and unbecoming thoughts, so that our feelings and actions may be pure and unpolluted. Thirdly, comes the c ... l, which points out that education and perseverance are necessary to establish perfection, and that the rude material of our natures receives its polish and refinement from repeated efforts alone.

In ancient Egypt rather a different signification was given to these tools - a little nearer to the original, since it is obvious that education and conscience are not exactly tools for a man to use. It will be noticed that all three are specially connected with the shaping of the stone. As the operative mason shapes the rough ashlar into the perfect ashlar by removing the excrescences and smoothing and measuring it, so must the E.A. in speculative masonry train himself perfectly in morality. In ancient Egypt the apprentice remained in that condition usually for seven years, until he satisfied those in authority that he was fit to pass on to the second degree. In the present day the qualifications have become little more than the lapse of time and the answering of certain questions.

In early Christianity there were three recognized stages through which everyone had to pass who wished to make progress - purification, illumination and perfection. St. Paul said: "We speak wisdom among them that are perfect." This is often misunderstood. Obviously, if the people were perfect in the modern sense of the term, they would not need to be taught at all. These words are not used in their ordinary sense; they are technical terms used in connection with the Mysteries, and well known by all educated people of that period as being so used. What St. Paul said was: "We teach the gnosis, the secret wisdom, only to those who have attained the degree of perfection," or, as a Mason would put it, the degree of the M.M., because those three stages correspond in a general way to the three degrees in Masonry. Nowadays, the Christian Church seems to stop at the first stage – purification - and to regard it as its greatest work to make people saints. That is indeed a very high and noble thing, but in the older days of Christianity, to make a man a saint was only a preliminary stage. St. Clement of Alexandria, one of the greatest of the Christian Fathers, says: "Purity - that is only a negative virtue valuable chiefly as a condition of insight." When the man had made himself perfectly pure and holy in his life, he was eligible for the second stage, that of illumination, and only after he was fully illuminated could he pass on to the stage of perfection, and so become a channel for God's power.

EGYPTIAN INTERPRETATION OF THE WORKING TOOLS

In ancient Egypt the t ... f ... r i ... g ..., or as it was then, the t ... f ... e i ... g ... or sacred cubit of the great pyramid, was nearly the same as ours. Their unit of measure, the inch, was derived from the accurate knowledge which the Egyptians had of the polar diameter of the earth, one five-hundred-millionth division of this being the pyramid inch. Our English inch of the present day was derived, through Greece and Rome, from this Egyptian measure, but it is not quite the same unit as that which was used in the building of the great pyramid. In the course of time it has been made a little shorter; it has lost about one thousandth part of itself, so that the pyramid inch is 1.0011 of the English inch. It is only in the last century that men have come to know the length of the equatorial diameter of the earth, but the polar diameter was known long ago.

Many countries still retain measures of length derived from the pyramid inch, but in France the decimal system was adopted. There they have the metre, which was intended to be one ten-millionth part of a quadrant of the earth, measured over the surface from the pole to the equator. Later they discovered that this measure was not perfectly accurate, so a metre is now a conventional length standardized by a bar kept in Paris, just as a standard yard is kept in London.

Scientific knowledge in that ancient land was in some respects fully as advanced as our own indeed even more advanced than was ours until very recently. The Mysteries included a thorough and liberal education, and especial stress seems to have been laid upon chemistry, astronomy and geodesy. In the very early ages when the great pyramid, the House of Light, was built, a vast amount of information was already in the possession of those who erected that stupendous monument, and they so designed its proportions as to enshrine within it in what they hoped was an indestructible form a great deal of this invaluable knowledge. For example, the perimeter of the base (36,524 pyramid inches) is to the height (5,813 pyramid inches) as is the circumference of a circle to its radius, i.e., mathematically 2π. It is interesting, too, that the base circuit measures in pyramid inches exactly the number of days in a hundred years. The exact size of the earth is also indicated there, as well as a number of other calculations connected with the solar system. Many of these have been carefully worked out by R. A. Proctor, the English astronomer, and Sir Gaston Maspero, the French Egyptologist, to whom I was introduced by Madame Blavatsky. Davidson and Aldersmith, in *The Great Pyramid*, p. 95, present a large amount of information on this subject. They remark:

The external features, dimensions and units of the Great Pyramid, when studied in plan, will be found to give precisely and accurately every essential value of the earth's orbit and its motions. This includes the values of the sidereal and solar years, the mean sun-distance, the sun's diameter, and the maximum and minimum values of the eccentricity of the earth's orbit.

The great pyramid was a house for initiations, and if some criminal Muhammadan fanatics had not destroyed the outer casing of it we should still have there, enshrined in stone, measurements of many astronomical phenomena more accurate than any that were available to us until the last century. It is only recently that reliable measurements have been obtained by European astronomers of the average distance of the earth from the sun. When I was a boy we were taught that it was ninety-six million miles; then they got it down to ninety-three million; later, calculations were made from very careful measurements of the mean equatorial horizontal solar parallax, taken at the time of the transits of Venus in 1874 and 1882, and they estimated it at ninety-two and a half million miles. I remember that Mr. Gladstone announced that in the House of Commons, and it aroused great interest at the time. In the eleventh edition of the *Encyclopedia Britannica* it is given as 92,998,000 miles. The ancient Egyptians made it 92,996,08 miles; who shall say that they may not have been nearer to the truth than we?

In ancient Egypt the t ... f ... i ... g ... was taken as the symbol of instinct. I am using there a word which is generally applied only to animals, and I do not want it to be misunderstood. By instinct was meant an inner feeling - the instinctive feeling that we have with regard to things. To this they attached a great deal of importance. They considered it as having two sides - the negative or the receptive, which gives us the feeling as to whether a thing is good or bad, or suitable or unsuitable for us - and an active side which we should now call taste; that is, the knowing exactly what is the right thing to have and to do, and what things will go together, will fit and harmonize. In relation to our fellow-creatures that would be tact. So the meaning of this idea of instinct was much wider than that of the present day.

In those days people - at least in Egypt, in Crete, in Greece - lived very close to nature, in the sunshine and fresh air, and they enjoyed those things in a way which we see now only perhaps among great poets and artists. They were nearer to the heart of things, and therefore their instincts were much more trustworthy than those of most people at the present day. Instinct was thus with them a definite tool to be used in the shaping and building of character. A good deal of that has been lost, as modern people have for so long led such artificial lives and have usually allowed their reason to override their instinct, even when that reason has had little material on which to found its judgments. I have myself had these instincts on many occasions, and I believe the experience is quite common; sometimes I have put them aside as not prompted by reason, as many men do, but in the long run I have always been sorry for not paying more respect to them. The instinct is not dead, and when encouraged can be revived by many people to quite a large extent.

The Egyptians took the c ... l to symbolize the intellect, which they regarded as a keen-edged instrument. They considered that the man who used his intellect would be able to remove the excrescences of superstition from the beliefs which presented themselves to him, until he became a perfect ashlar, when his thought would be well-defined and true. The c ... g ... was considered to be the divine force behind the c ..., and was interpreted as the will. This must not, of course, be confused with the Master's g ... 1, with which it has nothing in common, from which it differs even in shape. The distinction is also made clear by the fact that this tool is always spoken of as the c ... g ...

In his work, *The Magic of Freemasonry*, Major A. E. Powell has made an interesting study of the working tools of the first degree, in a chapter specially devoted to them. He takes the t ... f ... i ... g ... as a symbol of the wisdom of the R.W.M., who has to measure and plan as he rules, the g ... as an emblem of the strength of the W.S.W., it being the instrument for the transmission of force, and the c ... for the beauty of the W.J.W., it being the tool used for shaping the material. He points out that all our accurate or scientific knowledge is based on measurement, symbolized by the t ... f ... i ... g ..., that all our work in life is done by the movement of matter, effected by our energy which gives blows to it, for which the g ... is the symbol, and that the c ... is typical of the concentration of our purpose, as it cleaves through matter. Thus, he says, we know with the t ... f ... i ... g ..., we feel with the c ..., and we act with the g ... Each of these tools, he adds, must be taken as typical of a class - the t ... f ... i ... g ... for all measuring instruments, the g ... for all implements and machines for applying force, the c ... for all tools used for cutting and penetrating matter.

CHAPTER VII.
THE SECOND DEGREE. THE QUESTIONS

A PARALLEL has already been drawn between the three degrees of Blue Masonry and the three stages of progress recognized by the early Christian Church. Just as the conquest of passions and emotions is prescribed for the first degree, thus corresponding with the idea of purification, so in the second degree the idea of illumination is put before us in the reminder that its special object is to develop the intellectual, artistic and psychic faculties. As is stated in our ritual, the candidate for this degree must first give proof of his proficiency in the First Degree. I mentioned in an earlier chapter that in ancient days the E.A. remained at that stage for a period of seven years; and indeed in some cases the period was even longer, since the candidate was carefully watched in the conduct of his daily life by his superiors, and it was only when they were fully satisfied that he had fairly developed the necessary qualities within himself that he was permitted to pass on. In these days no time limit seems to be set, although in the Co-Masonic constitution it is understood that he shall have attended a certain definite number of Lodge meetings and also a special class held at regular intervals for the instruction of E.A.s. He is also expected to be able to repeat by heart the O. of the First Degree and to answer in open Lodge a few prescribed questions.

To the first of these we have already referred; it is of importance because it strikes the keynote of the whole, for when the candidate is asked where he was first prepared to be made a Freemason, he is instructed to reply: "In my heart", thus showing that the inner preparation is regarded as of even greater importance than the outer. He has then to describe the physical-plane preparation and to explain that he was initiated in the body of a Lodge just, perfect, and regular.* (*See p. 88.)

Then comes the quaintly expressed idea that the sun is always at its meridian with respect to Freemasonry, which may be interpreted that the Logos is always pouring forth His full power through each Masonic Lodge, wherever it may be situated. There seems to have been a stage in Masonic history in which it was the custom to divide the Lodge into three, or to hold it in three rooms, the outermost being that of the E.A.s, with the W.J.W. in the chair, while in the second room the W.S.W. presided over the F.C.s, and it was only in the third room that the R.W.M. sat in charge of the M.M.s. That has been given as a reason why the S.D., having conveyed the commands of the R.W.M. to the W.S.W., has to await the return of the J.D. from the outer room. According to that theory, as the W.J.W. presides over the Lodge of the E.A.s, and as he represents the sun at its meridian, it is fitting that the ceremony of initiation should be said figuratively to take place at midday.

Then comes Freemasonry's curious description of itself as "a peculiar system of morality, veiled in allegory and illustrated by symbols". This reply has always seemed to me somewhat misleading. It is not the Masonic morality which is peculiar, for that is the same which is proclaimed by every religion in the world; what is perhaps rightly to be claimed by Freemasonry is that its statement of the system is peculiarly felicitous, and that the method of its illustration is unique and forceful. Freemasonry is certainly one of the most interesting and influential of the secret societies of the world, numbering in its ranks some five millions of men pledged to observe the ties of brotherhood; and in its wonderful pageants of ceremonial - in the rituals of its many degrees, orders, chivalries and rites are enshrined splendid ideals and deep spiritual teaching of the most absorbing interest to the student of the hidden side of life.

Although today Masons do not call their Craft a religion, it has nevertheless a religious origin, as we have already seen, and it does religious work in helping its initiates and through them the rest of the world. To many of the Brn. it is the only real religion they have ever had, and certainly many of them put its principles nobly into practice: for masculine Masonry is a stupendous charitable organization as well as a "system of morality", and it offers a splendid training in practical kindliness and fraternity. In England and its colonies and in the United States of America Masonic charities are on a magnificent scale, and there are many exceedingly well-managed Masonic schools and orphanages. On this account, and because of the excellent character of its members, Masonry is highly respected, although in France and Italy it has lost caste to some extent because it has there allowed itself to become identified with anti-clerical political parties. Unfortunately Modern Masons have altogether lost sight of what might be called the inner charity - their power on higher planes. They would scarcely understand if one should say to them: "You ought to be sending out streams of thought-power; that should be one of your forms of charity." It is a pity that that inner work should be so much overlooked, for it is a tremendous agency for good, and one in which every Bro. can take part. External charity depends upon the private wealth of the few; but any Mason, however poor, can give his thought.

Naturally, Masonic Lodges are not all at the same intellectual level, and some spend far too much time in banquets and too little in study; but one has only to read the literature on the subject to see that, in English-speaking countries at least, the aims of the Craft have always been noble and uplifting. Note, for example, the following statements:

The real object of Freemasonry may be summed up in these words: to efface from among men the prejudices of caste, the conventional distinctions of colour, origin, opinion, nationality; to annihilate fanaticism and superstition, extirpate national discord, and with it extinguish the fire-brand of war; in a word - to arrive, by free and pacific progress, at one formula and model of eternal and universal right, according to which each individual human being shall be free to develop every faculty with which he may be endowed, and to concur heartily and with the fullness of his strength in the bestowment of happiness upon all, and thus to make of the whole human race one family of brothers, united by affection, wisdom and labour. (*History of Masonry*, Rebold, p. 62.)

The whole world is but one Republic, of which each nation is a family, and every individual a child. Masonry, not in any way derogating from the different duties which the diversity of States requires, tends to create a new people, which, composed of men of many nations and tongues, shall all be bound together by the bonds of Science, Morality, Virtue. (*Morals and Dogma*, Albert Pike, p. 220.)

That the sentiments expressed above have not remained mere theories is shown by the following extract from Dr. Churchward's *Arcana of Freemasonry*:

Only a few years ago we in this country went through great and acute tension - that danger which threatened war between us and the United States of America. That has passed, and will never return in an acute form again. Why? Because the Brotherhood sent their great representative, the Grand Master of Illinois, to this country, and I had the great pleasure to meet him at the Q. C. Lodge, when he gave the message of peace and brotherhood: "There shall be no war between the United States of America and England; we are of one Brotherhood, and the Freemasons of the United States have decided that there shall be no war, now or ever, between the two countries, and I am delegated to come here and tell you this, representing over a million of Brothers, and ask you in return to say there shall be no war." (Op. cit.., p. 75.)

This is a splendid testimony to the power of the Masonic tie. It is unfortunate that an attempt made later to prevent the great European war should have failed; for the Prussian Grand Lodges, when a similar appeal was made to them, refused to support the movement for peace.

The next question asked is as to the principles on which our Order is founded, which are usually given as brotherly love, relief and truth. Great prominence is rightly given to these three virtues in the ritual of the masculine Craft, and in the lectures officially prepared to be used in its Lodges they are described as follows:

By the exercise of Brotherly Love we are taught to regard the whole human species as one family, the high and low, rich and poor, created by One Almighty Being, and sent into the world for the aid, support, and protection of each other. On this principle Masonry unites men of every country, sect, and opinion, and by its dictates cultivates true friendship among those who might otherwise have remained at a perpetual distance.

To relieve the distressed is a duty incumbent on all men, particularly among Masons, who are linked together by one indissoluble bond of sincere affection; hence, to soothe the unhappy, sympathize in their misfortunes, compassionate their miseries, and restore peace to their troubled minds, is the grand aim we have in view; on this basis we establish our friendship and form our connections.

Truth is a Divine attribute, and the foundation of every Masonic virtue; to be good men and true is a lesson we are taught at our Initiation; on this grand theme we contemplate, and by its unerring dictates endeavour to regulate our lives and actions. Hence hypocrisy and deceit are or ought to be unknown to us, sincerity and plain dealing our distinguishing characteristics, while the heart and tongue join in promoting each other's welfare, and in rejoicing in the prosperity of the Craft.

The rest of the questions, though quaint, seem self-explanatory, and the various points which they raise have been already considered.

The p ... g . . . and the p ... w ... are then given to the candidate. In connection with these it is interesting to note that a sheaf of corn is often carved on the chair of the W.S.W. as his emblem; and this is probably connected with the fact that an ear of corn was shown to the aspirant as symbolical of the supreme mystery at Eleusis, indicating to him at the same time the universality of evolution and the indestructibility of life. "Except a corn of wheat fall into the ground and die, it abideth alone; but if it die, it bringeth forth much fruit." (John, xii, 24.) It is perhaps worth noting that the p ... g ... between the First and the Second Degree indicates the necessity for the conquest of that peculiar entanglement of the lower mind in the meshes of desire which in Theosophical literature is spoken of as kama-manas. Bro Wilmshurst *(The Meaning of Masonry, p. 119.)* remarks: *This [the p ... w ...] is meant to be descriptive of the candidate himself, and of his own spiritual condition. It is he who is an ear of corn planted near and nourished by a fall of water. His own spiritual growth, as achieved in the Apprentice stage, is typified by the ripening corn; the fertilizing cause of its growth being the downpouring upon his inner nature of the vivifying dew of heaven as the result of his aspiration towards the light.*

THE PREPARATION

It will be noticed that in the preparation of the candidate the same principle is followed as that which governed the corresponding ceremony in the first degree. The l ... a ... is made b ... because it is through that that the power is to be poured down, and also because during the ceremony of Passing the 1 ... e ... is to be supported by the s ... In the same way the r ... b ... is treated in a similar manner because the I.G. will touch it with the s ... on admitting the candidate to the lodge. As before, the r ... k ... is uncovered and the l ... h ... s ... p - s ... d, because these are the points in contact with the highly-magnetized floor or altar-cushion, during the taking of the O. and the actual conferring of the degree.

THE INNER PREPARATION

The inner preparation in this degree is in part the same as that in the first, for the C. hopes to obtain the privilege of being passed to the Second Degree by the help of G ..., the assistance of the s ..., and the virtue of a p ... g ... and p ... w ... The square here mentioned is the quadrilateral of the personality. Two things must happen with reference to that: it has been brought into subjection, as is implied in his treading upon it on entering the Lodge, but it has not lost its strength and activity thereby; it is as active as ever, but now all its energy is turned to the service of the real man, the higher self. That higher self incarnated in a personality for the sake of acquiring definiteness; the ego on his own plane is magnificent, but vague in his magnificence, except in the case of men far advanced on the road of evolution. Now, in the symbolism of this degree, the personality has seen with all clearness that the purpose of life is to serve the higher; he throws himself into the task with vigour and so gives some of his definiteness to make the purpose of the ego clear to himself; he makes a call to the Warrior within, to use the symbology of *Light on the Path.*

THE OPENING

While the preparation of the C. is taking place the R.W.M. once more calls upon the Brn. to assist him in opening the Lodge, but this time in the Second Degree; and yet again he begins with the universal question, but very slightly varied: "What is the first care of every F.C.F.?" And he receives the invariable answer: "To prove the Lodge close tyled." In the same form as in the First Degree he directs that that duty shall be done, and the inquiries and answers come just as before. Yet this tyling is not quite the same as the former. In each case the building of the enclosing wall takes place on all the planes; but in the First Degree attention is principally focused upon the astral world, and the defence set up at that level is incomparably stronger than the others, because that is most needed when a determined effort at astral purification and development is being made. It is as though in that purification the density of the candidate's astral body is reduced, and therefore the pressure on it from without becomes greater than usual, so that a special defence is required. In the effort made in the ceremony of the Second Degree it is upon the mental body that a similar pressure is exercised, and therefore the effort at strengthening the defences is centred in the mental plane. Thus the tyling of the Lodge in the opening of the Second Degree is not by any means a repetition of the previous ceremony, but gives rather an added security at a higher level.

Nevertheless it is eminently necessary that on the lower level also there should be no possibility of disturbance; consequently the next step is to reinforce the astral defences by calling upon the Brn. to stand to order as E.A.s, that action being as before a definite assertion of the power of the Brn. at that level and a calling together of its forces. When that is done the R.W.M, calls upon the W.J.W. asking whether he is a F.C.F. Although he is in essence the leader, the teacher and the mouthpiece of the E.A.s., he is also the representative of the higher mental; and consequently he answers immediately that he is a F.C.F., and asks that that fact shall be proved. The R.W.M. inquires by what instrument he will be proved, and he at once replies: "By the s ..."

The next question and answer as to the character of the square shows us that what is meant here is the tool of the working mason, the tool which symbolizes the spiritual will, not the quadrilateral. On the other hand, as the candidate enters the Lodge in this degree the other form of the s ... is also brought into requisition, for that upon which he treads as representing the lower nature, the personality, is certainly the geometrical figure. The Brn. are then asked to prove themselves as F.C.s, and when they have done so first the W.J.W. and then the R.W.M. repeat with emphasis the proof which has been given, thereby striking the keynote and expressing the peculiar quality of this degree. For just as the conquest of the passions and emotions is the prominent object of the E.A., so is the conquest and control of the lower mind the especial purpose of the Second Degree.

This is for most people a far more difficult conquest than the other; and in the case of many candidates the mental faculty has first of all to be aroused. We all believe ourselves to be at least capable of thinking; and yet the truth is that comparatively few people can think effectively. A person possessing a slight degree of clairvoyance can speedily convince himself of this if he will take the trouble to examine closely the thought-forms of those whom he meets in daily life. The vast majority of these are of vague and uncertain outline; it is among the rarest of phenomena to see clear and definite forms among the thousands that float about us. Thus before real progress can be made in the control of thought it is necessary for the average candidate to acquire the power of clear thought. As Ruskin remarks in *The Ethics of the Dust*: *The great difficulty is always to open people's eyes to touch their feelings and break their hearts is easy; the difficult thing is to break their heads. What does it matter, as long as they remain stupid, whether you change their feelings or not? You cannot be always at their elbow to tell them what is right; and they may do just as wrong as before or worse; and their best intentions merely make the road smooth for them - you know where. For it is not the place itself that is paved with them, as people say so often. You cannot pave the bottomless pit, but you may the road to it.*

So the first necessity for our candidate of the Second Degree is to control his mind, if he has anything worth calling a mind to control; and if he has not, to develop it. And this is the whole trend of the Degree and of its ceremonies; to that end he must study; to that end he must strive to open various centres in his higher bodies. He is told that it is his duty to make a daily advance in Masonic knowledge.

It will be remembered that the S.D. is the especial representative of the mental body, so naturally it is he who takes charge of the candidate, and bears the principal part in the work of this degree. It is interesting to note the change of colour that comes over the Lodge when it is opened in this degree - not that the distinctive hues of the light-globes of the various officers are lost, but that they are all modified by the admixture of a dominant tint which blends itself with them all. That master-colour was crimson in the E.A. degree, while in the F.C. it is yellow.

The chakra which we seek to awaken in this degree is a centre within the astral body which gives the power to sympathize with the emotional vibrations of others, so that the man instinctively knows their feelings; and when the corresponding etheric chakra is also stimulated it brings those experiences into the physical body, so that he becomes aware even on this plane of the joys and sorrows of his fellow-men. Forces from the spleen centre, such as have been described in Chapter V, are playing through this chakra also, but this time it is the yellow ray which goes to the heart, and after doing its work there passes to the brain and permeates it, directing it principally to the twelve-petalled flower in the midst of the highest force centre at the crown of the head. The connection of this especial centre with the Second Degree is obvious when we remember its characteristics of companionship and service, its association with T.G.G.O.T.U., the second member of the Trinity, and the buddhic principle in man.

The prayer which is offered just before the Lodge is declared open is that the Craftsmen may be enlightened in the paths of virtue and of science, and the Lodge is declared to be opened on the s ... for the instruction and improvement of F.C.F.s.

It is of deep significance that in the invocation of this degree the R.W.M. uses for the Logos the title of the Grand Geometrician. Long ago Plato said that God geometrizes, and a study of crystallography will show vividly how true that is with regard to the building up of beautiful mineral forms. In the higher kingdoms also the student finds the same wonderful evidence of order and regularity. Indeed, the more deeply we study the processes of nature the greater in every direction becomes our admiration for the wonderful work of Him who made it all.

THE E.A.'S LAST WORK

The candidate having once more proved himself as an E.A. has to perform his last work in that capacity. On this occasion it is the S.D. who leads him, as he is now especially concerned with the lower mind, which must be controlled and developed by the F.C. He brings him first to the pedestal of the W.J.W., gives him a mallet and chisel, and instructs him to k ... on his l ... k ... and give three blows with the mallet, striking the chisel on the rough ashlar. The stone taken from the quarry has all its sides irregular. Strictly speaking, it is not an ashlar until the A. has made it regular in form, and at this point he puts the finishing touches to that work; but still the stone will have to be smoothed and polished before it is ready for lifting into the edifice, and that is part of the work of the Second Degree. Looking over with the inner sight a number of people gathered together, such as the audience at a lecture or theatre, or the congregation at a church, one sees that most of them are astrally and mentally very much out of shape, like rough stones, or even like twisted, stunted trees, that have grown in an unfavourable clime. Such are not yet apprentices in any kind of Lodge.

THE FIVE STAGES

The five stages are journeys round the Lodge, at the end of each of which the candidate is given certain instructions, from a printed card and by word of mouth, while he carries the tools appropriate for their practical realization. The journeys are outward signs of the raising of the candidate's consciousness through the planes.

In the first stage he carries the mallet and chisel, and learns about the five senses-touch, hearing, sight, taste and smell. This is the physical stage, for the physical body is not valuable in itself, but only as the vehicle of the senses, through which a man gains knowledge of the physical world with which to direct his work. It is these senses in his body which must now receive his attention, that they may serve him well.

On the journey of the second stage the A. carries a rule and compasses, and learns something of the Arts. These are classified as architecture, sculpture, painting, music and poetry - all forms of beauty - a sufficient indication that all true work produces what is beautiful. The rule and compasses are to remind him to apply the principle of geometry to his feelings, guiding and controlling his astral body, so that his work will express high emotion and arouse it in others.

In the third stage the A. is supplied with a rule and level, and he reads and hears about natural science - mathematics, geometry, philosophy, biology and sociology. He is now dealing with the mental plane and his bodies thereon, and the rule and level tell him of the order, balance and common sense that are necessary in this work.

At the next stage the candidate finds himself no longer dealing with the things of his personal nature, but looking upwards to that higher part of himself which will come to flower in the later part of his path. He sees such matters first of all in the lives of great men and women who have adorned the pages of history. He carries a pencil and book, and learns of the benefactors of humanity - sages, artists, scientists, inventors and legislators. All of these exemplify the unity of mankind, since they live not for themselves alone, but with a clear consciousness of the happiness and sorrows of mankind, and a great desire to help and to give. Here is expressed that quality of human nature which springs from the principle of *buddhi* on the plane beyond the mental, where there is direct intuitional vision of the unity of life.

Beyond this is the last and fifth stage, which the candidate treads with his hands free, ready to take up any instrument that is required at any moment. In this he learns of service - that the highest ideal of life is to serve. Well do the brethren sing:

Thou shalt show me the path of life; in Thy presence is the fullness of joy; and at Thy right hand there is pleasure for evermore.

I will behold Thy presence in righteousness: and when I awake up after Thy likeness, I shall be satisfied with it.

For this is the path of the spirit, the One behind the many, the first cause. Of that first cause the Christ said, "My Father worketh hitherto, and I work," and Shri Krishna, speaking as the Deity, explained in the *Bhagavad Gita* that were He to abstain even for a moment from His activity, His service of the world, everything would fall into ruin. The rule that service is the highest ideal in life was thus initiated by the Most High, and it is the plain duty of those who would be His faithful servants to follow in His steps.

THE FIVE S ... S

The candidate must now advance to the east by the proper s ... s. These are five, and are taken as though ascending a winding staircase, which in the t ... b ... brings the F.C. to the door of the middle chamber of the temple. With regard to the middle chamber Major Meredith Sanderson writes as follows in An Examination of the Masonic Ritual, p. 31:

This term is a misreading of the original Hebrew, and is admitted as such by all authorities. The correct reading of I. Kings vi., 8, is as follows: "The door for the *lowest row of chambers* (not '*for the middle chamber*') was in the right side of the house, and they went up with winding stairs into the middle row, and out of the middle into the third." That is to say there was a row of chambers on each storey and the winding stairs reached from the ground floor to the top storey (cf. v. 6, where the word chamber should read storey, and Ezek. xli, 7.)

The F.C.s pass into that chamber, says the explanation of the t ... b ..., to receive their wages, which they do without scruple and without diffidence. The F.C.s have no scruple about taking that which they have earned, and have no doubt that they will be paid exactly what they deserve. This refers not only to the perfect fairness and absolute justice of the Masters of the Great White Lodge (one of whom once said, "Ingratitude is not one of our vices"), but also to the great law of karma. That is a divine law relating living beings to their environment in this world, so that a man shall be given that for which he has worked, neither more nor less. It is therefore God's will that every man shall have what is his due; he need not fear to take what comes to him (which embodies an opportunity for greater service) and he need not imagine that anything which he deserves can be stolen from him or mislaid. "Be not deceived," said St. Paul, "God is not mocked; whatsoever a man soweth, that shall he also reap."(Gal. vi, 7.)

Not only will he receive in the future the exact result of what he does now, but it also follows that what he is receiving now is the exact result of what he has done in the past, either in other lives or in the earlier part of this life. Therefore if suffering comes he knows that he has deserved it, for otherwise it simply could not happen.

Another interesting point is that we are told, in the explanation of the t ... b ... that the F.C.s were paid in specie, which symbolizes the reward of toil not directly remunerated by its results, but that the E.A.s received *their* wages in corn, wine and oil.

Corn and wine at once call to mind the sacred elements in the Christian Eucharist, and also the myth of the sun-god, who rises into mid-heaven to ripen the corn and the grape, and thus gives of his life for the benefit of others. These are types of the things most valuable to man; and to say that anyone is paid in corn and wine thus means that the richest of earth's treasures are the reward of his work, and that at the same time they carry with them the blessing of God.

The oil typifies the great gift of wisdom. As oil is expressed from the olive, so is wisdom culled by the soul of man from all his experiences on earth. When all the material results of work have perished, as in the case of the dead and gone civilizations of antiquity, still the wisdom resulting from all the efforts made and the experiences suffered remains in the heart of man. The reward of work in the world is not only outward, in the things that are gained, but also inward, in the heart and mind of man himself. All these rewards came to the E.A. as the natural result of his work, according to karmic law, he feeling and enjoying them all, and learning without special intention; but the F.C. is more wide awake to what is happening. He uses discrimination, and should have completely controlled his feelings, so that he is in a position to decide for himself what he will have as the result of his labour, what shall be his eating and drinking, his giving and taking, his reading and companionship. He takes his pay in specie, and buys what he will - no longer a child, but a responsible man. He seeks experience and wisdom; it need not be thrust upon him or given from the outside.

But in all that use of his wealth and power and opportunity, the C ... n's ideal should be service. He has to be as an ear of corn by a fall of water for others, so that his presence shall always be a blessing to them, a source of their spiritual nourishment, their happiness and true prosperity.

The winding form of the staircase may be thought to indicate that evolution is always in the form of a spiral, not of a straight line. We are constantly coming round again to the kind of work and knowledge and duty that we have done before, but always at a higher level. So in successive incarnations on his human pilgrimage each man will go again through childhood, youth, maturity, ripening and fruitful age, but as he evolves each of these stages will be more perfect than it was before.

The spirals of evolution are still more far-reaching, so that the successive divisions of human life give us an epitome of the kingdoms of nature. The human embryo in the course of its growth takes on the appearance of each of the earlier kingdoms in succession; and besides that, in the development of the human body the gestation period reflects the downward course of the elemental kingdoms mentioned in Theosophical literature; from birth to about the age of seven we have a time in which the wisest educationists consider that the child's physical nature should receive more attention than the emotional and mental; next up to the age of about fourteen there is an epoch in which the right development of the emotions should have chief consideration; then follows another term to the age of about twenty-one when the teacher should appeal especially to the unfolding powers of the mind.

The last three ages may be taken to correspond to a certain extent to the mineral, vegetable, and animal kingdoms; in the first of them consciousness is in the physical plane, in the second it is developing in the emotional plane, and in the third the lower mind gradually gains ground, and leads on to the stage when man becomes the true thinker. There is then a long period of middle life - the real human career. That is followed in turn by the epoch of old age, which ought to bring wisdom; this is as yet often imperfect in most people, being but an adumbration of the superhuman heights of future attainment.

When the Lord Buddha walked the earth He was once asked by a disciple to sum up the whole of His teaching in one verse. After a moment's thought He replied:

Cease to do evil;
Learn to do well;
Cleanse your own heart;
This is the religion of the Buddhas.

We may surely trace here some correspondence to the teaching of the three degrees in Masonry. The teaching of the First Degree is that of purification, of the purging from the nature of all that might lead the man to selfish and ill-considered action. That of the Second Degree instructs the man to seek knowledge - to acquire the mental development which will not only preserve him from evil-doing, but will clearly prescribe for him a definite course of altruistic action. The first makes the man negatively good, while the second is positive; but both refer to actions upon the physical plane. The third instructs the man to rise to a higher level and to consider not merely outward action but the inner condition of which all outer manifestation should be an expression.

THE O.

This brings us to the O. of the candidate, which however contains singularly little that can be thought of as applicable to the special study and development of the Degree. He pledges himself to act as a true and faithful C ... n, to acknowledge s ..., obey s ... s, and maintain the principles inculcated in the First Degree.

The R.W.M. then proceeds to create, receive and constitute precisely as in the First Degree; but anyone who possesses the inner vision will notice a more decided widening of the link between the ego and the personality, so that it is opened up as a definite channel for the downpouring of force - a channel which the candidate can utilize with marked effect if he sets himself to work upon it and through it. Unfortunately most candidates receive no instruction as to the inner side of the ceremony, and are consequently unable to avail themselves of the really wonderful privilege. In this respect also, as in the former degree, there is a certain parallel between the passing of a F.C. and the ecclesiastical ordination to the diaconate; and at the same time a link is made between the C ... n and the H.O.A.T.F. in those Lodges where He is acknowledged.

As in the case of the widening of consciousness which we have just mentioned, this wonderful link with the great M.O.T.W. is for the candidate exactly what he likes to make of it. It may be of the very greatest benefit to him; it may change the whole of his life and enable him to make rapid progress along the path of initiation; or on the other hand, if he entirely neglects it, it may make but very little difference to him. When such a link is made with the Lord Christ for the deacon at his ordination, the very work which the deacon has to take up keeps the possibilities of his destiny before him; but with the uninstructed Freemason this is usually not so, and he often continues to live his ordinary life all unaware of the magnificent opportunity which has opened before him. We see therefore how heavy is the responsibility of the Master of the Lodge when the duty is laid upon him to employ and instruct his Brn. in Freemasonry.

Bro. Ward, in his *F.C.'s Handbook*, p.31, strongly emphasizes the idea that in this degree we are dealing especially with the preservative Aspect of the Deity. He writes: *The s ... of f ... implies not merely fidelity to his O ..., but obedience to the rules of T.G.G.O.T.U. We can hope to be preserved only if we conform to those rules laid down by Him for our preservation ... The h ... s ... is said in our rituals to be the sign of p ... y ... r or p ... r s ... e, but in its essence it is the sign of preservation, the sign associated with God the Preserver, under whatsoever name He is called, throughout the world.*

He goes on to explain that it is found in this association in Egypt, in India and in Mexico, and that it was so used by the Roman Collegia and the Comacini. He also draws attention to the fact that the distinguishing badge of this degree has on it two blue rosettes, symbolizing the rose. Blue was the colour of Isis, and is that of the Blessed Virgin Mary, whose emblem is the rose. The triangular flap, which in the First Degree was worn with the point upward, to indicate that the spiritual had not yet entered into control of the material, is now turned down to show that the higher is supposed definitely to be taking charge of the lower. We shall see this same symbolism carried further still when we consider the sublime degree of the M.M.

Just as the g ... of the First Degree showed the necessity of the conquest of the desire nature, so does that of the Second Degree show the need at this stage of full control of the lower mind. We may compare the instruction implied here with that given in Light on the Path on the killing out of various kinds of desire, and that in *The Voice of the Silence*: "The mind is the slayer of the real; let the disciple slay the slayer."

In the Co-Masonic ritual the R.W.M. tells the neophyte twice over in almost the same words that he is now expected to make the hidden mysteries of our science his future study; but Bro. Ward remarks that in the masculine ritual the second statement is that he is now permitted to do so. He attaches great importance to this, as showing that the compilers of the ritual were well aware of the danger, both for themselves and for others, which exists for men who attempt to develop and use higher powers without having first given proof of exalted moral character in the previous degree.

THE WORKING TOOLS

The working tools of this degree are the same as the movable jewels, and we have already dealt fully with them under that heading.

The new F.C. is now promoted from his seat in the N. E. to another in the S.E. of the Lodge. He is following the path of the sun which (in the northern hemisphere), rises in summer north of east and proceeds through the east to the south, giving more and more service to the world as he advances, until he rises to his highest point in the south, and then goes towards his setting in the west, and his resurrection to a new day, of which we shall hear more in due course.

CLOSING THE LODGE

In the closing of the Lodge in the Second Degree there is only one matter that calls for special mention. The R.W.M. asks the J.W. what he has discovered, where it is situated, and to what it alludes, and he receives the reply: "A s ... d S ... l, in the c ... of the building, alluding to T.G.G.O.T.U." There seems to be considerable diversity of opinion as to what this sacred symbol should be. All are agreed that it is set underneath the Blazing Star, and is in some sense a reflection of it. Since the letter G appears within the star, the same letter is sometimes inlaid in the floor. This is thought by Major Sanderson to be merely a modern substitute for the all-seeing eye, to which in the masculine ritual the R.W.M. makes reference in explaining the symbol. Bro. Ward, however, prescribes that the point within a circle limited by two straight lines should be inlaid in the floor in brass. Both these arrangements seem open to the objection that the symbol would be always present, and could therefore hardly be described as discovered in the working of the Second Degree only. It has been our practice in a certain Lodge to use the movable seven-pointed star as the symbol, and to lay it on the floor only during the working of the F.C. Degree. In the Co-Masonic ritual the comment that the R.W.M. makes is as follows: *Brn., let us remember that, as He is the c ... of His Universe, so is His reproduction of Himself the c ... of ourselves, the Inner Ruler, immortal, and that our whole nature must be conformed to That whereby it lives.*

CHAPTER VIII.
THE THIRD DEGREE.
THE OPENING OF THE LODGE

WHEN all is ready for the opening of the Lodge in the Third Degree the R.W.M. once more commands the W.J.W. to see that the Lodge is properly tyled. This time the forces with which we have to deal in the work of the meeting will be mainly on the higher mental plane, so the defences of the Lodge are now reinforced at that level by the invisible hosts, and therefore a blue tinge henceforward predominates, though the lower levels are by no means neglected.

The Brn. are then called to order as Craftsmen, and the R.W.M. turns to the W.J.W. again, with the question: "Are you a M.M.?" On his replying that he is, the Master asks him by what instrument in architecture he will be proved, and he replies: "By the square and compasses."

This means that a M.M. may be tested and known by the fact that both the higher self and the lower self are in working order, are functioning together and in harmony. The M.M. is symbolical of the Initiate of the fourth degree, whom the Buddhists call the Arhat; at that stage of attainment on the occult path the battle against the lower quaternary is practically over, and the latter has become an obedient instrument in the hands of the higher triad, which is awake and active in all its three parts.

Next the R.W.M. puts a number of questions alternately to the W.J.W. and the W.S.W., and they answer as acting together. A little later on it will be seen that they act together also in the work of raising an F.C. to the degree of M.M. On the present occasion the W.s tell the R.W.M. that they have come from the east and are going to the west to seek the genuine s ... s of a M.M., which were lost by the untimely death of the Master H.A., and that they hope to find them on the c ...

THE C ...

It will be remembered that at the closing of the F.C. Lodge it was asked of the J.W. what the brethren had discovered while in the position of F.C.s, and the reply was that they had found a s ... s ..., in the c ... of the building, which stood for God. The consummation of the F.C. work was to discover that c ...; but the M.M. has his eye upon it all the time as the place where he hopes to find the lost truth.

It is on the c ..., the officers now say, that they hope to find the genuine s ... s of a M.M. It is by finding in himself that deeper Self which is the

Monad, beyond even the higher triad, that the M.M. will at last discover the supreme secret of life, and will then find in very truth by his own living experience that he is and always has been one with God. There is something almost Vedantic in this Masonic conception of lost s ... s, for the Vedantins say that in this maze of life men have lost themselves, as it were, in a great and terrible forest, and now their entire aim in life is to escape from it and to find that real happiness which is the very nature of their own true and essential being.

A study of the meaning of the working tools of a M.M. throws much light on this subject of the c ...; we will therefore treat of them here, instead of later on in the chapter.

The working tools of the third degree are the s ... t, the p ... and the c ... The s ... t is an implement which acts on a centre pin, whence a line is drawn to mark out the ground plan of the intended structure. Pith the p ... the skilful architect delineates the building in a plan for the instruction and guidance of the workmen. And the c ... enable him to ascertain with accuracy and precision the limits and proportions of its several parts. So runs the ritual.

But there is a meaning deeper than this, for these are the tools with which the Arhat is to become an Adept. In earlier degrees his consciousness had to be raised from the s ... to the c ..., that is, from the quadrilateral to the triangle, from the lower to the higher self; but now it has to be raised from the triangle to the point, from the higher self to the Monad. The Monad is now beginning to work its will in the higher self, as before the higher self worked its will in the lower. The s ... t represents the action of that Monad, as it turns upon a centre pin, and sends out a line from its own body as it spins the web of life, just as a spider spins its web from its own body. The p ... marks that chosen path or ray of the Monad, the line of life and work which the Arhat must discover and on which he must specialize in order to make rapid progress. And the c ... once more represent the triangle, the powers of the triple spirit which he must use in his work.

The conversation between the R.W.M. and the W.s goes on to define the c ... as a p ... within a c ..., from which all parts of the c ... ce are equidistant, and to say that it is a p ... from which a M.M. cannot err. I have already written on this subject in Chapter II, but I could here add that there is a great distinction between the things of the natural world and those of the inner life of consciousness. All material objects are characterized by boundaries - they are delineated; but the inner life always proceeds from a centre, so that it is quite impossible to set bounds to love or thought. They take their rise in and stand upon a centre, and radiate from that. The circumference of their circle is nowhere, but the centre is within the man. When he has risen to the fullness of his divine nature the circumference will still be nowhere, but the centre will be everywhere; no life whatsoever will be excluded from his sympathies. That is what is symbolized by the statement that all parts of the c ... ce are equidistant from the c ... The M.M. who keeps his eye on that c ... and acts from that p ... cannot err. It is on that c ... that the R.W.M. opens the Lodge.

Still one point in the conversation remains for consideration. The officers state that their journey is from the east to the west. This may be taken to refer to the path of the sun, which is typical of the path of the Initiate. Here we have the well-known solar myth again. The sun is new-born at the beginning of the year in the darkness of winter; he struggles through the clouds of the early spring, which seem to threaten his life; in the summer he rises to his highest point in the sky, giving freely of his life to ripen the corn and the grape. But now enemies close around him; autumn hems him in with its shadows, and at last he falls stricken before the onset of winter. Yet, passing through a figurative death in the west, he discovers the secret of renewed life, and rises once more in the east and ascends again into the mid-heaven. So in many successive lives he has to deal with the world, and gradually to disperse the clouds of ignorance which resist the unfoldment of his potentialities, before he can rise into the high noon of his glory at the completion of his work of temple-building, when he finally travels onward into the west and finds the secret of perfect immortality. Then he need journey no more, for he has reached the centre and is at rest; he has become a pillar in the temple of God, and he shall go out therefrom no more.

But in the preparation for this high consummation both East and West take part. Although the East has always been the place of light, whence comes all knowledge, yet when the sacred word was lost men journeyed westward in the hope of finding it, and the chivalry of the West joined with the philosophy of the East in that high quest. The East contributes the spiritual teaching, but the West provides the accuracy and definiteness which make it readily assimilable, and the practicality which enables us to apply it to the helping of the outer world.

THE PREPARATION

In the preparation of the candidate both a ... are made b ... because in the due-guard both are raised in blessing; both b ... are laid open to the double influence of the c ..., which have always at the same time a positive and a negative quality, conferring simultaneously power and sensitiveness, one point being always at rest in the centre, while the other describes a circumference.

However far we may travel from God, and however long and hard the journey, the divine spark within us can never be truly separated from Him, or err from that Centre.[5]

Both k ... are b ..., because both are used in the ceremony, and both h ... are s ... p - s ... d because in this way the fullest advantage is taken of the very concentrated magnetization of the mosaic pavement.

THE INTERNAL PREPARATION

In this degree the candidate seeks his object by the united aid of the s ... and c ..., which may be taken to signify that his development depends upon the right use both of the body and the soul, the square and the triangle. In the method of symbolism adopted the candidate is always required to look forward to that which shall be, rather than to rest content with that which is. The perfection at which the M.M. is aiming will be attained in its fullness only when the three points of the triangle, the spiritual will, the intuition and the intelligence shall be fully aroused and in entire control of the four lower vehicles - the mental, astral, etheric and dense physical bodies.

As Bro. Powell has said in *The Magic of Freemasonry*, p. 92.:

In the Third Degree in Freemasonry we find an appeal quite different and distinct from those of the two preceding degrees. The M.M. comes within the range of a fresh influence, entering a new world, piercing through another of the veils which separate him from a true understanding of life - and death. Perhaps the most characteristic feature of the Degree is this atmosphere which it creates, so real and yet so elusive in description - a sense of mystery.

ENTERING THE LODGE

As he enters the Lodge he is received upon the points of the compasses, and through them he gains the first touch of this higher

---

[5] *The M.M's Book*, by Bro. J. S. M. Ward, p. 22

atmosphere, this new influence of the M.M, degree. The raising of the Lodge to a higher degree changes the dominant vibrations, not only of the Lodge as a whole, but of every Bro. present. That is why it is necessary that a Bro. who was not present at the opening of the Lodge in a higher degree - as for example the candidate for passing or raising - needs a special pass-word, a word of power, which is intended to do quickly for his vibrations what the opening ceremony has done more gradually for those of his Brn. In the p ... g ... leading from the Second to the Third Degree is shown the necessity of extending self-control still further, and gaining some mastery over that strange intermediate tract beyond the lower mind which in a certain school of thought is denominated the subliminal consciousness.

In this Degree, as in the others, he kneels under a triangle made by the crossed wands of the deacons while the blessing of T.M.H. is invoked; indeed, it is noteworthy that all the O.s in Craft Masonry are taken within that same triangle, indicating that the whole of the threefold man, body, soul and spirit, is engaged in the work that is being done. Bro. Ward (*The M.M.'s. Book*, pp. 28- 29.) draws attention to the fact that the candidate now takes three symbolical journeys, as in the First Degree, but with a different object: *He first satisfies the W. J.W., representing the Body, that he is an E.A. - i.e., a man of good moral character. He next satisfies the W.S.W., representing the Soul, that he has benefited by the lessons of life and acquired intellectual knowledge. Then comes the third journey, when he is once more challenged by the Soul, who demands the P.W. ... Let us combine these meanings. He comes laden with worldly possessions, which in themselves carry the seeds of death, unconsciously representing in his person the worker in metals who made the twin columns and is about to be entombed. Therefore the Soul presents him to the Spirit as one properly prepared to carry out the part of his great predecessor.*

THE SEVEN S ...

In all the Degrees the candidate advances towards the East, the place of Light, but in each Degree more than in the previous one. In the first he takes three s ... s - though even then they steadily increase in length - 9, 12, 15; in the second not only are there five instead of three, but they tend definitely upwards and form a staircase. In the third there are seven, and furthermore, the first three are symbolically over an o ... g ..., showing that, on the higher plane to which the winding staircase led him, the candidate has triumphed over death, and marches on unwaveringly along his path of progress on the other side of it. Some writers think that in taking these s ... s over the o ... g ... the candidate should after the first s ... face due north, after the second due south, and after the third due east, looking thus at the three entrances to the temple, through which H.A.B. endeavoured to escape.

THE O.

He then takes the M.M.'s O. - perhaps one of the finest and most far-reaching that have ever been written. If only every M.M. kept his pledge to the uttermost, in spirit as well as in letter, this earth of ours would soon become a veritable heaven. To quote again from Bro. Powell:

"Faithful unto death" may well be taken as the motto of the M.M., and if this were truly the keynote of his whole life, then indeed would Freemasonry have performed a splendid service to all men, and its name would be honoured above all other names from generation to generation. If every M.M, could carry out his O ... without evasion, equivocation or mental reservation of any kind, and prefer to suffer death rather than slander a Brother's good name or fail to maintain at all times the honour of a Brother as his own, then indeed would there be, right in the heart of humanity, such a brotherhood as would bring the completion of the H.T. almost within range of our earthly vision. Such a standard of fidelity amongst M.M.'s would in time lead humanity to so high a level of goodwill that not only would men cease from injuring one another, but even inaction in a deed of mercy would become action in a deadly sin. This, and nothing else, is the true meaning of the F ... P ... of F ..., to uphold which the M.M. is pledged. It is no light matter to enter the First Portal and become a Freemason; it is an even more serious undertaking to take the O ... of a M.M. and swear to be faithful unto death. Let every M.M. ponder this well and re-affirm to himself, by all that he holds sacred, his determination, in all cases of trial and difficulty, to follow the noble example of the great symbolic figure who suffered death rather than be false to his oath.* (*The Magic of Freemasonry, p. 98.)

The O. needs no comment, save perhaps a reference to the promise to attend meetings when called "if within the length of my c ... t ..." It has apparently been the custom to interpret this as meaning "within three miles"; it probably was originally equivalent to "within convenient walking distance". Assuredly no M.M. who understands how great is the privilege of taking part in the work of the Lodge will be likely to disregard any such call if it is in any way possible for him to respond to it.

In this case, as so often in others, Bro. Wilmshurst gives us a beautiful mystical interpretation, taking the c ..., t ... to represent the "silver cord" which links the subtler part of the body to the denser, and suggesting that a Bro. who for some good reason cannot obey a summons physically may yet attend astrally and take part in the ceremony on a higher plane. If this explanation be accepted, the length of the c ... t ... would be the distance to which the M.M. finds himself able to travel astrally. It is perfectly possible and even eminently desirable that the M.M. *should* attend Masonic meetings astrally, in this way giving his strength and his blessing to many Lodges, and doing much more work for the Craft than he can do by confining himself to his own Lodge. A closer study of the physics of the higher life will show him that the actual "silver cord" is observable only when etheric matter is withdrawn from the dense body, as in the case of a medium and that the connection between the astral and physical vehicles of the ordinary man is a wonderfully exact sympathetic vibration; perhaps better symbolized by a chord of music than a cord of silver; but the interpretation is nevertheless quite permissible.

THE ETHERIC FORCES

The O ... being taken, the R.W.M. proceeds to the actual ceremony of admission, the external ritual of which is the same as in earlier degrees, except for the k ... s and the name of the degree; but the inner effect is very different.

In each of the previous Degrees I have referred to certain currents of etheric force which flow through and around the spine of every human being. Madame Blavatsky writes of them, in *The Secret Doctrine*, vol. iii, p. 503, as follows:

The Trans-Himalayan school ... locates Sushumna, the chief seat of these three Nadis, in the central tube of the spinal cord, and Ida and Pingala on its left and right sides. Ida and Pingala are simply the sharps and flats of that Fa of human nature, which, when struck in a proper way, awakens the sentries on either side, the spiritual Manas and the physical Kama, and subdues the lower through the higher. ...

It is the pure Akasha that passes up Sushumna; its two aspects flow in Ida and Pingala. These are the three vital airs, and are symbolized by the Brahmanical thread. They are ruled by the will. Pill and desire are the higher and lower aspects of one and the same thing. Hence the importance of the purity of the canals. ... From these three a circulation is set up, and from the central canal passes into the whole body... (p. 537.)

Ida and Pingala play along the curved wall of the cord in which is Sushumna. They are semi-material, positive and negative, sun and moon, and they start into action the free and spiritual current of Sushumna. They have distinct paths of their own, otherwise they would radiate all over the body (p. 547).

It is part of the plan of Freemasonry to stimulate the activity of these forces in the human body, in order that evolution may be quickened. This stimulation is applied at the moment when the R.W.M. creates, receives and constitutes; in the First Degree it affects the *ida*, or feminine aspect of the force, thus making it easier for the candidate to control passion and emotion; in the Second Degree it is the *pingala* or masculine aspect which is strengthened, in order to facilitate the control of mind; but in this Third Degree it is the central energy itself, the Sushumna, which is aroused, thereby opening the way for the influence of the pure spirit from on high. It is by passing up through this channel of the *sushumna* that a yogi leaves his physical body at will in such a manner that he can retain full consciousness on higher planes, and bring back into his physical brain a clear memory of his experiences. The little figures below give a rough indication of the way in which these forces flow through the human body; in a man the *ida* starts from the base of the spine just on the left of the *sushumna*, and the *pingala* on the right (be it understood that I mean the right and left of the *man*, not the spectator); but in a woman these positions are reversed. The lines end in the *medulla oblongata*.

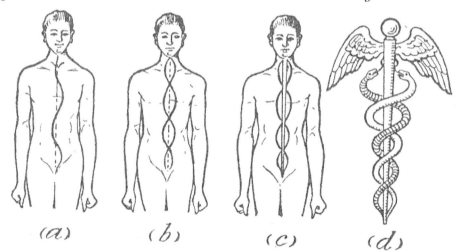

(a)   (b)   (c)   (d)

Figure 14

The spine is called in India the *brahmadanda*, the stick of Brahma; and the drawing given in Fig. 14(*d*) shows that it is also the original of the caduceus of Mercury, the two snakes which symbolize the *kundalini* or serpent-fire which is presently to be set in motion along those channels, while the wings typify the power of conscious flight through higher planes which the development of that fire confers. Fig. 14(*a*) shows the stimulated *ida* after the initiation into the First Degree; this line is crimson in colour. To it is added at the Passing the yellow line of the *pingala*, depicted in Fig. 14(*b*); while at the Raising the series is completed by the deep blue stream of the *sushumna*, illustrated by Fig. 14(*c*).

The stimulation of these nerves and the forces which flow through them is only a small part of the benefit conferred by the R.W.M. when he wields the sword at the moment of admission. I have already referred to the widening of the connection between the individuality and the personality, and to the formation of a link between certain principles of the candidate and the corresponding vehicles of the H.O.A.T.F. The changes induced are somewhat of the same nature as those which I have described on page 319 of *The Science of the Sacraments*, but of a less pronounced character.

I cannot emphasize too often or too strongly that while these effects are absolutely real, unmistakable and universal, their result in the spiritual life of the candidate depends entirely upon himself. The link made with the H.O.A.T.F. and the widening of the channels of communication offer the man an opportunity quite unparalleled in the ordinary life of the layman; but they in no way compel him to take that opportunity. If through ignorance or sluggishness he makes no attempt to utilize the new powers bestowed upon him, they remain dormant; if he uses them intelligently they steadily increase in effectiveness as he becomes more familiar with them. As Bro. Ward remarks in *The M.M.'s Book*, p. 3: "The spiritual benefit a man receives from Freemasonry is in exact proportion to his desire and ability to comprehend its inner meaning."

HIRAM ABIFF

It is only after the candidate has received this wonderful outpouring of spiritual strength that he is subjected to "the greater trial of his fortitude and fidelity" which is involved in the symbolical part of the Degree. A most remarkable drama now unfolds itself before him, and he finds himself quite unexpectedly enacting the part of its hero. The setting of the piece is well-arranged and effective; the darkening of the Lodge, the verses which are sung, the music which is played, the special vestments adopted both for the officers and the candidate - all the surroundings are admirably calculated to enhance the general impression which it is desired to create. Under such circumstances the newly-made M.M. hears for the first time the traditional history which plays so important a part in the Masonic scheme.

The name commonly given to this extraordinary narrative is perhaps somewhat inappropriate, for a little consideration soon shows us that it cannot seriously be considered as historical in the ordinary sense of the word; but if we accept it as a legend, and invest it with a moral significance, we shall find that it has much to teach us. We need not doubt that its central figure Hiram Abiff really lived, nor that he was sent by his namesake, Hiram, King of Tyre, to work for King Solomon in connection with the decoration of the temple. He is described in Jewish scripture as a clever worker in metals, and those of us who investigated the making of the pillars fully confirm that statement, though they do not find him suffering the sanguinary death which the legend asserts. As I mentioned in an earlier chapter, King Solomon himself appears to be responsible for introducing into Jewish Masonry the original form of the story, but not for the insertion of the name which we now use for its hero. Moses brought from Egypt the myth of the death and resurrection of Osiris, and that persisted in a modified form until the time of David. Solomon for patriotic reasons transferred the theatre of the drama to Jerusalem, and centred its interest round the temple which he had built, winning popularity at the same time by bringing his ritual into accordance with that of surrounding peoples, who were mostly worshippers of the Phoenician deity Tammuz, afterwards called by the Greeks Adonis.

Although he recast the legend, and made it wholly Jewish, it was not he who imported into it the name which we know so well, for we find Hiram Abiff acting as what we should now call W.J.W. at a great private ceremony of consecration and dedication at which Solomon's new ritual was performed for the first time. On the same occasion Hiram, King of Tyre, took the part of W.S.W., though for some obscure reason his visit was kept secret, and he returned home almost immediately, his place being taken for the public ceremonies by Adoniram. Rehoboam, Solomon's son, seems to have taken an intense dislike to Hiram Abiff, who had more than once reproved him for arrogance and unworthy conduct; so when after Solomon's death he came to the throne, he took a curious, perverted revenge upon Hiram by decreeing that the victim of the 3° should bear his name for ever. Exactly why this should have afforded satisfaction to Rehoboam it is difficult to see; but perhaps we should hardly hold him responsible for his actions, as he was obviously a decadent, a degenerate of the worst type. His enmity may possibly have shown itself in other ways also, for Hiram Abiff presently found it desirable to return to his own country, where he died full of age and honour.

I am told that only a few years ago a Javanese prince imitated Solomon's procedure, for much the same reasons as actuated the Jewish monarch. He and his people were at least nominally Muhammadans; but he said to them: "Why should you turn towards Mecca for your devotions? I have a very fine temple here; turn to it and not to Arabia when you recite your prayers." They seem to have accepted the suggestion, and in this way arose a variation - in the cult which may well puzzle the historians a century later.

Bro. Ward, in his recent book *Who was Hiram Abiff?*, p. 74, argues that the whole legend is nothing but an adaptation of the myth of Tammuz, that Hiram Abiff was one of a group of Priest-Kings, and was slain by the others as a voluntary sacrifice at the dedication of the temple, in order to bring good fortune upon the building. He adduces much evidence in support of this theory, and displays a vast amount of erudition and research, gathering together an amazing collection of the most interesting facts. I strongly recommend his book to the perusal of our Brn., even though I personally still cling to the idea that Masonry originally reached the Jews from Egypt, however much it may afterwards have been influenced, as it certainly was, by the Tammuz-worship of neighbouring nations. Bro. Ward cites instances of the survival of traces of the cult of Adonis in the most unexpected quarters; for instance, he writes:

When the Pope has died, a high official, armed with a small ivory hammer or gavel, goes up to the dead man and lightly taps him once on each temple and once on the centre of the forehead. After each knock he calls on him to arise, and only when the third summons has been made in vain does he officially proclaim the sad news that the Pope is dead, and therefore a successor must be elected. Bro. Ward further identifies Hiram Abiff with Abibaal, the father of Hiram, King of Tyre, and even suggests that Hiram was not a personal name at all, but a title of the Kings of Tyre, just as Pharaoh was of those of Egypt.

From another source comes the somewhat fantastic suggestion that Solomon also was not a personal name, but is capable of the subdivision Sol-om-on; *sol* meaning the sun, *om* being the sacred word of the Hindus (a substituted word, because the real word is a Name of Power, the Name of the Logos, to pronounce which would shake the world and destroy the speaker) and *on*, from the Greek to on, the absolute existence. This interpretation may be fanciful; but it seems true that the King's compatriots called him Solomon, pronouncing his name as an amphibrach, not as a dactyl, as we do.

The name of Hiram Abiff is somewhat altered in higher degrees, and even in the Bible it sometimes appears as Huram. A further modification is Khairum or Khurum. Khur by itself means white or noble. There is a variant Khri, which under certain circumstances becomes Khris. This would suggest some possible connection with Krishna and Christ. There are certain passages in the Book of Job where he speaks of the orb of the sun, and the word he uses is Khris. It is on record that Hiram, King of Tyre, was the first man who offered the sacrifice of fire to the Khur, who afterwards became Herakles. Plutarch tells us that the Persians of his day called the sun Kuros, and he connects it with the Greek word Kurios, which means Lord, which we find in the Church service as "Kyrie eleison". Khur is also connected with the Egyptian name Horus, who was also Her-Ra and Haroeris, names of the sun-god. The Hebrew word Aoor also means light or fire or the sun, and from that we get Khurom, which is equal to the Greek Hermes. Bro. Wilmshurst in The Masonic Initiation, p. 100, also regards the name Hiram as identical with Hermes, and thinks that a connection can he traced between the form Huram and the Sanskrit word Guru, which means "spiritual teacher". He therefore takes Hiram Abiff to signify the Father-Teacher, or the Teacher from the Father. That Hiram was a widow's son is also a significant fact. Horus as the child of Isis was the reincarnation of his own Father Osiris, and so as a posthumous child might well be described as a widow's son.

Though of the tribe of Naphtali, he was born and resided in Tyre, and may well therefore have learned from the Dionysian fraternity which had a centre there.

DEATH AND RESURRECTION

Whatever we may think of the traditional history as a story it is clear that it is a myth of death and rising again. The expression of it is perhaps somewhat clumsy, for no reference is made to the soul; it is merely the body which is raised to its feet, but it is obviously implied that when this was done in the proper manner life returned to it, as was said to be the case when Anubis raised Osiris from the bier with the very same gesture.

In the exoteric religion of Egypt two prominent features were the mourning for the dead Osiris and the universal rejoicing over his resurrection. Both of these are commemorated in the Co-Masonic ritual; the former by the various readings prescribed for the Orator, and the latter by the little anthem "Thanks be to God, who giveth us the victory".

In the exoteric religion of Egypt two prominent features were the mourning for the dead Osiris and the universal rejoicing over his resurrection. Both of these are commemorated in the Co-Masonic ritual; the former by the various readings prescribed for the Orator, and the latter by the little anthem "Thanks be to God, who giveth us the victory".

Apart from the instruction given as to life after death, there is in this strange story an allegorical lesson which should be taken to heart by every M.M. Once more Bro. Wilmshurst expresses it for us, explaining that just as: ... *the turning away from the attractions of the outer world ... the purification and subdual of the bodily and sensual tendencies ... the work of detachment and self-purification is our Entered Apprentice's work ... [just as] the analysis, discipline and obtaining control of one's inner world - of the mind, of one's thoughts, one's intellectual and psychic faculties - is the extremely difficult task of the Fellow Craft stage ... [so] the "last and greatest trial" lies in the breaking and surrender of the personal will, the dying down of all sense of personality and selfhood, so that the petty personal will may become merged in the divine Universal Will, and the illusion of separate independent existence give way to conscious realization of unity with the One Life that permeates the Universe. For so only can one be raised from conditions of unreality, strife and figurative death to a knowledge of ultimate Reality, Peace and Life Immortal. To attain this is to attain Mastership, involving complete domination of the lower nature, and the development in oneself of a higher order of life and faculty. (The Masonic Initiation, pp. 19, 20.)*

This realization of absolute unity is perhaps the most wonderful experience that comes to man in the course of his evolution-a depth of bliss which is utterly indescribable. No person, no thing is separate from any other, and yet everything is perfectly clear; all are "partial expressions of a single, sublying, inexpressible unity". Lord Tennyson wrote of it thus:

All at once, out of the intensity of the consciousness of individuality, the individuality itself seems to dissolve and fade away into boundless being; and this is not a confused state, but the clearest of the clearest, the surest of the surest, where death is an almost laughable impossibility, the loss of personality (if so it were) seeming no extinction, but the only true life. I am ashamed of my feeble description. Have I not said the state is utterly beyond words? This is the most emphatic declaration that the spirit of the writer is capable of transferring itself into another state of existence, is not only real, clear, simple, but that it is also infinite in vision and eternal in duration.

Another Bro. of the Craft has written: You know everything and understand the stars and the hills and the old songs. They are all within you, and you are all light. But the light is music, and the music is violet wine in a great cup of gold, and the wine in the golden cup is the Scent of a June night.

THE STAR

Even after the symbolic resurrection has taken place we are still warned that any light which can penetrate to these lower planes is but darkness visible, and that for true light and fuller information we must lift our eyes to that bright and morning Star whose rising brings peace and salvation to the faithful and obedient among men. There is no doubt that in the myth as taught in ancient Egypt the star to which reference was made in these terms was originally Sirius. Bro. Ward remarks:

The association of these ideas with the Dog Star is undoubtedly a fragment which has come down from ancient Egypt, for the rising of Sirius marked the beginning of the inundation of the Nile, which literally brought salvation to the people of Egypt by irrigating the land and enabling it to produce food. (*The M.M.'s* Book, p. 50.)

For us, however, the star is invested with a symbolical meaning, and reminds us of the Star of Initiation which marks the assent and approval of the Lord of the World when a new candidate has joined the mighty Brotherhood which exists from eternity to eternity. So we endeavour to carry out the precept of our ritual:

Let that Star be ever before your eyes, and let its light illumine your heart; follow it, as did the Wise Men of old, until it leads you to the gateway of Initiation, where it shines above the portal of that glorious temple, eternal in the heavens, of which even King Solomon's was but a symbol. (*The Masters and the Path*, p. 157.)

THE RAISING OF HUMANITY

Humanity is but one stage of the mighty ladder of evolution. The divine life which is now manifesting through us has in long past ages animated in succession the elemental, mineral, vegetable, and animal kingdoms. Now that particular life-wave has reached the human kingdom. It entered that kingdom by the gate of individualization ages upon ages ago; it will leave that human kingdom by the gateway of initiation - that Fifth Initiation which makes a man into a superman or Adept. Humanity is slowly - very, very slowly - treading a great broad road that winds round and round a mountain, ever rising gradually until it reaches the summit. The process is deliberate and often irregular, until the soul suddenly realizes the purpose of his evolution, God's plan for man, and resolves to use all his power to reach the goal as soon as possible. Then he begins to climb straight up the mountain side, and each time that his path crosses the winding road he achieves a definite stage of his progress; at each such point there is an Initiation.

The great Initiations are five; the first marks the soul's stepping off the beaten path, and the last his entering the Temple at the summit of the mountain. To make this shorter but steeper path a living reality should be the effort of every M.M.; and the three degrees undoubtedly typify stages on this road.

The E.A. should as a personality be employed in organizing his physical life for higher use; but at the same time as an ego he should be developing active intelligence in his causal body, exactly as does the pupil of the Masters who is preparing himself for Initiation. I do not of course suggest that each E.A. is doing this, or even as yet can do it; but the Degree is intended to put that development before him as a goal, and the sooner he begins his upward climb, the better. In the same way the F.C. is organizing his emotional life at the lower level, while he unfolds intuitional love in his buddhic body; and the M.M., while arranging his mental life down here, should as an ego be strengthening his spiritual will.

FIRE, SUN AND MOON

We encounter in the Indian scriptures certain tests which seem to approach the same ideas from a different angle, and so should be of interest to Masons. The navel, heart and throat centres in the human body are mentioned as the places of fire, the sun and the moon respectively, and it is said that he who meditates in those centres will find there the Devis Saraswati, Lakshmi and Parvati or Girija, in that order. Those Devis are outward-turned powers or *shaktis* of Brahma, Vishnu and Shiva, the three Persons of the Blessed Trinity, and have respectively the qualities of giving knowledge, prosperity and self-control - in other words, of helping the man to reach his highest mental, astral and physical aims; for the physical, astral and mental principles are a reflection (inverted, like that of a mountain in water) of the three principles of the higher triad.

Saraswati is the patroness of learning and practical wisdom; Lakshmi fulfils desires and makes life rich and full, and when she is truly worshipped she sanctifies all material prosperity; Girija or Parvati blesses the physical body and makes its powers holy. The E.A. has to bring his physical body to perfection, so the aid which he needs is precisely what is symbolized by Girija's will; the F.C, has to do the same for his astral body, with the help of Lakshmi's love; the M.M. repeats the process for the mental body, aided by Saraswati's *kriyashakti* or power of thought.

To conquer and organize the physical nature for the use of the higher self the E.A. must use his will, the power of Shiva, the First Person, reflected by his Devi Girija. To transmute the passions of the astral body the F.C. must use his intuitional love that comes from Vishnu, the Second Person, through Lakshmi. To conquer the wavering mind and make it a perfect instrument for the higher self, the M.M. must use the power of his thought, the divine activity of Brahma, the Third Person, reflected by Saraswati. Madame Blavatsky said that the aspirant should make a bundle of the lower things and nail them up to the higher self; when he has done this he will have fulfilled the destiny which is indicated for him - he will have stepped with t ... s ... over his o ... g ...

This allusion is similar to that of the k ... s in the three Degrees, and in no way affects the fact that the E.A. is at the same time learning to control the emotions, and the F.C. is gaining mastery of the mind. The Mason is simultaneously doing two pieces of work - developing and advancing on higher planes, and yet controlling and perfecting his personal instruments.

How are these connected with fire, the sun and the moon? Remember the three lesser lights: (1) the R.W.M., (2) the sun - the W.S.W., and (3) the moon - the W.J.W. In their capacity of lesser lights these officers correspond to the Devis. It is the W.J.W. who especially helps the E.A., the W.S.W. the F.C., and the R.W.M. the M.M.

It is interesting to note that in the above explanation fire corresponds to the mind. Another aspect of the same truth is seen in the fact that it is the power behind modern science. Without fire chemistry, physics, geology, astronomy and all the practical applications of these sciences could not exist. The M.M. is symbolically a wielder of this power; he is a worker in metals, a caster of pillars, hollow within, to contain the archives of the soul and spirit. In his hand is *kriyashakti*, the creative power.

The path of the moon is said to typify the life of the ordinary man, who clings to objects of desire and parts with them reluctantly at death. After a period in the astral and heavenly worlds he returns to earth, to repeat the process. It is the path of rebirth after intervals. The path of the sun is that of the occult aspirant, the man of spiritual desires, who values life only for what it can give to the higher self in others as well as himself. He also is reborn, but usually without an interval, or after a very short one. The path of fire is the path of ascension, from which there is no longer any rebirth under the law of necessity, but only at the choice of the ego - only for the helping of the world.

THE VILLAINS

Little need be said of the remainder of the traditional history. We may note the curious similarity between the names given to the three villains, and the fact that the three terminations when put together make the sacred word Aum or Om. Jubel or Yehubel is said to signify "good and evil"; or it may be interpreted as containing the two names of Jah (Jehovah) and Bel or Baal - which to a Jew of that period would have been simply good and evil over again.

THE INSCRIPTION

Lastly, we may mention the mysterious inscription on the plate of the c ... n on the t ... b ... of this degree, written in the Masonic cipher. In its ordinary straightforward form this cryptogram is known to almost every schoolboy; but it is capable of a number of permutations. In this case its letters are arranged in a somewhat unusual manner, and it must be read from right to left. Treated in this way, it yields the initials of our Master, the alleged date of his death, and the word and password of the degree. But none but a Mason is likely to decipher it.

CHAPTER IX.
THE HIGHER DEGREES

THE majority of masculine Freemasons hold that the Craft comprises only the three Degrees of E.A., F.C., and M.M., though in English Masonry they allow the Mark Degree and the Holy Royal Arch as nominally extensions of the Second and Third Degrees respectively, and they have also a ceremony of Installation for the Master of a Lodge which is practically an additional Degree though it is never called so.

Among the masculine Masons only those who belong to the Ancient and Accepted Scottish Rite work the higher Degrees, though various other small bodies of Masons use some of them. The Rites of Memphis and Mizraim used to have a list of 97 degrees, but have now reduced them to 33. Nevertheless though many Masons do not admit them, these higher Degrees are definitely part of the great scheme of Freemasonry, standing out as landmarks upon the upward Path which leads to conscious union with God, enshrining in their ritual and symbolism a series of pictures of the successive stages of spiritual attainment, and conferring sacramental power calculated to quicken the growth of man's inner faculties at various levels and in various ways.

Therefore in the Co-Masonic Rite we recognize both sets of Degrees, and regard them as constituting a coherent whole, leading those who work them properly to a very high stage of development. But they are clearly intended to provide for two distinct types of people - for the many and the few. For the ordinary man of the world the three Degrees of Craft Masonry are all-sufficient; when he has learnt the lessons which they have to teach, he is no longer the ordinary man; he stands high above the average. If he can supplement them by the knowledge conveyed by the Mark Degree and the Holy Royal Arch, he has a rule of life and a philosophy which will carry him creditably through the rest of this incarnation, and ensure for him a good opportunity of progress in the next. In the Royal Arch he passes beyond the substituted secrets and learns the genuine Word which has so long and so unhappily been lost. For the true Word is the Name of God, and those who entertain an unworthy conception of the nature and attributes of God are in ignorance of that true Nature.

THE MASONIC PLAN

The Masonic plan is obviously meant to develop the principles of man in regular order. The work of the Blue Lodge is concerned primarily with the transitory personality, the temporary instrument of the soul. If the tongue of good report is heard in a man's favour, we may assume that he has his physical vehicle fairly under control; but in the Degree of E.A. he is instructed to bring it completely into subjection, to smooth and polish the rough ashlar, and at the same time to keep his emotional nature within due bounds, repressing its lower aspects and developing its higher side. As F.C. he learns absolutely to control those emotions, while he is working at the gradual unfoldment of the powers of his mental body, the awakening and training of his intellectual faculties.

As M.M. he is taught to live up to that sublime title by gaining complete mastery over the personality, the mind as well as the emotions, to develop a magnificent attitude of brotherhood and altruism which compels him ever to take the standpoints of the ego, so that never again may the square be allowed to obscure the compasses, and leads him through the Valley of the Shadow of Death to the threshold of that heavenly world where the immortal Self for ever dwells. For the mystic death and raising again relate not only to the contained existence of man's personality in the astral world after the death of the physical body, but in a higher sense typify a death to all that is transitory and impermanent, and the attainment of an eternal Reality beyond the veils of space and time.

THE CEREMONY OF INSTALLATION

It has always seemed to me a matter of great regret that in the workings of Continental Masonry the beautiful ceremony of the installation of the Master of a Lodge should be so greatly truncated or even entirely omitted. The position of R.W.M. is one of great difficulty and responsibility, and to hold it successfully requires a combination of qualities not often exemplified. Firmness and perfect justice must be conjoined with tact, adaptability and persuasiveness. The R.W.M. should have an enthusiastic interest in Masonic work, a strong determination to maintain its immemorial traditions and the sanctity of its landmarks, and an earnest resolve ever to uphold the dignity of the Craft, yet never for a moment to forget that gentleness and brotherly love are the very essence and foundation of all its labours.

The Bro. whose duty it is to develop these characteristics within himself manifestly needs all the help that can be given to him, and he unquestionably receives more power from on high from the use of a stately and impressive ceremony than from the mere fact of being elected by the Brn. and taking his seat in the Master's chair. Apparently the

H.O.A.T.F. accepts and endorses the custom of the maimed rite in those countries where it prevails, for the succession is passed on, even though there is quite a different feeling about the effect produced. (See p. 175.)

The actual conferment of the authority occurs at the moment when the R.W.M. is solemnly placed in his Chair with a certain s ... and w ... of power, but there is also a charming and appropriate symbolism hidden behind the other s ... s. The b ... s ... is that of a mighty and dignified monarch singling out one upon whom he is about to bestow a favour; the p ... l ... and the s ... of s ... give most valuable hints as to what should be the behaviour of the Master in the Chair, and the s ... of a m ... of a ... and sc ... well expresses the courtesy and dignity which should characterize his every action.

THE MARK DEGREE

In the Mark Degree the aspirant is encouraged to add to that general growth which is expected of all Masons the disclosure of whatsoever special talent or power he may happen to possess, in order that his abilities may thus be at the disposal of his brethren and be used for the benefit of his Lodge, so that such work as passes through his hands may bear upon it the mark of his private characteristics, and thus be recognized from all others. Thus to develop his talent, not for self-glorification but for the good of his Brn., is the special duty of the Mark Mason; while the work of the Mark Master is to find in those under his charge talents as yet unsuspected even by their possessors, and to draw them out under his kindly and fostering care.

At the same time the neophyte is taught by the ritual the necessity of humility and patience. He makes a k ... s ..., a beautiful and excellent piece of work, but one for which the builders are not yet ready, and consequently it has for the present to be thrown aside. The candidate in his disappointment feels at first that his life-work has been wasted; but he is exhorted to exhibit patience and fortitude, and in due course the time comes when his work can be accepted and utilized. Such experience is inevitable in the life of one who is striving to serve humanity; the student must be prepared to find that ideas, unquestionably good in themselves, have yet to be rejected when put forward prematurely; he must learn to subordinate his will to that of T.G.O.O.T.U., to work at the task prescribed for him, and to play the part assigned to him in the great plan of which he is but an infinitesimal though necessary fraction.

However full the world
There is room for an earnest man;

God hath need of me, or I should not be;
I am here to aid the plan.

We may see in the Degrees of Craft Masonry a prophecy or adumbration of the True Initiations that lie far ahead on the Path of the neophyte, taking the E.A. Degree as imaging the entry upon the Probationary Path, the F.C. as representing that entering upon the Stream which is the First of the Great Initiations, and the M.M. as typifying the Fourth Step, the Initiation of the Arhat.

The characteristic of the F.C. Degree is Service; all its five stages are forms of service, and they lead up to that condition in which the candidate's hands are perpetually free to take up whatever tools may be needed at the moment in the work of helping others. As the Mark Degree is recognized as having originally been part of the F.C., Ex. and Perf. Bro. Wood takes the Mark Man and the Mark Master as respectively symbolizing the Second and Third of the Great Initiations, thus leading up very satisfactorily to the M.M. Degree, which is obviously a foreshadowing of the Arhat Stage.

He also finds in the Hindu system an interesting analogy to the teaching of the Mark Degree. The man who has entered upon the First Stage of the Path proper is called *parivrajaka*, the Wanderer, and this is taken to signify that the Initiate has no real home, no foundation or anchorage in this physical world. As it is expressed in a hymn: "I'm but a stranger here; heaven is my home." He has realized the first part of that quotation, but not quite yet the second; he feels as though he were merely a visitor to these mundane regions where most people settle themselves and make themselves at home, yet he is not definitely established in spiritual work. When he has cast off the three fetters of self-centredness, doubt and superstition, he is called *kutichaka*, the Hut-Builder; he is now no longer a wanderer, unsettled in both worlds, for he has found for himself a definite place and work on the buddhic plane. When this is achieved a Mark is given to him, typified in Masonic and biblical phraseology as a white stone, upon which a new name is written - the true name of the ego.

The Hindu term for the man who takes the Third great step is *hamsa*, the Swan; and this name is supposed to be founded upon an ancient fable which endowed that bird with the apocryphal faculty of separating milk from water after they had been mixed. He is therefore taken as a symbol of the man whose discrimination is perfect, who can distinguish what is worth doing and do it, and therefore "marks well".

The Officers in a Mark Lodge represent the seven principles in man, as they do in the ordinary Lodge, but we have in addition three Overseers, who guard the South, West and East Gates. These also are in their right place in the series of principles if we take them to typify the *antahkarana*, which in the Initiate has becomes an active channel between the ego and the personality. As the Lords of Karma select the portion of accumulated karma to be worked out in one lifetime, and this is expressed in the man's bodies and his environment, so does the ego, says Bro. Wood, select a portion of himself to be the internal agent (*antahkarana*) between himself and the personality. (This is explained in his book *The Seven Rays*.) This antahkarana, which is triple, thus contains the plan of work of the incarnation, and the Overseers, as agents of the Lords of Karma, guard that plan.

When the man has passed the Second Initiation, having cast off three fetters aforesaid, he begins to see and to act upon the greater plan of the ego, which is superior to the portion incarnated. But the Overseers will not permit him to follow his vision to the neglect of the lower work in the inferior part of the plan which he has still to do. He must not lose sight of his vision, but yet must humbly submit himself to the duties which remain to be done on ordinary lines.

THE HOLY ROYAL ARCH

As the Mark Degree is an extension of the F.C., so is the Holy Royal Arch of Jerusalem a logical continuation of the M.M. Degree. I am intentionally putting aside all consideration of the elaborate confusion of its history, though I have introduced a few notes about it into my second volume, *Glimpses of Masonic History*. Suffice it to say here that all the higher Degrees, to which I am referring in this book, have their roots in the Ancient Mysteries of the remotest past. They have not been, as is often supposed, created anew by ceremonialists of the Middle Ages, but have been revived and re-introduced at the direct or indirect suggestion of the H.O.A.T.F. when He thought their re-emergence desirable. Let it never be forgotten that all through the ages He (or His predecessor in Office) has been "The Hidden Life in Freemasonry", and that that Life has manifested itself in many ways and through many unexpected channels when and where it seemed best for the carrying on of the Great Work.

To explain, to such an extent as is permissible, the wonderfully illuminative teaching of this truly sublime Degree of the Holy Royal Arch I shall borrow freely from the exposition given in the Mystical Lecture of the Co-Masonic Ritual of the Degree, reserving only such points as are necessary to guard the secrets.

Having symbolically reached in the 3° the threshold of immortality, the aspirant finds a quest opening before him, a quest for the G ... S ... of a M.M., which were lost by the untimely death of our Master H ... A ... It may be noted that through the teaching given in this Degree of the H.R.A. we see for the first time why and how the Sacred Word was lost because of that death. It was not that it was forgotten, but that the Three Principals had sworn to pronounce it only when they met together. For these lost secrets all M.M.s are pledged to seek until they are found. These are the secrets of man's eternal being, the secrets of that Divinity which he has forgotten because of his shrouding in the veil of matter; and it is said that they may be found by following the guidance of a Star, as did the Wise Men of old. That Star is the Star of Initiation, the Star of God's presence in our hearts.

The Degree of the H.R.A. leads the neophyte a step further in his quest, and is thus a fitting sequel to the Sublime Degree of M.M., being indeed an integral part of the same Hebrew tradition. The symbolical time of the R.A. is that of the commencement of the building of the Second Temple, the Temple of the man's soul, even as the Temple of King Solomon represents that of his transitory personality. But before the inquirer can find the lost W ..., that Hidden Light which dwells in all created things, which is buried deep in the Temple of Solomon the King, his vision must be so purified that he can behold His presence with eyes unveiled. This attainment of true spiritual vision is symbolized by the Passing of the Four Veils on the road to the Heavenly City, the Sanctuary of Light and Peace; for the Veils represent those limitations of consciousness which blind his vision of the Truth. The P ... W ... s of the Veils explain the means by which he may lift the barriers that hold him back, and show him the qualities that must be developed if real spiritual progress is to be made. Such is the work of the Excellent Master's Degree, and it is undertaken in the power and the light of the Star.

In the Chapter of the H.R.A., the quest for the W ... is carried to a temporary conclusion. By a seeming accident the Candidate is led to discover the Secret Vault of Solomon the King, buried deep below the surface of the earth; in that Vault he finds the s ... and m ... N ... of T.M.H., and for the first time in his Masonic work gains direct vision of the Divine Presence. The sacramental power outpoured in this Degree is intended to quicken the growth of the Divine Spark within him, so that a conscious realization of the truth of God's immanence may be gained by those who live its teaching rightly, and the Candidate may be enabled thereby to recognize the presence of God in all things, however deeply that presence may be veiled from the eyes of the flesh.

The teaching of the H.R.A. is beautifully epitomised in the words of the Psalmist in Psalm cxxxix, 7-12:

Whither shall I go then from Thy Spirit, or whither shall I go then from Thy Presence?

If I climb up into heaven Thou art there; If I go down to hell, Thou art there also.

If I take the wings of the morning, and remain in the uttermost parts of the sea, even there also shall Thy hand lead me, and Thy right hand shall hold me.

If I say: Peradventure the darkness shall cover me; then shall my night be turned to day.

Yea, the darkness is no darkness with Thee, but the night is as clear as the day; the darkness and the light to Thee are both alike.

Certain emblems which are brought prominently before us in the ceremony of the H.R.A. are for us full of solemn signification and valuable suggestion. The meaning of the Divine N ... which is discovered in the Secret Vault of Solomon the King is at once simple and profound. It teaches that God is one and the same God, by whatever Name men call Him, and that He is immanent in the lowest as well as in the highest. Proclaiming thus the universal Fatherhood, it maintains also the universal Brotherhood, and sets before our Companions the noblest of ideals. The entire symbol is surrounded by the Circle, the emblem of God Himself, the eternal Reality behind and within all things unchanging, yet containing all the elements of change. Of this circle it may be truly said that it has its centre everywhere and its circumference nowhere; for it is Omnipresence made manifest in symbol. Furthermore, the circle enshrines a profound truth of creation. It is generated by radiation from a centre; that is to say, its circumference is determined by the limits of the rays going out from the centre in all directions. It is this radiation which in the deepest sense constitutes the circle itself; for centre and circumference are but alternating moments in the process of radiation. By this we may understand that Creation, or the radiation from the Divine Centre of all living things, is not an action performed at some particular moment by God, but is continuous; it is His very Being; creation is co-eternal and co-existent with God.

All creation truly goes forth from the Divine Centre. The countless rays move each in its own direction towards the circumference; but whereas in the centre they are all One, on the circumference they are manifold, each ray being distinct from all others. Thus in God both unity and multiplicity are simultaneously contained; at the Centre all is One, on the circumference all is manifold. In the outer world we live on the circumference of the Everlasting Circle, and all is in separation and therefore in pain; the Royal Art of Masonry teaches us that we must travel along our own ray of manifestation towards that Centre from which a M.M. cannot err, in order to re-discover the truth of the unity of Divine Life in all things. When we move on the circumference, we move in time; yet when we behold the circle as a whole, we see its circumference simultaneously in all its parts, and thus are led to realize that time is but our distorted vision of Eternity.

Again, the symbol of the circle teaches us the mighty Rhythm of Creation; all things go forth from the centre of Unity to the circumference of Multiplicity, and then return once more to that Unity whence they sprang. This is the Eternal Breath of God, the Breath of Creation which is manifest throughout the entire universe, in the life of man with its cycle of existence from childhood through manhood to old age, and in Nature with its alternations of day and night and the rhythmic flow of seasons. In this connection it is of interest to note how many words denoting Spirit in different languages primarily mean Breath - *spiritus* in Latin, *pneuma* in Greek, *ruach* in Hebrew, atma in Sanskrit. It is this Divine Breath, the Holy Spirit, the Creative Fire of God, whom we especially invoke in the Degree of the H.R.A.

Within the circle the triangle is placed, teaching us that God, though One in essence, manifests as a Trinity - Power, Wisdom and Love. The Divine Will is the Centre of the circle resting in Itself in eternal and unchanging peace; the Divine Wisdom is the process of radiation, the Holy Spirit who is the Source of Divine Activity, creating the manifoldness of things as it goes forth from the Centre; the Divine Love is shown forth in the circumference of the circle, uniting all separated creatures in the very bond of peace. This threefold nature of the Divine is present throughout all Creation, in every object and in every creature. In our own consciousness it is manifest in the Spiritual Will, the Intuitional Wisdom and the Creative Intelligence which are three aspects or modes of the Spirit of man, made in the image and likeness of his Creator. In the universe around us we see it as the three qualities of manifestation - inertia, mobility and rhythm, known in Hindu philosophy as the three *gunas*, and in Western philosophy as space or extension, time or change, and rhythm or qualities which give to each thing its distinct and essential nature.

Another symbol of creation is the cross inscribed within the circle, showing how the Divine in manifestation is crucified upon the cross of limitation, willingly suffered that the world might come into being. In that process of creation the Divine as life and the Divine as form seem a duality, even though they are but manifestations of the one eternal God. This interplay or apparent duality in the universe is also symbolized by the cross, which thus becomes the emblem of the Fourfold Name of God. Amongst the medieval Rosicrucians the four arms of this cross were taken to symbolize the four elements, water, fire, air and earth, called in Hebrew Iammim, Nour, Ruach and Iabescheh, corresponding yet again to the Four Beasts about the throne of God, symbolized for us by the Four Great Banners of the Order.

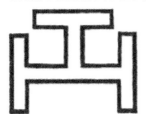

Figure 15

Since thus we learn that all life is the Divine life, it follows also that the brotherhood of that life is in truth universal, and is by no means confined to the human species. Not only is every man our brother, of whatsoever race, colour or creed he may be, but the animals and the trees around us - yea, even the very rock under our feet - are all our younger brethren, all part of the same mighty evolution. When we realize all that this knowledge implies, when we see how great a difference it makes in our attitude towards the world around us, and how great a change the practice of the truth here taught should make in every Companion, we shall not wonder at the high regard in which Masonic writers hold this Degree of the H.R.A. of Jerusalem, which they consider as the crown and completion of Freemasonry, because of the knowledge of God which it gives to us.

A curious but most instructive symbol characteristic of this Degree is that called the Triple Tau, formed out of three levels, one standing upright and two lying horizontally and joined in the centre. The Tau in ancient Egypt was the symbolic equivalent of the cross; it signified the crucifixion of the Divine Life in the world of manifestation. It was also emblematic of the androgynous nature of the Deity; it typified God as Father-Mother. On the Installed

Master's apron we find three Taus in separation; in the Holy Royal Arch we see them conjoined, for here the teaching given is the unity to be found in this entire threefold universe, conveying also the meaning that each Person in this Trinity has its male and female aspect - precisely the same idea which is expressed in the Hindu religion by the statement that each Person has his Shakti, commonly described as his consort. Thus the Three-in-One becomes Six-in-One, and, with the surrounding circle which indicates the unmanifested Totality, we have the Mystic Seven.

The Triple Tau is also called in Royal Arch Masonry the Key. It contains eight right angles, and is used as a measure or mnemonic whereby the Platonic Solids can be calculated. Taken alone, it is commensurate with the Tetrahedron, the sides of which, being four equilateral triangles, are together equal to eight right angles, because the interior angles of any triangle are together equal to two right angles. It is said that this solid was used by the Platonists as a symbol of the element Fire.

Two of these Keys are equivalent to the Octahedron, which contains sixteen right angles, and was considered to represent Air. Three Keys are commensurate with the Cube, the sides of which contain twenty-four right angles; this figure was supposed to typify Earth, because it is of all these figures the firmest and most immovable upon its basis.

Five of these Keys give us forty right angles, which are equal in amount to those contained in the twenty equilateral sides of the Icosahedron. This solid was taken to express the element Water.

The remaining Platonic Solid, called the Dodecahedron, has for its sides twelve regular pentagons. It is a rule in geometry that the interior angles of any rectilinear figure are equal to twice as many right angles as the figure has sides less 4 right angles; thus the interior angles of a pentagon are $10 - 4 = 6$ right angles; therefore the dodecahedron is contained by seventy-two right angles, and consequently is represented by nine Keys. So it will be seen that this Key is the greatest common measure of all these Platonic Solids, and that is why on the scroll round it in the Jewel of the Holy Royal Arch Degree we find the Latin phrase: *Nil nisi clavis deest*, "Nothing is wanting but the key", teaching us on the one hand that without the inner knowledge all these symbols are but lifeless, and on the other that, great as is the teaching given, there is yet more to be found as we move along on the path of Masonic progress.

There is a method by which, by sub-dividing the triangles and the Seal of Solomon into smaller triangles and adding up the total number of degrees formed by all their angles, we can yet again work out the number of right angles equivalent to those of the Platonic solids. This process is complicated, and is of little practical value, so I do not give it here; although it is true that the Platonic Solids have a profound meaning in connection with that process of Divine Creation, upon which the Degree of the Holy Royal Arch contains such priceless teaching.

STILL HIGHER

In endeavouring to give such idea as may lawfully be given of the splendour and the immense practical value of the higher Degrees I must briefly recapitulate something of what I have already written in *Glimpses of Masonic History*. Though the H.R.A. so satisfactorily rounds off the system of Masonic teaching for most men, there are still deeper wells of wisdom for the student who is determined to win his way to the ultimate goal, whom nothing but the highest can satisfy. Gradually such a man comes to understand that, although he has indeed in the H.R.A. found the Divine Name, and contacted for himself at least one aspect of the Hidden Light of God, there is a further search still before him, in which he can penetrate even deeper into the consciousness and being of the Deity. Great and marvellous indeed is the revelation already given to him - a revelation which has changed for him the whole aspect of life, and made the selfish and miserably limited existence of the profane for ever impossible for him. Yet he now begins to see that he is as yet touching only one circumference of a vast circle - nay, more, that he is working only on the surface of an infinite sphere.

THE ROSE-CROIX

It is then that he begins his second great quest, which leads up through a number of stages, during which different attributes of the All-Father are studied and to some extent realized, until it culminates in the magnificent illumination given in the Eighteenth Degree, that of the Sovereign Prince of the Rose-Croix of Heredom, through which he finds the divine Love reigning in his own heart and in those of his Brn. He also learns that God has descended and shared our lower nature with us expressly in order that we may ascend to share His true nature with Him.

The Name of T.G.A.O.T.U. which is revealed to the aspirant in this most wonderful 18° was the central and innermost secret of the ancient Egyptian mystery-teaching. The H.O.A.T.F. in His incarnation as

Christian Rosenkreutz translated the Word into Latin, most ingeniously retaining its remarkable mnemonic character, all its complicated implications, and even a close approximation to its original sound. Naturally it cannot be given here, but the general character of the instruction which it conveys in so skilful a manner may be indicated by a sentence quoted from one of the patron saints of Freemasonry: "God is light, and in Him is *no darkness at all*." It further teaches us that God sits enthroned in every human heart, that the inmost Spirit of each man is part of God Himself, a spark of the Divine; and that therefore all men are one in Him, and there is no height to which man may not aspire.

From this great central fact a whole system of philosophy may be deduced, and also a rule of life; when men are really convinced of it, there is brotherhood, peace and progress, but when this Word is lost, chaos reigns and evil stalks abroad. Each Knight should meditate upon it and try to realize all that it involves, for the knowledge which it gives should permeate the whole fibre of his being, should literally become part of his very essence, if he is to do the duty which is expected of him. The deep reverence and thankfulness which that sublime thought inspires must be his constant attitude; he must live in the light of that glorious truth; it must never be forgotten even for a moment. For the man who really knows this, all life is one great glad song of triumph and of gratitude. All this he acknowledges, in all this he rejoices every time that he remembers that wondrous Word of power.

It is the clear duty of every Knight of the Rose-Croix to spread this light abroad - to preach by word when possible, and always by action, this true "gospel of the grace of God". In the Co-Masonic form of this Degree he is instructed to offer himself as a channel for the Divine force and to make efforts to cooperate with T.G.A.O.T.U. By this daily work his buddhi or intuitional principle, the hidden wisdom which in Egypt was called Horus, the Christ dwelling in man, should be aroused and greatly developed, so that he becomes, to the limit of his capability, a living manifestation of the Eternal Love, a veritable priest who is its instrument for the helping of the world.

In this Degree also we find certain symbols of deep significance. The flower of the Rose has the threefold connotation of Love, Secrecy and Fragrance, while the Cross bears also the threefold meaning of Self-sacrifice, Immortality and Holiness. So when these two emblems are taken in conjunction, as they always are in the name Rose-Croix, they betoken the Love of Self-sacrifice, the Secret of Immortality, and the sweet Fragrance of a Holy life.

The Serpent represents Eternity; the Double Triangle, Spirit and Matter; the Pelican is another ancient symbol of Self-sacrifice, as the Eagle is of Victory.

It is significant that up to this point the aspirant, having complied with certain requirements, may apply for advancement, may demand recognition of his progress. But now that he is coming in sight of higher Degrees he may no longer make demand - he must wait for invitation from those who have already attained. It is not for him, but for them, to decide when he is ready to make a further effort. At the levels which he must now approach, the brotherhood is so close, so perfect, that there must be no risk that its fullness may be marred by the introduction of a discordant element.

Not only do these higher Degrees carry on further the same process of development which was begun in the lower, they may be said in a certain sense to repeat it at a higher level. The E.A. controls and uplifts emotion in the astral body; the Rose-Croix of Heredom develops far higher love in the buddhi which corresponds to it. The F.C. tries to strengthen his intellect to comprehend the hidden mysteries of Masonry; the Knight K.H. unfolds within him that grander intellectual quality which gives him always perfect balance and a sense of absolute justice, so that he understands the working of karma. The M.M. combines within himself and carries farther qualities of the Degrees below him; the due-guard of his Degree shows that he is intended to be shedding blessing and help around him wherever he goes; and of course this is true to a far greater extent and at a far higher level of the Sovereign Grand Inspector General of the 33°, for he should have love, wisdom and power equally manifesting in him, so that in him the true essence of governance may be set forth.

In Blue Masonry and in the Degree of the H.R.A. we call in the assistance of certain Seventh-Ray Angels to assist the officials in conducting the work of the Lodge or Chapter; in this 18° and in other still higher Degrees we do that, also, but the type of Angels who respond is different, for each Degree has its own kind of Deva-attendant. In these cases, however, the support of the Angelic kingdom is much more fully extended; not only have we the aid of the Devas in the performance of our ceremonies, but to each Prince of Heredom at the time of his Perfection a special Angel is attached, to help him in his private and individual work for the cause. This will be more readily comprehensible if I mention first the characteristic of the other Degrees.

BLACK MASONRY

Few need anything further than the splendid revelation of the indwelling Love of God which they receive in the Eighteenth Degree. But there are those who feel that there is yet more to learn of the nature of God, who eagerly wish to understand the meaning of evil and suffering, and its relation to the Divine plan; for them Black Masonry exists - the teaching and progress comprised in the Degrees from the nineteenth to the thirtieth. This section of the Mysteries is especially concerned with the working out of karma in its different aspects, studied as a law of retribution, and so from one point of view it is dark and terrible. This is the inner kernel lying behind the vengeance-elements in the degree of Knight K.H. The darker aspects of karma are largely connected with man's ignorance of the nature of God, and with confusion with regard to many forms in which He reveals Himself, and thus the s ... s of the 30° contain the heart of its philosophy. That Degree would not be fully and validly conferred unless these s ... s were duly communicated, since they express its inner meaning and purpose.

In the ancient Egyptian instruction, corresponding to this group of Degrees, it was taught that whatsoever a man sowed that also must he reap, and that if he sowed evil the result would be suffering to himself. The karma of nations and races was also studied, and the inner working of the law upon the different planes was investigated by the inner sight, and shown to the student. The whole of what we now call Black Masonry led up to an explanation of karma, as Divine justice, this having been preserved for us in shadow in what is now the 31°, that of the Grand Inspector Inquisitor Commander, whose symbol is a pair of scales. In Egypt this pair of scales was taken as an emblem of the perfect balance of Divine justice; the aspirant learnt that all the horror sometimes associated with the working out of karma was indeed based on absolute justice, although it appeared as evil to the lesser vision of the profane.

Thus the first stage of the higher instruction, that of the Rose-Croix or Red Masonry, is devoted to the knowledge and assurance of good, while to the Second stage, that of the Knight K.H., is assigned the knowledge of apparent evil and its explanation. Next, in the first steps of White Masonry, the crown of the whole glorious structure, the aspirant learns to see the underlying justice of the great and eternal God, called in Egypt Amen-Ra, who stands behind all alike, whether it seems to us evil or good. We are told that in older days, before the *Kaliyuga*, in which the apparent evil predominates over the good, the Knight K.H. wore regalia of yellow instead of black.

The 30° links the Knight K.H. to the ruling rather than to the teaching branch of the Great Hierarchy. He should become a radiant centre of perennial energy, which is intended to give him strength to overcome evil and to make him a real power on the side of good. Though the sash is black, the prevailing colour of the influence is an electric blue (that of the First Ray, quite different from the blue of the symbolic or Blue Masonry of the early Degrees) edged with gold, including and yet not drowning the rose of the 18°°. A higher level of the same energy is transmitted to the Chair of the Sovereign Commander, who has the ability to pass on the sacramental grace of the Degree to others.

WHITE MASONRY

The highest and last of the sacramental powers of the Ancient Mysteries which have been transmitted to us is that of the Sovereign Grand Inspector General of the 33°. The Brn. of this high Order should have passed on from a conception of the Divine justice to the certainty of knowledge and the fullness of the Divine Glory in the Hidden Light. The 33° links the Sovereign Grand Inspector General with the Spiritual King of the World Himself - that Mightiest of Adepts who stands at the head of the Great White Lodge, in whose strong hands lie the destinies of the earth - and awakens the powers of the Triple Spirit as far as they can yet be awakened. This highest of all Degrees is given to but few, yet even among those few there can have been but a handful who had the least conception of what they had received, or of the powers given into their hands. Most of those to whom it comes probably regard it as chiefly an administrative Degree, and have no idea that it has a spiritual side at all. The actual conferring of the Degree is a very splendid experience when seen with the inner sight; for the Hierophant of the Mysteries (the H.O.A.T.F.) stands above or beside the physical initiator, in that extension of His consciousness which is called the Angel of the Presence. If the recipient of the Degree happens to be already an Initiate, the Star (called in Egypt the Star of Horus) which marks the approval of the One Initiator once more flames out above him in all its glory; while in any case the two great white Angels of the rite flash down in splendour from the heavenly places, showing themselves as low as the etheric level, that they may give their full blessing to the new Ruler in the Craft.

The H.O.A.T.F. makes the actual links both with Himself and with the reservoir of power set apart for the work of the Masonic Brotherhood, and also through Himself with that Mighty King whose representative He is for this work, while the great white Angels of the Order remain as the guardians of the Sovereign Grand Inspector General throughout life. This stage combines the wonderful love of Horus the Son with the ineffable life and strength of Osiris the divine Father and Isis the eternal Mother of the world; and this union of love with strength is its most prominent characteristic.

It confers upon those who open themselves to its influence power similar to and only a little way below that of the First great Initiation, and those who enter the 33° should assuredly qualify themselves for that Step before very long. Indeed, in the great days of the Mysteries this stage was accessible only to Initiates, and one feels that it ought to be given only to such now just as it would seem appropriate that the marvellous gift of the episcopate should be conferred only upon members of the Great White Brotherhood. The power of the Degree when in operation shows itself in an aura of dazzling white and gold, enfolding within it the rose and the blue of Rose-Croix and K.H.; and yet it is also strongly permeated with that peculiar shade of electric blue which is the especial sign of the presence of the King. The Sovereign Grand Inspector General is the "Bishop" of Masonry, and if the life of the Degree is really lived he should be an ever-radiating centre of power, a veritable sun of light and life and glory wherever he goes.

Such was the highest and holiest of the sacramental powers conferred in the Mysteries of ancient Egypt, such the highest Degree known to us in Freemasonry today, bestowed in its fullness upon very few. The opportunity to draw down its sublime glory is offered to all who receive the Degree; how far it is taken and what use is made of the power is in the hands of the Bros. alone, for to use it, as it should be used, needs high spiritual development and a life of constant humility, watchfulness and service. If he calls upon it for the service of others, it will flow through him mightily and sweetly for the helping of the world. If he neglects the power, it will remain dormant and the links unused - and Those behind will turn Their glance away from him to others more responsive. The influence of the 33° is a veritable ocean of bliss and splendour, strength and sweetness, for it is the power of the King Himself, the Lord who reigns on earth as Viceregent of the Logos from eternity unto eternity.

HOW TO USE THE POWERS

It must of course be understood in all cases that, though the conferring of the Higher Degrees puts certain definite powers in the hands of the recipient, it does not instantly endow him with the knowledge of how he is to employ them; he must grow into that by long and careful practice, and full comprehension of them is the first step.

To gain such full understanding is no easy matter. Those of us to whom these powers are entrusted have to wield the forces of a new and higher world; we have to learn to do in a small way what our Masters are doing all the while on a far larger scale; and that means that we must consciously lift our lives much nearer to Them. A definite piece of Their work is being turned over to us, to set Them free for other and higher activities; we must not fail Them, we must not disappoint Them by showing ourselves unable to do it.

Clearly our task is of the same nature as one with which we are all of us already theoretically familiar. All who have worked in the Liberal Catholic Church or in the earlier Degrees of Co-Masonry know that the chief object of those great organizations is to draw down spiritual influence from on high, and to radiate it out upon the surrounding world in a form in which that world can readily assimilate it. But in each of those bodies the actual work of radiation, of distribution, is done by non-human entities - by the great Angels or Devas whom we invoke - our part in the work being rather the provision of the material which they employ. Ours is the intensity of the devotion and of life and good will which calls down the response from the Logos; theirs is the labour of sorting out, of classifying and directing the manifold varieties of that Divine response, and applying it where it is most needed.

But now in this work of the higher Degrees we are called not only to collect but to direct - not only to provide material but to distribute and apply it. We are to exercise the functions of the Angels on some of the lower planes, thus leaving them free to concentrate their energies on higher levels where as yet we are less effective. The great Angels of our respective Degrees will assuredly work with us; it is for that purpose that they have come to us; but we on our part must do our share of the work so that the machine as a whole may act at its highest efficiency.

This is indeed a prodigious privilege which has been conferred upon us, and it involves a correspondingly weighty responsibility. None of us, I am sure, would intentionally use our power wrongly; there is no danger of that; but there is the possibility that through ignorance we may fail to make sufficient use of these new talents of ours. We were told long ago that "inaction in a deed of mercy may become action in a deadly sin". Since the Great Ones have entrusted us with powers so portentous it behoves us to try to understand them fully, to study their working, so that we may learn how to use them to the best advantage, how to do with them what our Masters intend us to do.

A second point is that, having received a great accession of strength from our connection with the Angel, we must keep a doubly careful watch over our words and thoughts, and guard ourselves most strictly from even a momentary flash of irritability. With us, after our years of self-training, such a feeling passes so quickly that, though of course it is always undesirable, it may not previously have mattered very much; but now it becomes far more serious, for even its rapid passage may do considerable harm to the object of our wrath.

OUR RELATION WITH THE ANGELS

We must consider heedfully the relation with the Angelic kingdom into which these higher Degrees bring us, for it is a matter of the utmost importance. At the moment of his Perfecting, there is attached to the Sovereign Prince of the Rose-Croix a splendid crimson Angel - a Being of beauty, dignity and power beyond the utmost stretch of our imagination.

What is the nature of this attachment, and what will be the practical effect of this beautiful partnership? The Angel links himself with the higher principles of the man, most of all with the buddhi or intuitional wisdom, and the result should presently show itself in two ways. The indescribable vitality and versatility of the Angel's mind will constantly impress themselves upon the mental body of the novice, stimulating it into far greater activity, suggesting new lines of thought and action for the benefit of humanity, strengthening the quality of love within him and offering it ever new channels through which to flow.

Conversely, whatever ideas may arise in the neophyte's own mind will at once be seized and intensified by the Angel, and all sorts of hints will be offered as to methods of putting them into practice. But it cannot be too often reiterated or too strongly impressed upon the aspirant that all this will happen only if he makes a definite effort to lay himself open to the Angelic influence, only if he fills himself with the fiery love which is the common factor and line of communication between the two evolutions which otherwise differ so widely.

If we are at all to understand these wondrous denizens of a higher world, which is yet a part of our world (and it is clearly our duty to try to understand them), we shall need to widen out our entire conception of life. Our studies in earlier Degrees should have given us a loftier point of view, and endowed us with a wider outlook than that of the uninstructed man; but we are still confined within our human rut, and we must learn to transcend it. As compared to the unimaginable reality, our ideas are at the best personal and limited - even mean and sordid. They are good of their kind, but they are restricted to that kind; effective in some directions, but utterly unaware that there are other directions of greater importance.

The kingdoms of nature are curiously related to each other, and mutual comprehension is extraordinarily difficult. Think how far it is possible for even the most intelligent of our domestic animals to understand our own life. He sees us sitting reading or writing for hours together; how can he have any real idea of what we are doing? The very large section of our existence which depends upon our possession of those powers is altogether beyond his grasp, and we can never explain it to him. Just so are there many activities of the Angelic kingdom which are incomprehensible to us.

Yet when one of these bright Spirits is attached to us by a Masonic ceremony we must not think of him either as director or as an attendant, but simply as a co-worker and a brother. Our self-centredness is so ingrained that when we hear of such wonderful association we at once think, however unconsciously, what zee can gain by the relationship. What can we learn from this resplendent being? Will he guide us, advise us, protect us? Or, on the other hand, is he a servant whom we can send to do our will? It is just because we are creatures of that sort, just because we think in that way, just because we are at that stage of evolution, that admission to the 18° has to be by invitation only. A person who is still in that condition of what might be called latent selfishness is not yet ready to be linked with a radiant entity who does not know what selfishness means.

Here is a great and powerful Being, of an order quite different from our own, but in certain ways complementary to it; if we two can work together in a union so perfect that there shall be but one will, one purpose, one thought - and that the Divine thought - between us, we can achieve very far more, we can be of enormously more use to the Logos, than we could ever be when labouring separately, no matter how strenuous might be our endeavours. Such a union is part of God's intention for us; if we can attain it, it will be an incredible advantage to us; yet if we desire it because of that personal gain, we are unworthy of it and shall fail to realize our hope. We must accept such magnificent comradeship only because of the benefit which will accrue to the world; as regards ourselves we must be absolutely impersonal, we must have forgotten ourselves utterly, yet we must be filled with the Divine fervency of love for humanity.

A man may feel: "These things are too high for me; who shall be sufficient for them?" If karma puts the opportunity in his way, the achievement is within his power, even though it may mean harder work than he has ever yet undertaken. And the fiery love which is the very essence of the life of his Seraph will awaken ever more and more of the latent quality in himself, until what now seems impossible has been realized, has become a part of his daily existence.

The 30° brings its Angel also, of appropriate character - a great blue Deva of the First Ray, who lends his strength to the Knight K.H., somewhat as the crimson Angel assists the Ex. and Perf. Bro. of the Rose-Croix. The 33 ° gives two such splendid fellow-workers - Spirits of gigantic size as compared to humanity, and radiantly white in colour. Among the Angels there is no sex as we understand the word; yet these two Great Ones differ in a sense which is best expressed by saying that one of them is predominantly masculine and the other predominantly feminine. He who stands usually on the right hand of the Sovereign Grand Inspector General has an aura of brilliant white light shot with gold, and represents Osiris, the sun and the life, the positive aspect of the Deity; she who stands on the left has an aura of similar light veined with silver, and represents Isis, the moon and the truth, the negative or feminine aspect of the Divine Glory. They are splendid beyond all words, and radiant with living love, though most of all they convey a sense of irresistible, though benevolent, power; and they give strength to act with decision, accuracy, courage and perseverance on the physical plane.

They belong to the cosmic Order of Angels, who are common to other solar systems besides our own, and their permanent centres of consciousness are on the intuitional plane; though whenever they think fit they draw round themselves mental and astral matter (as, for example, at all the greater ceremonies in Lodge) and they are always ready to give their blessing whenever it is invoked. They are inseparably one with the Sovereign Grand Inspector General, linked to his higher Self, never to desert him unless by unworthiness he first deserts them and casts them off. The symbols of the sun and moon are usually represented on the gauntlets of the holder of this sublime position, and they are intended to refer to these great Angelic Powers, who bear a close resemblance to those magnificent members of their kingdom who attach themselves to a Bishop at the time of his consecration, and thereafter remain always in connection with him.

This last phrase requires a little further explanation, for the association is of an unusual character. This shining retinue of the heavenly host does not visibly accompany either the Bishop or the Sovereign Grand Inspector General at all times, yet the consciousness of these high Angelic comrades is never out of touch with his own, though the link is not easy to explain. The Angel keeps a line of communication always open, and the end of this line, which rests in the aura of his human partner, floats there like a star or tiny point of light. If the Bishop or the Prince-Mason calls upon his inner friend, the latter is instantly there; indeed, a call, is not necessary - the merest flash of thought is enough. The link must be of a very remarkable nature, for I myself have found that the intention to perform any episcopal act - even to give the most ordinary blessing - at once attracts the attention of these noble collaborators, though I have not consciously thought of them at all.

I have wondered whether it would be irreverent to see in that tiny point of light in the aura which represents the Angel, some sort of analogy at an infinitely lower level to the Host in the Tabernacle which is the vehicle of the Lord Christ. How often have I seen, in some small village church on the Continent, the gentle glow which indicates the Holy Presence; and when some humble peasant-woman comes in on her way to market, puts down her basket in the porch, and kneels for a few moments of prayer, how often have I seen that glow flash out into a sun-like radiance in immediate response to her earnest thought of devotion! The Holy Presence is never absent, but It certainly exhibits Itself in greater activity in answer to an appeal. Is the Angel's force-centre something like a faint reflection of that?

Perhaps another analogy may be found in the twelve stars which, following the beautiful description in the Apocalypse, are so often shown in medieval paintings round the head of the Blessed Virgin Mary. All these represent powers; perhaps they correspond in some way to the points of light which the Angels leave in our aura. The Star always floating over the head of an Initiate betokens the Power of the King, upon which he can draw at any moment, while the star upon his forehead is the symbol of his own acquired power.

CHAPTER X.
TWO WONDERFUL RITUALS.
THE WORKINGS IN EGYPT

IN Chapter VI we have commented upon the procedure adopted in Lodge when there is a candidate to be initiated. Naturally this is not always the case, and when it is not, after disposing of any business that may arise it is usual for the R.W.M., or some expert Bro. called upon by him, to give some instruction to the Brn. along Masonic lines, or to deliver a lecture on some historical point of Masonic interest. Sometimes the formulated "Lectures" of the Masculine Craft are rehearsed - a very interesting set of documents arranged in the form of questions and answers, which recapitulate and explain the ritual, and contain a good deal of miscellaneous Masonic information. Sometimes the official explanation of the t ... b ... is recited, with any comment or further elucidation which occurs to the R.W.M.

In ancient Egypt this was the point at which in the ordinary Lodges the special teaching of the Mysteries was given. It seems to have consisted of somewhat informal talks by the R.W.M, on the various sciences which were included in their rather extensive curriculum. The Brn. were permitted to ask questions, but everything was done with the greatest possible decorum, and with a certain archaic and formal but very real reverence that was charming to see. What we must call examinations, though they were very different from ours, were held when convenient, and no Bro. could pass into a higher degree without satisfying the officials as to his full knowledge and capability with regard to the stage in which he was then working. Whenever it was at all possible a special point was always made of the copious illustration of any subject under consideration, and this was effected sometimes by pictures and models, sometimes by dramatic representations (as of important scenes from ancient history), and sometimes by actual materialization of objects and materials which could not otherwise be procured.

In the three Grand Lodges the procedure differed. Their members had already acquired the necessary scientific knowledge, so they were able to devote themselves entirely to the great purpose for which they existed - the pouring forth of spiritual power over the country. This was done by means of a ritual perhaps as magnificent as any ever known to man - a ritual of which I will here give a free translation, though I feel it entirely impossible to reproduce in words the majesty and splendour of the original.

As already stated, the Grand Lodges were limited to forty members, but these Brn, were especially and essentially picked men, and each one had it as a duty to take up some particular quality or activity and fit himself to be a representative of that. One man, for example, represented perseverance, and was called the Knight or Lord of Perseverance; another was the Knight or Lord of Courage; another took up the virtue of tact, and so on. A list of these qualities is appended; but I am not satisfied with it, for it is often exceedingly difficult to find English equivalents for the Egyptian ideas, and in many cases a whole sentence would be needed folly to explain the latter.

It was, then, the duty of each brother to fit himself to expound or express his quality or activity - not for himself, but as a part of the whole. A man cultivated courage, not that he might be brave, but that he might represent courage in that group, regarded as a composite entity, which was in a very real sense a unity. Each one of them must know his quality not only from his own point of view, but also by an odd system of cross correspondences. Each person was supposed to be able to deliver a sermon about his quality from the point of view of each of the other qualities. Courage tempered by humility; courage affected by love, and so on; there were many quaint and interesting combinations. These were first-rate men - and they needed to be to do their work efficiently.

Love and Wisdom	R.W.M.
Strength	W.S.W.
The Power to discover and appreciate Beauty	W.J.W.
	I.P.M.
Discernment (Good Judgment or Discrimination)	Orator or Mouthpiece
	Secretary (Recorder and Librarian)
Eloquence	
Truth and Accuracy	Administrator (Treasurer)
Industry (Diligence)	Director of Ceremonies
Efficiency	Director of Music
Sense of Unity (Sympathy)	S.D.
Courtesy	J.D.
Tact	I.G.
Decision (Promptitude)	Tyler
Courage	
Cheerfulness	
Confidence	Columns
Calm	
Balance	
Perseverance (Steadfastness)	
Reverence	
Devotion	
Foresight (Calculation or Prescience)	Columns
One-pointedness	
Sense of Honour	
Impartiality (Unprejudicedness)	
Justice	
Desirelessness	
Control of Thought	
Control of Emotion	
Control of Body	
Judicious Speech	
Control of Memory (Knowing what to remember and what to forget)	
Meditation	
Purity	
Patience and Gentleness	
Persuasiveness	
Adaptability	
Tolerance	
Eagerness for Service (Humility)	
Study	
40. Perspicuity	

THE FORM OF THE TEMPLE OF AMEN-RA

The performance of the beautiful ceremony called "The Building of the Temple of Amen" was the principal work done by these great Lodges; and, as I have said, the Brn. regarded it as the chief reason for their existence. As explained in Chapter I, they held that the Hidden Light of God dwelt within the heart of every man, however unevolved he might be; and they considered it the duty of the enlightened one, first, so to live as to let that Light shine unobstructed through him, and secondly, to try by every means within his power to help to arouse and unveil that Hidden Light in his fellow-men.

They found by experience that one of the most efficient modes of giving such help to large numbers simultaneously was to afford a channel for the outpouring of a vast flood of spiritual force over the surrounding country, and that was what they endeavoured to do in the ceremony which I am about to describe. They said: "All Light comes from the Great One; but because men shut themselves away in the caves of ignorance and misunderstanding, our earthly mirrors can reflect that Light where otherwise it would not penetrate, and so the Great One accepts our help, and condescends to use in the work that part of Himself which is manifesting through us." They looked forward to this ceremony with the utmost eagerness and thought no pains too great to take to prepare themselves for it; and they threw themselves into its performance with an unsurpassable enthusiasm.

They met for this function in a subterranean hall of vast size, resembling in appearance a great cathedral. The Lodge was a small area in the midst of this prodigious cave, like the *cella* in a Greek temple. The mosaic floor, the tessellated pavement and the usual Masonic arrangements were there, just as we have them now. For the performance of this particular rite the altar stood in the middle; but the usual form of the Lodge in Egypt was the double square - an oblong about twice as long as it is broad - and in that case the altar stood at the middle point of the eastern square; but for "The Building of the Temple of Amen" the altar was absolutely central. In all Lodges in Egypt they attached very great importance to the altar, saying that the altars of Masonry had from time immemorial been the beacon - lights of liberty, and the Lodge a city of refuge.

Just outside the area of the Lodge on the north side was a row of nine subsidiary altars, somewhat like little round-topped tables. Each was a highly carved stone pillar, rising to a height of a little more than three feet and then spreading out into a round table-top, perhaps a couple of feet in diameter. On each of those was the name of one of the great Archangels. These were the altars of the Nine Orders of Angels, and that which now we represent under the name of the Archangel Michael was the central point of the nine. Below on the floor round each of these was a kind of shallow trough in which during the ceremony incense was burning all the time. I am not quite sure how the fire was kept up, for in the Egyptian Mysteries they had means of producing exceedingly bright light and intense heat which were quite different from ours - probably something we have not yet discovered. They had thus a thin veil of incense rising round each of these little altars.

The altar in the centre of the Lodge was peculiar, and requires a little explanation. It was built on the same general plan as those of the Angels, but it was considerably more massive. Its edge was thick, and not strictly speaking circular; it was really a polygon with forty sides - a side for each person present. The altar-top was perhaps about seven feet in diameter, and each of the forty little facets was square. The altar was made of some kind of obsidian or possibly jade-glass-like, not black, but dark blue or green. In the centre of this thick altar-top there was hidden a very bright light, quite invisible when all the mechanism was closed.

In the upper surface of this hollow altar there was a circular opening, closed by a little door, the two halves of which could slide apart so that the light could shine out upwards towards the roof through that hole in the top of the altar. Apart from this, each of the facets had a little door that drew up. One could take hold of the projecting frame, and draw up the little door, so that a pencil of light shone out horizontally towards the far-distant wall through the little slit which was thereby opened. Inside each of these little doors was coloured glass, so that different rays came forth from each of these forty slits when they were opened. These colours were chosen to represent the various qualities, or at least to distinguish one from another. Some were simple colours, but most were combinations. I mean that a pencil of light would be divided - half yellow and half blue, let us say; sometimes such a division would be diagonal, and sometimes horizontal, so that the resulting beams were readily recognizable.

Over the altar in the centre of the roof was the Blazing Star, which at full power was a really splendid light, equal to several big electric arcs put together. It was however, capable of being dimmed down gradually, and could be used at various degrees of power. Each of the Brn. brought to this ceremony a private light of his own, which was practically a dark lantern. It was a rather clumsy-looking bog of blue earthenware, but it had a tube corresponding to that of a bull's-eye lantern, so that it could shoot out a powerful pencil of light which stood out clearly in the incense-laden air. Each person's ray of light was different, corresponding to one of those from the altar in the centre. Another feature which is quite foreign to our modern ideas was the presence of two attendant acolytes at the ceremony - a boy and a girl of about twelve years of age, most beautiful children, chosen for their beauty out of the whole land of Egypt. They were sworn under the most sacred oath (the oath by Amen, which none would ever dare to break) not to speak outside of what took place in the Lodge. Certain vessels and other paraphernalia were kept under the R.W.M.'s pedestal, and solemnly fetched thence by these little acolytes when required.

THE BUILDING OF THE TEMPLE OF AMEN-RA

When the ceremony of the Building of the Temple of Amen was to be performed the Lodge was opened in the ordinary way, and raised straight to the Third Degree by the shortest method in due and ancient form. The Blazing Star flashed out at the moment of opening, but not to its highest possibility. After inquiries as to business, the R.W.M. gave one k ... which was answered as usual, and said:

"Brn., we have met to perform the greatest of our duties - to build the Temple of the Great One, the Great Architect, the Grand Geometrician, the Most High."

As he uttered the first title, all present raised the back of the right hand to the forehead, and at each of the other titles the appropriate salutes were given, exactly as we know them now. Remaining at the salute the R.W.M. continued:

"May we be found worthy to serve Him."

All present repeated the words, chanting solemnly in reply:

"May we be found worthy to serve Him."

In the same way the following sentences were repeated:

R.W.M. - May our work be guided by His wisdom.

All - May our work be guided by His wisdom.

W.S.W. - May our work be inspired by His strength.

All - May our work be inspired by His strength.

W.J.W. - May our work show forth His beauty.

All - May our work show forth His beauty.

R.W.M. - May our work be acceptable in His sight.

All - May our work be acceptable in His sight.

That last sentence meant more than is conveyed in the English words, for it also included the idea that while He saw it, and approved it, He might also be seen in it, might shine through it and manifest Himself.

Then the R.W.M. said:

"Brn., let us prepare ourselves by a few minutes of meditation."

He made a sign with his hand, and the Blazing Star was extinguished, leaving the Lodge in total darkness. Each brother had his lamp lit, but the light was perfectly concealed. At each man's seat was a sort of socket or stand into which his lamp fitted, and when it was laid on that socket its tube was accurately aimed at the corresponding facet of the central altar. Each brother (or sister) retained always the same seat, and the coloured glass in the tube of his lantern exactly resembled that in the facet of the altar to which he was opposite.

THE UNVEILING OF THE HIDDEN LIGHT

After a few minutes of meditation in the darkness the R.W.M. gave a k ..., which was answered as usual, and the W.S.W, said:

"R.W.M., is it your will that we pray the God Ra to unveil the Hidden Light?" (The God Ra is the Solar Logos, manifesting through the sun).

The R.W.M. replied:

"Ra unveils His light when we unveil ours. So give that you may receive."

Then he left his seat in the darkness, and walked down to the altar, with his two little attendants, and stood with his back to his own throne, but close to the altar. He also had a lamp like all the rest, and he now carried it in his hand. He drew up the slide of his lamp and showed his light, as he said: "I give the Light of wisdom," and aimed that light at the altar in front of him, and as he did so he stretched forth his hand and drew up the corresponding little door. There was a little ledge on which it hitched so that it remained open, and so in response to the coloured ray from his lamp a similar coloured ray shone upon him from the altar. He then handed his lamp to his little acolyte, who carried it back to his chair, and set it in its socket; and then the R.W.M. walked round the table to the other side.

Then the W.S.W., from his place, said: "I give the Light of strength," and uncovered his light, which also was set in its socket so that the ray of light fell on the edge of the table exactly opposite to him. The R.W.M. slipped up that little door, and the corresponding light shone out. Then the W.J.W. unveiled the light of beauty, and after him each member in turn mentioned his own quality, saying: "I give such and such a light," and each time the R.W.M. raised the little door opposite to the speaker, and the corresponding colour shone forth - always the double ray, that which the man gave and the ray from the centre which answered it.

When all the forty members had uncovered their lights in that way, the R.W.M. said:

"The circle is complete; let the light shine."

With these words he opened the top of the table, sliding back the two semi-circular doors, so that a strong cylindrical beam of white light flashed up to the roof. The coloured rays of the qualities were perhaps four inches in diameter, but this beam measured a couple of feet through - a great funnel of light shooting up to the ceiling, which was very lofty - at least seventy feet high, I should think; and then in response to that, the Blazing Star was unveiled at its fullest power.

The symbolism here is obvious and beautiful. Each person first gives his quota and gets his response. When all have done their respective parts they have built up the perfect man. Then the white light which includes all shoots up, and down comes the Light of the Logos in reply. When the whole vast hall was flooded by this splendid light from the Blazing Star, the people closed their lamps, all the little doors in the sides of the altar were dropped down again, and those on the top of the table slid back into place.

THE OFFERINGS

The next part of the ceremony was a hymn to Ra, the Logos, the Sun-God, thanking Him for His response, giving glory to Him and saying: "Let us bathe in His Light, and pay Him due reverence." That was the general effect of it, but there were many verses. When that was finished, the R.W.M. said: "Bring in the offerings"; and his acolytes went off to his pedestal and produced them.

The children brought him two golden vessels, which bore some resemblance to those used in the Christian eucharistic service, and evidently to a certain extent corresponded to them. This ceremony long antedated Christianity, so it is by no means impossible that some of its features may have been absorbed by the later religion. We may clearly regard this as the Egyptian form of the Eucharist, for its object was identical; the Brn. offered themselves, body, soul and spirit, to God, He entered into them in an especial manner in return, and they then acted as the channels of His bounty to the world.

The boy returned from the Master's pedestal bearing in his hands a circular golden dish with a domed cover perhaps twelve inches in diameter; in fact, it was in shape and size by no means unlike some that are used to hold vegetables at a modern dinner table, but made apparently of solid gold, richly chased and evidently very heavy. The girl bore a cup of similar manufacture - not quite the Christian chalice; more like the two-handled loving-cup of mediaeval times. These vessels were treated with the utmost reverence, as of immemorial antiquity; they were scarcely in the Egyptian style, and may quite possibly have been Atlantean. The girl carried also a curious triangle of gold, in the centre of which was realistically engraved a human eye. A slight bowl-like depression at the apex of the triangle enabled the officiant to use it as a kind of spoon, as will presently be explained.

These vessels were placed on the altar before the R.W.M., who extended his hands over them and said:

"O thou Most High, Most Strong, Most Wise, Thou ever-shining Light, from Whom all light forever comes, we return to Thee herein the light and life that Thou hast given us. Our life is in this offering; we lay it at Thy feet, we pour it forth before Thee. As it bears our life to Thee, so may it bear Thy Life to us. Flood Thou our offering with Thy Life, that it may awaken Thee in us."

All stretched forth their hands and chanted the Egyptian equivalent of: "So mote it be."

The R.W.M. then drew over himself a wonderful golden robe, which his acolyte had brought from the pedestal, gave a k ... and, turning slowly round, with his arms extended towards the columns, said:

"Brn., you have given yourselves to our Lord Osiris-Ra; now Osiris-Ra will give Himself to you."

And once more all chanted: "So mote it be."

Then the R.W.M, removed the covers from the vessels. In the dish there lay a curious-looking flat cake, perhaps six inches square and half an inch in thickness, which was scored into squares like a chess-board - not cut through, but half cut by six lines parallel to each of the sides, so that it could easily be broken into small squares. The marking was heavier round the nine squares in the centre. The cake was of flour, with a slightly sweetish taste, but the top was covered by a thin layer of whitish-grey material, not unlike the icing on some modern cakes. The cup contained a colourless fluid.

THE DESCENT OF OSIRIS

As soon as the R.W.M. had uncovered the vessels, he raised his arms towards the Blazing Star, and cried three times: "O LORD, descend!" When that tremendous flood of light fell upon the offerings, a remarkable chemical change was at once set up, presumably by the actinic action of the light-rays, and the greyish-white icing grew crimson. It would appear that the same sensitive chemical was in solution in the cup, for the colourless liquid also became a deep rose. The change of colour was obviously intended to symbolize the descent of the Divine Life, and when it was completed, the R.W.M. gave seven k ... in a peculiar sequence (which were repeated by the W.W.s, the I.G., and the Tyler) and said:

"The Lord gives Himself to us; thank we the Lord."

All the Brn. repeated these words, chanting them over and over again in a kind of anthem with many parts, which was evidently very well known to all.

THE DISTRIBUTION OF THE SACRAMENT

When this was finished the R.W.M. beckoned to the D.C., who marshalled in order eight members from the south-east corner of the Lodge, and brought them to the altar with him. These nine grouped themselves around the R.W.M. as he stood at the altar. He then, facing the altar, broke off the little square at the north-east corner of the cake, and dropped it into the cup; taking up the strange golden triangle, he dipped the apex into the cup, brought out the little square in the spoon-bowl, and reverently consumed it. Then, as he turned from the altar to the nine Brn, standing round him, they bowed slightly to him, all saying together: "Thou art Osiris."

The R.W.M. broke off another fragment of the cake, and dropped it into the cup; then the D.C. stepped forward with the salute and handed him a small spoon made of that beautiful blue highly glazed earthenware which we often find in ushabtis. The R.W.M. took the spoon, picked up the fragment in it, and administered it to the D.C. As soon as the latter had received it, the whole group, including the R.W.M., bowed slightly to him, and said simultaneously: "Thou art Osiris." Each Bro. in turn produced his spoon, received his fragment of the cake and the grave bow and salutation from his Brn.

When the group of nine had all partaken, the D.C. conducted them to their seats, and brought up to the altar the W.J.W. and nine others - the south-west corner in fact - who went through precisely the same ritual. Then the W.S.W. and nine from the north-west corner came, and finally the Secretary and nine from the north-east. Each Bro. brought his little spoon and, after using it for administration to him, the R.W.M. dropped it into a large golden bowl which was held at his side by his young attendants. An important point noticed was that they held out the bowl in front of the R.W.M. every time he administered a fragment, lest a drop of the liquid should fall. As the R.W.M. gave the fragment to each man, he said: "Receive the Light; thou art Osiris; let the Light shine." And the nine brethren bowed gravely and repeated: "Thou art Osiris."

It will be seen that when all the forty had received and returned to their places, the central block of nine squares still remained. The R.W.M. broke off one of these, dropped it into the cup, took it out in his own golden triangle-spoon, and carried it to one of the Angel-altars in the north. He was accompanied by his young acolytes, who walked one on each side, holding a cloth stretched before him to catch any drop that might fall from the triangle. On each altar was a small square of linen with a tiny blue saucer upon it, and in this the R.W.M. laid the fragment of the cake, saying: "The gift of Osiris to ..." (mentioning the name of the Angel). The Brn. chanted in response: "Praise to the holy ..." using the same name. The R.W.M. did this at each of the nine altars, passing back to the large altar each time; and the last fragment, which was the central square of the original cake, went to the altar of the Archangel whom we call St. Michael.

The children then brought from the pedestal a flagon containing water, and the R.W.M. carefully washed the dish, cup and triangle, the water being poured into the large bowl into which the blue spoons had been thrown. The vessels were wiped with the cloth which the acolytes held in front of the R.W.M. He then proceeded with his attendants to the nine altars of the Angels, carefully removed from each the tiny saucer with the fragment of cake, and threw both saucer and cake into the bowl. Then he took up the little square of linen, wiped the top of the altar with it, and threw that also into the bowl. It is evident that each Angel was supposed to have extracted from the offering whatever he wished, so that the outer symbol might now be removed. The R.W.M. did not in this case make a separate journey for each, but began at the west end of the line and moved straight along. When he returned to the central altar he threw into the bowl the cloth with which the vessels were wiped. The cover of the bowl was then placed upon it, and the R.W.M. sealed it in two places with his seal. It was then set aside by the acolytes until the end of the ceremony.

THE REUNION OF OSIRIS

This being done, the R.W.M. returned to his chair with his attendants, and all were seated. Then he gave a k ..., and said:

"Brn., the body of Osiris is broken and buried within you. How shall Osiris rise again?"

And the Brn. took up the same words:

"The body of Osiris is broken and buried within us; how shall Osiris rise again?"

They chanted them over and over again antiphonally. It was an anthem, yet set to a strange weird minor melody which was wonderfully impressive. This music grew gradually softer and more melancholy, and as it did so, the light slowly faded until there was complete darkness. Then the music died down altogether, and there was a period of silence during which the Brn. meditated upon the death and life of Osiris.

Out of the silence there presently arose soft, faraway fairy-like music, which swelled and drew nearer by imperceptible degrees. Though so soft it was no longer sad, but calm and happy, with a lovely haunting refrain; and after a while a voice emerged, but so gradually, so skillfully that it was scarcely possible to say when it began. At first it seemed to be humming the air; then words somehow shaped themselves little by little, and before one knew it the voice was singing ever more and more strongly and clearly: "Osiris is immortal, unchanging; Osiris is broken, divided into thousands of parts, yet ever reunited; though He may be many, yet is He ever One. We are Osiris; through us shall He rise again; through us shall He be reunited; for we be one, even as He is One." Then the Brn. joined in and sang the same words in gradually swelling chorus.

As their chant ceased the R.W.M. gave the k ... and his voice rang out:

"Rise, Brn., you who are Osiris; as you have received, so give."

He himself rose, turned to the East and uncovered his lamp, throwing its light on the far-away eastern wall of the great hall, saying as he did so:

"I, Osiris, give the Light of wisdom." All the Brn. now faced outwards towards the walls, and the W.S.W. uncovered *his* lamp and said:

"I, Osiris, give the Light of strength."

Then the W.J.W. in the same way sent out the Light of beauty, and each brother in turn uncovered his light and sent out his especial quality with all his might into the dim vastness of the cathedral, which typified the darkness of the outer world. So flexible was the language that "the Light of beauty" could just as well be taken to mean "the beauty of the Light".

The scene at this point was most impressive, the pencils of light shooting out in all directions into the dim surrounding vastness. When the last brother had spoken, the R.W.M. added:

"As the truest wisdom is love, I send out also the Light of love, which enfolds and includes all."

THE SHINING OF THE LIGHT

After a few minutes of intense silent concentration, the R.W.M. repeated the special sevenfold k ..., which was answered by the Wardens and Guards, all the Brn. faced inwards, and immediately a chant of triumph rang out:

"Osiris hath risen again; Osiris is One; we are all one in Him. Rejoice, O brothers, rejoice! for Osiris hath conquered death and fear. There is no death, there is no fear; Osiris lives forever, and we live in Him."

This was re-echoed anthem-wise, and finally culminated in a great triumphant shout:

"Shine forth, Osiris-Ra; let the Light shine!"

And at that the R.W.M. turned on the Blazing Star so that the whole immense hall was flooded with light once more. All the Brn. then extinguished their lamps, and drew round themselves beautiful shimmering festal robes in honour of the resurrection of Osiris; and when they were ready the R.W.M. gave a single k ..., and said:

R.W.M. - W.S.W., is Osiris one or many?

W.S.W. - Osiris is ever One, R.W.M., yet shows Himself in many forms.

R.W.M. - W.J.W., when does He show Himself in many forms?

W.J.W. - When He divides Himself and descends into the lower worlds, R.W.M.

R.W.M. - W.S.W., why does He thus descend?

W.S.W. - For our sake, R.W.M.

R.W.M. - How for our sake, W.J.W.?

W.J.W. - Because without Him we could not be, R.W.M.

R.W.M. - W.S.W., are we then Osiris?

W.S.W. - We are Osiris, R.W.M., and through us His Light should shine.

R.W.M. - W.J.W., whence comes that Light?

W.J.W. - From the Eye of Osiris, R.W.M., when He looks upon His world.

R.W.M. - W.S.W., what if He turned away His glance?

W.S.W. - The world would cease to be, R.W.M.

R.W.M. - W.J.W., is His light then in all?

W.J.W. - It is, R.W.M., but in some it is hidden through ignorance.

R.W.M. - W.S.W., what then is our work?

W.S.W. - To unveil that Hidden Light, R.W.M.

R.W.M. - W.J.W., how can we do this work?

W.J.W. - R.W.M., the more clearly the Light shines in us, the more will it call forth the Hidden Light in others.

R.W.M. - W.S.W., why is that so?

W.S.W. - Because Osiris is one, R.W.M., and Osiris within us calls to Osiris in our brethren.

R.W.M. - Then, Brn., let us ever express our gratitude for what He has done for us by making

His Light to shine upon others, as we have done today.

R.W.M. (continuing) - And let us now join in recognition of Him.

THE PLEDGE AND THE BLESSING

A procession was then formed, all Brn. wearing their gorgeous festal robes, and they marched round the great hall, singing joyous hymns with tremendous enthusiasm. Having completed their circumambulation, they divided into four groups, one taking its position at the middle point of each of the four walls of the hall; then at a given signal, they all moved simultaneously towards the centre, and took up their original positions in the Lodge. When these were reached, the R.W.M. gave the peculiar sevenfold k ..., and raising his arms above his head, said:

"Brn., we have built again the Temple of Amen-Ra, who creates, sustains and ends the worlds. Osiris, Isis, Horus, all are One in Him. We pledge our lives to Him from whom we receive them; let us invoke His blessing."

In response, all the Brn. raised their arms towards the Blazing Star, and solemnly repeated: "We pledge our lives to Amen-Ra, to Him from whom they came." Then, lowering their arms, they broke out into a wonderful finale, an anthem in which the Sacred Name was repeated many times, much as it is in the Amen Chorus in Handel's Messiah, though the music was more reminiscent of Bach's fugues: "Praise to Amen, thanks to Amen; Amen, Amen, Amen-Ra." The happiness and enthusiasm of the Brn. were indescribable.

When the last glad chord had died away, the R.W.M. raised his arms again and said with deep feeling:

"Blessing and Peace and Love and Life be yours from Amen for ever."

And all stretched forth their hands, and replied: "So mote it be."

Then the Lodge was lowered and closed in due and antient form.

* * * *

At a convenient time after the whole ceremony was over, the R.W.M. and some of the Officers took the golden bowl to the bank of the Nile. They embarked upon a boat, and were rowed out to the middle of the river, and there the R.W.M. broke his seals, and emptied out the entire contents of the bowl into deep water. Then he carefully washed it and it was borne back to the sanctuary.

THE CEREMONY OF THE HOLY ANGELS

THE H.O.A.T.F. holds a Lodge of His own in one of the halls of His castle, and we have at various times been privileged to see some of His workings. One beautiful ritual that I witnessed there I am allowed to describe, as it is so unlike an ordinary Masonic meeting that there can be no infringement of any O.

It is a special ceremony performed annually on the Church festival of St. Michael and all Angels. It is worth the notice of the Masonic as well as of the ecclesiastical student that a number of these festivals of the Christian Church are much more than mere commemorations; they are definitely occasions on which, for various reasons, heaven and earth draw nearer together, and communication between the seen and the unseen worlds is noticeably easier than is commonly the case. Often there is an astronomical basis for the phenomenon, as in the case of the festivals of the two St. Johns who are said to be the patron saints of Freemasonry - one occurring on June 24th, and the other on December 27th - obviously aiming respectively at the summer and winter solstices, though wrong by a few days because of the maladjustment of the medieval calendar. Michaelmas Day is evidently an attempt to mark the autumnal equinox, though now it is a week behind time; still, it is one of the occasions which I have mentioned, and each year advantage is taken of that fact to make the wonderful interchange of forces which I am about to try to describe - though again, as in the former case, this is one of the many instances in which words seem hopelessly inadequate.

THE LODGE AND OFFICERS

At the eastern end of a large hall there was a beautifully carved throne of white marble raised upon several steps; and upon it sat the H.O.A.T.F., dressed in a splendid crimson robe like a cope, fastened on the breast by a design of brilliantly flashing jewels, diamond and amethyst, in the form of a seven-pointed star. Underneath the cope-like vestment he wore a suit of golden chain-mail, which was once the possession of a Roman Emperor. At each side of Him, standing upon one of the steps which led up to His throne, was an attendant dressed in silver chain-mail, holding his sword upright at the carry. At the western end, facing Him, sat the Chohan of the Third Ray, magnificently robed in green and gold; but the clasp of His robe was a golden triangle studded with diamonds and emeralds, and His throne was of polished porphyry. He was evidently acting as W.S.W.; and for the W.J.W. on the southern wall, midway between Them, was set a third throne, of rose-coloured marble, upon which sat another well-known Adept, dressed in a white garment not unlike a chasuble, heavily ornamented with blue and gold. On the front of it was embroidered a Corinthian column, extending from neck to knees, and foliations sprayed out upwards from it over the shoulders, as do the orphreys of a Gothic chasuble. On His breast hung by a golden chain a five-pointed star of sapphires, and from it in turn depended a ruby cross.

The whole central part of the Lodge was left empty, though a number of Brn. robed in brilliant colours sat in the columns. The lozenges of the mosaic pavement were pale rose and pale blue, and there seemed to be some additional design faintly indicated upon it by lines. There were also lines of different colours round the edge of it, as is not unusual in Co-Masonic Lodges.

THE TRIANGLE OF ADEPTS

The H.O.A.T.F. was clearly in charge of the proceedings as R.W.M., and He began the ceremony by interchanging some rapid sentences with the other Adepts. There were also some singing and a number of quick simultaneous movements. Then the R.W.M. chanted some solemn sentences that sounded like a prayer, and came down from His throne and stood on the floor at a certain point a little distance in front of it. As He left the throne, the two attendants, facing each other, saluted Him with their swords as He passed between them, and then stepped down to the floor and stood in front of the throne awaiting His return. The W.S.W. also chanted a prayer and came down, and then the W.J.W. did exactly the same thing, so that They were standing on the floor in a right-angled triangle, all facing towards the centre. After exchanging ceremonious salutes They chanted together antiphonally, and seemed to throw flashes of fire towards one another, till the triangle was marked out by lines of brilliant golden light.

THE ARRIVAL OF THE ANGELS

Then the R.W.M. turned towards the W.J.W. and chanted a sentence. The W.J.W. replied, and then They both turned Their backs on the centre and stood facing outwards at right angles to the line of fire that joined Them - facing south-east. Then simultaneously They chanted an invocation, throwing Their arms forward; and suddenly two great Angels appeared facing Them, standing so as to make a square with Them. They exchanged certain signs as though in greeting, and then They again chanted and threw out lines of fire, so that the square was marked out in lines of golden light like the triangle. Then the W.S.W. turned towards the W.J.W., and They chanted together, facing outwards at right angles to the line which joined Them - facing south-west. They too chanted the invocation and repeated the movements which the R.W.M. and the W.J.W. had made before. Again two Angels appeared facing Them and forming a square with Them, and again the square was traced in lines of light. Each time when an Angel came a cry of welcome (H ... B ... B ... H ...) was raised by all present and some kind of salutation was given.

Then the W.J.W. raised His arms and chanted an invocation, and immediately there stood beside Him a great Angel dressed at He was. When the Angel appeared, the Adept and He clasped each the other's right hand, and raised Their left hands above Their heads. They exchanged some rapid salutations, the assembly uttered its cry of welcome, the Angel took the W.J.W.'s place, and the latter returned to

His throne. Next the W.S.W. went through the same ritual, and was also replaced by an Angel dressed just like Him; and finally the R.W.M. did as the others had done. As the R.W.M. left the floor and prepared to go to His Throne, He drew His sword and made a certain sign in the air, replaced it in its scabbard and then returned to His seat. His attendants saluted Him as before, and resumed their previous places on the step. All the Adepts left Their chairs by the left-hand side, and returned to them by the right-hand side. We had now the Angels representing the seven Rays of our solar system arranged in two squares meeting in a point, and standing upon the two sides of the triangle which were adjacent to the right angle.

THE BUILDING OF THE TEMPLE OF THE ANGELS

After some further singing the R.W.M. rose from His throne and, extending His arms upwards, commenced a mighty invocation, in which, after He had sung the first sentence, all the Angels and the two W.W.s joined. Then the three officers and all the Angels turned sharply to the north, and joined in chanting a longer invocation, as a result of which two other Angels appeared, completing the third square. But these two were cosmic Angels, of the types which are not limited to one solar system; so that now all the nine Angelic Orders were represented; and when they had outlined their square of golden light we had before us on the floor a fiery delineation of the forty-seventh proposition of the first book of Euclid - with the preparation of which the Adept who was acting as W.J.W. was so closely associated in His incarnation as Pythagoras.

Again the Angels wove their lines of light, but this time throwing them upwards into the air, so that upon each of the three squares they erected a pyramid, and upon the original central triangle a tetrahedron. They then threw their lines downward into the earth, and thus produced a set of inverted pyramids. The entire figure was thus a nest of four prisms (one hexahedron and three octahedra), the floor upon which the Angels stood representing the central plane. A "bird's eye view" of this form is attempted in Fig. 15, and Plate XI is another effort to show it in perspective in colour.

THE CEREMONY IN THE TEMPLE

Having thus built for themselves a temple of this strange form, the Angels proceeded to perform a most interesting ceremony inside it. They moved in a wonderful choric dance, arranging themselves in various figures much as the Adepts do at the Wesak ceremony, which I have described in *The Masters and the Path*, though the figures were no the same.

Figure 16

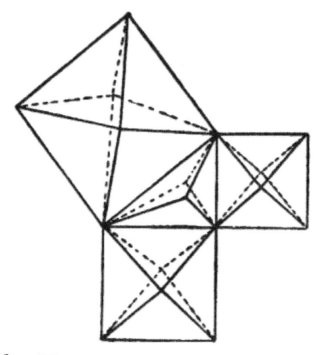

Plate XI

THE TEMPLE OF THE ANGEL

They made a seven-pointed star, a swastika, a cross, and many other figures, but it was very difficult to see them on account of the dazzling radiations of coloured fire from the points of the figure. After many such changes they all joined in a sort of hymn - a most marvellous outburst of music, in which the voices pealed out like trumpet-calls, like the chiming of mighty bells. The multiprismatoidal temple was transparent like crystal, and yet somehow permeated with fire, so that in watching it one realized the meaning of the strange description in the Revelation of a sea of glass mingled with fire.

As the angelic chorus swelled out the glow of this temple grew brighter and brighter, and lines of dazzling light shot out into the empyrean, bearing messages and greetings to worlds far away in space. And unmistakably there came a response to this wondrous call - even many responses. Strange to us beyond all words in magnetism and in feeling were these replies from other worlds; but that they were replies there was no question. Some came from other planets of our system; others just as surely came from worlds of which we at present know nothing.

The end of the ceremony was dramatic. The prisms glowed with greater and greater intensity, until the whole figure seemed a mass of living fire, and with a final grand outburst of triumphant song it suddenly swept upwards and vanished - caught up in a chariot of fire like Elijah of old. Then a hymn was sung, the H.O.A.T.F. solemnly blessed the assembly, and all filed out in procession, singing, the three Officials bringing up the rear as usual.

THE EFFECT OF THE FESTIVAL

The Festival of St. Michael and All Angels, on which, as I have said, this Masonic meeting is held every year, is an anniversary which long antedates the Christian era, though Christianity quite rightly adopted it, as it did so many of the festivals of earlier religions. It is an interchange of joyous greetings and hearty good wishes - a kind of 'happy new year' among the Angels. The ceremony is, however, not merely a celestial greeting, but has other functions as well, many of which are quite impossible to understand. It was evident, for example, that forces were being discharged into the interior of our earth; we were in some way being loaded or charged, and were in turn imparting to other worlds something of which they had need. I am sure that we are as yet far from fully comprehending the significance of this magnificent ritual. I remember that Madame Blavatsky once spoke to us of it, and I also once wavy years previously heard a reference made to it by one of the Adept Brotherhood.

CHAPTER XI.
CLOSING THE LODGE. THE GREETINGS

JUST as at the opening of the Lodge we gathered together all our forces for the evening's work, so now in the closing of the Lodge we marshal them once more for the final effort of outpouring the Masonic blessing. The ceremony of closing begins when the R.W.M. asks if any Bro. has any proposition to make, specifying that such propositions must be for the benefit of the Order in general or for the benefit of humanity. All business and all proposals connected with business should have been done at an earlier period in the evening, before the Lodge has commenced the special work of the meeting. The only matters with which we deal at this stage are the proposal of candidates for initiation, and the reception of greetings from other Councils, Consistories, Chapters or Lodges.

The greetings then given are by no means formal. Each greeting received is a very distinct contribution to the force which is produced during the working of the Lodge; it brings with it the peculiar mental atmosphere of the Lodge whose greeting is given. Every Lodge exists on the mental plane as a definite mental object - a real thing in the realm of thought. When, therefore, one of its members gives a greeting in another Lodge, there comes to him from his own a spear of light, bearing good influence, which radiates through him. When a Bro. is in his own Lodge, a certain aspect or facet or segment of his aura, which represents his relation to that Lodge, is galvanized into activity; some portion of his potential being is vivified because he is part of that Lodge.

The Lodge as a mental entity is made up of such sections of all its members, welded together to form a whole, and it is from that whole that the spear of light comes and flashes out when the greetings are given. When we speak of a Lodge as a mental entity we do not mean something existing merely in mind or fancy; on the mental plane each Lodge is a definite thing, a great sphere, with a precise allocation in space, over the place where the Lodge meets. In the case of a hall where a number of Lodges meet on different evenings, the several spheres are to be seen floating above the building; these spheres are then not intermingled at all, but clustered together over the premises in such a way as to remind one of a collection of toy balloons.

The mental forms made by different Lodges vary very greatly. In some cases such a form is a very fine thing indeed, upheld by a number of people who are intensely in earnest, whose Lodge is a very real thing in their lives. When the members have considerable knowledge of the occult meaning of the Lodge and its work, that makes a splendid form on the higher mental plane; but if the Lodge is composed of members of little intellectual ability, whose thoughts are for the most part centred upon good fellowship and banqueting, the astral counterpart of the Lodge will be strong, but the mental portion of its form deficient. It follows from this that the greetings from some Lodges are of far more effect than those from others.

The highest greetings of all are those from the Supreme Council. The R.W.M. asks the question which leads to the greetings three times. Therefore the force which the Lodge receives through the greetings is divisible into three groups, each quite distinct from the others. Sometimes there are answers to all the three questions, but often there are not. The first group brings the benison of White Masonry. That greeting can be given only by members from the 31° to the 33° inclusive, and it has distinctly the character of a blessing from on high; for this reason its communications are dated always from the Zenith, signifying that its benediction descends impartially upon all.

In this same section greetings may be received also from an Encampment of the 30°. Regalia of that degree are black; its special teaching is concerned with the working out of karma, whether it be good or evil, and its special function in Masonry is the inculcation of order, justice and discipline. For that reason it is established in an Encampment on the hills, so that it can see all round any subject which is submitted to it.

The second class of force comes from Red or rather rose-coloured Masonry. This group comprises all Masons from the 4° to the 29°, and includes also the Masons of the Holy Royal Arch. Its central point is the 18° or Rose-Croix, and its special characteristic is love. Because of its quality of love it dates its communications from the valleys - the fertile valleys running down from the mountains, yet descending towards the teeming plains of every-day life.

The greeting of the first group may be compared to the blessing of a great guru or religious teacher, while the second is more like the affection which parents give to children, or that which the pitris or ancestors shower upon mankind. In the 33° each man exercises a power of blessing not unlike that of a Bishop in the Christian Church, for the great white Angels who are especially engaged in the work of the 33° have very much in common with those who exercise similar functions in that Church.

Then comes the third group of greetings, from Mark Lodges and from Blue Masonry, given by members of the three degrees. These bring a great stream of brotherly encouragement and strength from other Lodges, which stand at the same level Masonically as that to which the greetings are given. These Lodges are all on the plains, which extend far into the blue distance. So we have three distinct types of greetings, giving blessing, love and encouragement respectively.

Sometimes a Mason is requested by a Lodge other than his own, with which he happens to be personally connected, to convey its greetings to his own Lodge and other Lodges which he may visit. In such a case he becomes a kind of envoy for that Lodge, although he does not belong to it, and he is thereby empowered to carry its greeting just as effectively as a member of that Lodge could do it.

At this stage of the proceedings, should it happen that no proposition is forthcoming, the W.S.W. announces: "The c ... s are silent, R.W.M." Here we have the use of the word c ... s in another sense, referring not to the pillars that stand upon the pedestals, but to the members who are not in official position, and are sitting in the north and south. These Brn. are literally in the position of c ... s in the building of the temple, as will be seen in the large coloured Plate which accompanies this book, and it is their work that supports the Lodge. It is not that the Brn. make up a c ..., horizontally, being in a row, but that each one is a separate perpendicular c ..., helping to support the roof; they stand as brothers, equal in their work. I will quote here an account of a very beautiful and most instructive vision which came many years ago to an intimate friend of mine. He writes:

One day when meditating on brotherhood there suddenly leaped into existence before my internal vision a magnificent temple, apparently Egyptian or Grecian in style. It had no outer walls, but consisted of a large number of pillars supporting a graceful roof, and surrounding a small walled shrine, into which I did not see. I cannot express the vividness with which I felt that the building was instinct with meaning - impregnated, as it were, with magnetism of intelligence which made it no mere vision, but an object-lesson containing the very highest teaching. Simultaneously an explanatory sonnet unfolded itself, and described in a few terse, compact lines how this was a symbol of true brotherhood - how all these pillars, all in different places, some bathed in the glorious sunlight, some for ever in the half-shade of the inner lines, some thick, some thin, some exquisitely decorated, some equally strong yet unadorned, some always frequented by devotees who used to sit near them, others always deserted - how all of them silently, ungrudgingly, perseveringly and equally bore together the one roof, protecting the inner hall and its shrine-all different and yet so truly all the same. And the sonnet ended: "In this see brotherhood."

I could not reproduce that sonnet now, but the richness and the fullness of its meaning, the deep wisdom so neatly wrapped up in those few words made me see as if in the gleam of a searchlight what true brotherhood really means - the sharing of service, the bearing one's part regardless of all else but the work to be done.* (*Some Occult Experiences, by Johan van Manen, p. 20.)

There is much to be learnt, I think, from such a vision as that.

The greetings are concluded by the rising of all the Brn. of the Lodge, and their exchange of hearty good wishes with the R.W.M., thus bringing to a focus their feeling of love and loyalty to him and to the H.O.A.T.F. behind him.

PREPARATION FOR CLOSING

Then inspiring verses are read by the Orator from the V.S.L., and the R.W.M. calls upon the Brn. to assist him in closing the Lodge. We have already seen what a large part the Brn. play in the opening of the Lodge, by the power of their thought and devotion. All through the ceremony the thought-form made by the visible and invisible Brn. and workers has been increasing in the richness and strength of its content; now all turn their attention to the distribution of that force to the world around.

I may perhaps illustrate the nature of this effect by reference to the construction of a certain type of Hindu mantras. Some years ago I was requested by our noble brother Sir S. Subramania Iyer of Madras to investigate a mantra which he had been using for many years, which had been given to him by Swami T. Subba Rao, a great South Indian occultist. I looked into the matter with considerable care, and also made use of it afterwards, for it was very remarkable.

This mantra is found, I am told, in the Gopalatapani and Krishna Upanishads, and is composed of five parts, as follows: (1) Klim, Krishnaya, (2) Govindaya, (3) Gopijana, (4) Vallabhaya, (5) Swaha. As one meditates upon this with intent each syllable makes a line in such a position that a five-pointed star results, as in Fig. 17.

And as the mantra is repeated these stars pile up behind one another to form a tube having this five-pointed form of cross-section, which makes a channel for spiritual force coming from Shri Krishna, who is the same Being as the Lord Maitreya, the present Bodhisattva or World-Teacher, the Great One who entered into the body of Jesus as the Christ. With this force coming through it the mantra can be used for many purposes, such as healing, or the removal of fire and other elementals, as well as for general good.

Figure 17

I found, however, that there were three stages in the process. With the recital of "Klim", which it is said is called "the seed of attraction" by the Hindu occultists, the attention of the Source of the force is attracted and what may be called a kind of downward door or valve is opened; then, throughout the body of the mantra the force pours into the form; and finally, with the sound "Swaha", that force is sent out to do its work.

Our work in the Lodge is of the same nature as that done by means of such ancient mantras. During our meeting we have been enriching the form by our devotion and thought, and now we prepare to let the accumulated force burst forth as a blessing on the surrounding world.

THE CLOSING

The closing, like the opening, begins with the momentous question as to the first and constant care of every Freemason to see that the Lodge is close t ... d. With the general purpose and effect of t ... g I have already dealt in Chapter V. The special reason for putting this query again at this stage is that we are now especially collecting and generating force which is intended to be used not within the Lodge, but for projection along certain definite lines outside it. We therefore see carefully to the t ... g of our Lodge, just as a man who has inserted a cartridge into a breech-loading rifle is careful to close the chamber hermetically, so that the whole force of the explosion will be directed only along the barrel, but of course the explosion in this case is not of destruction, but of blessing to the world.

The next command is that the Brn. should come to order as Freemasons - not this time in order to see that no intruders are present, because our doors have been guarded all through the ceremony, but because this coming to order with the s ... p and s ... n is the method appointed to call out the special power of the degree, to increase to the fullest extent the activity of the chakra concerned, so that each member may realize and express fully the power conferred upon him as an E.A. When this is done one may see the chakra light up and glow, flash and scintillate, and often increase in size.

Then the R.W.M. turns to the W.S.W. and asks once more what is his situation in the Lodge and why he is so placed. This is in effect a call upon the W.S.W.'s Angel representative to do *his* duty, to see that each Bro. is filled with strength, not only to take his share in the present work, but to carry on through life until the next meeting. Again, with the same object, having done everything possible to stimulate the Brn. and to increase the spiritual power available - by drawing in help from the Craft, by arousing the loyalty of the members, by the inspiration of the S.L., by the most careful t ... g, by the use of the special power of the degree in which they are working, and by a call upon the Angel for assistance - we now turn to the Logos Himself, expressing our heartfelt gratitude for the blessings we have received and our hope that the Order may continue to deserve His help by doing its duty of expressing every moral and social virtue. Still further enthusiasm is evoked by the beautiful words and thoughts of the closing hymn, and then the R.W.M. sums up our Masonic duty to our neighbour in the comprehensive injunction that we should meet upon the level, act upon the plumb, and part upon the square, each officer raising the symbol attached to his collar as the word is pronounced.

We meet in perfect equality and friendliness, showing no preference or prejudice, but doing justice to all. We act always with absolute truth and uprightness, showing ever the keenest sense of honour; and though the Lodge is now closing, and we are about to separate on the physical plane, yet we part on the square, never forgetting the close adjustment which it secures, so that our brother's interest is our own in his absence as in his presence, and there can be no selfishness or forgetfulness, for we are all stones builded together into one divine temple to the glory of T.G.A.O.T.U.

Then the R.W.M., raising his hands, speaks the fateful words which release all this splendid accumulation of force, and send out a vivid pulsation of energy to every member of every duly constituted Lodge throughout the world. What each Bro. can receive of this stupendous outpouring depends upon himself, his degree of advancement, his knowledge, his attitude of mind; but that the gift is one of enormous value, that the privilege of belonging to the Order is very great, there can be no question in the mind of any student of occultism.

The elemental hosts which have been gathered together rush outward to all points of the compass, only their captains, the representative Angels of the officers, still remaining in their respective places. When at the command of the R.W.M. the W.S.W., who typifies Shiva, the destroyer of forms, utters the formula of closing, the Angels of the assistant officers also fade away, leaving only the three principals and the august thought-form of the H.O.A.T.F. The R.W.I.P.M., in the solemn utterance "And the word was with God", reminds the Brn. that even when manifestation ceases the Christ still remains within the bosom of the Father, ready to spring forth again, the Alone-born, the Self-begotten, when He, the Eternal Word, shall deign to speak once more.

The principal Officers now extinguish their candles in rotation, each decreeing as be does so that the quality which he personifies shall nevertheless remain enshrined within the hearts of the Brn.; and the R.W.I.P.M. explains how this is possible by reminding them yet again that "His light shineth even in our darkness". As the candles are extinguished the representative Angels disappear, each as he goes bowing profoundly to the Presence of the M.O.T.W., who raises His hands in blessing, and vanishes only when at the closing prayer for the preservation of the Craft all turn with uplifted hands towards His portrait.

So ends one of the most wonderful ceremonies in the world - a ceremony which has survived, practically unchanged in its essential parts, from an antiquity so remote that history has forgotten it. Misunderstood, only half appreciated, maimed in many cases of the glorious and dignified rites which are its true expression, it is nevertheless still doing its appointed work in an ungrateful and uncomprehending world. Founded many thousands, perhaps millions, of years ago, by order of the Spiritual King of the World, it still remains one of the mightiest weapons in His hands, one of the most efficient channels of His blessing. Some of us have the wisdom to grasp this, the good karma to be employed in this department of His service; may we never forget how great is our privilege; may we never fail to take the fullest advantage of this opportunity which He has given us!

S ... M ... I ... B ....

THE END.

Printed in Great Britain
by Amazon

78267866R00129